Phil Tufnell played 42 Test matches and 20 One-Day Internationals for England between 1990 and 1997. In a 17-year first class career, he took more than 1,000 wickets with his left-arm spin. Following retirement in 2002, Tufnell became a hugely popular TV personality. He was the winner of *I'm a Celebrity, Get Me Out of Here!* in 2003, and enjoyed a long run in *Strictly Come Dancing* in 2009. Current broadcasting commitments include being team captain on *A Question of Sport* and regular features on *The One Show*. Since 2003 he has been a star turn on *Test Match Special*. In 2011, he was awarded an honorary doctorate from Middlesex University.

Justyn Barnes, who collaborated with Phil Tufnell on the writing of this book, is the editor and author of more than 20 books, including *The Reduced History of Cricket, Freddie Flintoff: England's Hero* and *Four More Weeks: Diary of a Stand-in Captain* with Mark Ramprakash. A Tavare-esque 36 not out in 30 overs for London Schools Under-11s represented the height of his cricketing achievements and his strike rate deteriorated thereafter. He bonded with Phil over their shared interests in quirky human behaviour, fine wines and homemade minced meat-based lunches.

PHIL TUFNELL

Where am I?

my autobiography

With Justyn Barnes

headline

First published in 2015 by
HEADLINE PUBLISHING GROUP

First published in paperback in 2016 by
HEADLINE PUBLISHING GROUP

8

Cataloguing in Publication Data is available from the British Library

Paperback ISBN 978 1 4722 2937 3

Typeset in Bliss by Palimpsest Book Production Limited, Falkirk, Stirlingshire

Printed and bound in Great Britain by
Clays Ltd, St Ives plc

Headline's policy is to use papers that are natural, renewable and recyclable products and made
from wood grown in sustainable forests. The logging and manufacturing processes are expected to
conform to the environmental regulations of the country of origin.

MIX
Paper from
responsible sources
FSC® C104740

HEADLINE PUBLISHING GROUP
An Hachette UK Company
Carmelite House
50 Victoria Embankment
London EC4Y 0DZ

www.headline.co.uk
www.hachette.co.uk

To my dad, R.I.P.
Thanks for all the advice, love and support . . .
and fillet steak.

ACKNOWLEDGEMENTS

Thanks to:

Justyn Barnes – for yet again making everything so easy and thoroughly enjoyable for me and producing another cracker.

My Dawnie – for all the experiences we've enjoyed together, many of which we've relived for this book. Fourteen fantastic years and counting. . .

My brother Greg – for his perfect eulogy for our dad.

Matt Dawson, Nick Hancock, Eleanor Horne, Dom Parker and all the *Test Match Special* team – for jogging my memories of everything from meeting the world's oldest barmaid through quiz/commentary capers to the horrors of *The Jump*.

Mike Martin – for taking care of business (and keeping a record of all the weird and wonderful jobs I've done over the past fifteen years).

Jonathan Taylor – for giving your wholehearted support to this project from day one.

Richard Roper and Humphrey Price – for getting this book to the finishing line.

CONTENTS

PROLOGUE: DAD

'Thank you everyone for coming this afternoon. Dad would have enjoyed complaining that you shouldn't have taken a day off school, or a day off work, or had to worry about setting the satnav.

I am simply unable to deliver a tribute to Dad today that will remotely do justice to the best dad in the world. I have, though, made one observation throughout these last few painful weeks. Dad was a great raconteur and poet, and a voracious correspondent with almost anyone. So although we are all feeling sad today, remarkably, there are others that are quite pleased. . . Arsène Wenger, Roy Hodgson, Middlesex County Cricket Club, the ECB, Swaffham County Council, Norfolk County Council Parking Fines Department, David Cameron, the Tory Party, Her Majesty's Immigration Service, the NHS, Greenpeace, The Sun, the Daily Mail, the BBC, Radio 5. . .

So whether it's that lot, or those that are sad like us, or all the people that I have spoken to over the last few days, everyone will be saying the same thing: how much Alan – our dad, our grandpa, our husband, our friend – will be missed.

And that's the key. Because by being missed by so many it has become very clear to me that Dad certainly lived his life and made his mark.

Well done, Dad, for a life well lived.

Phil and I could not have asked for more.

You're the best, Dad.'

Eulogy by Greg Tufnell at the funeral of Alan Tufnell (1926–2014), Golders Green Crematorium, London, 3 December, 2014.

My dad, born in 1926, was a silversmith by trade. He followed his grandfather and father into the family business before being conscripted into the British army to fight in the last year or so of the Second World War. He never liked to talk too much about what he saw on the battlefield. I do know that he was regarded as a good shot with a rifle, but, like many ordinary people called up to fight, he had no desire to kill people. A couple of his mates lost their lives in the conflict, and he didn't want to die as well. He was just a teenager, a kid, and back home in north London, he had a childhood sweetheart called Sylvia.

So when he saw a poster pinned up in the mess advertising a vacancy for a trumpeter in his regiment's band, he thought, 'I'll have a go at that'. Dad could play the trumpet. This could be his ticket to a life of touring around well behind the front line, entertaining the troops, helping to keep spirits high, and drinking plenty of spirits along the way.

This was the era of swing music, of legendary big-band musician Glenn Miller and Dad loved all that. (In December 1944, the same year that Dad was called up, Miller was killed when the aircraft taking him across the Channel to play for American troops in France went missing.) All he needed to do was pass the audition, but his hopes start to fade when he heard that another lad he knew in the regiment, who went by the nickname of 'Johnny Fingers', was also going for the job. He'd never heard Fingers play the trumpet, but he was supposed to be good.

At the audition, the sergeant major and a couple of members of the band called the hopefuls to stand up and play one by one.

'Okay, Private Tufnell – let's hear what you've got.'

So my dad toots away on his trumpet.

'Very good, Tufnell, thank you.'

Then it's Johnny Fingers' turn. Sure enough, he lives up to his nickname, playing a mind-boggling, note-perfect trumpet solo.

The 1940s army equivalent of the *X Factor* panel are smiling, nodding their heads and tapping their feet along to his performance. My dad's heart sank: 'That's me done. . . There's only one spot for a trumpeter and this bloke's amazing.'

A couple of weeks later, Dad receives an official letter. To his astonishment, it's an invitation to join the band. Fantastic. So he spends the last year of the war playing for the band and having a good time, well out of the line of fire.

He never quite knew why he'd been chosen ahead of Johnny Fingers –

whose fate on the front line I don't know – but had an inkling that *his* dad, Bill Tufnell, might have had something to do with it. It was only when his dad was poorly and dying, that he found out for sure.

'Dad,' he said. 'I've always wondered how I got that place in the band, because Johnny Fingers was brilliant – how did I get that gig?'

'Well, son, I went down to see the sergeant major. . .'

'Oh, did you, Dad. And what did you say to him?'

'Well, son, I made him an offer he couldn't refuse. . .'

I'm guessing that offer was money, because he had made a few quid from the silver business. I suspect he gave him a year's wages in return for getting his son in the band so he would survive. Or maybe a lump of silver?

What he did may seem wrong, but my granddad had lived through the carnage of the Great War, where he saw his mates shot and blown up in front of his eyes, and he was prepared to do everything in his power to ensure that his son didn't suffer the same fate.

As soon as my dad heard the real reason why he was chosen for the band, he could clearly visualise old Bill Tufnell going down to see the sergeant major, because Bill was a big believer in meeting in person, looking someone in the eye, squeezing the flesh and getting the deal.

Dad told me that he was the master at getting the business done. When you went out with Bill, the deal was guaranteed. There would be long lunches filled with anecdotes and laughter, he became their mate, not just a client, plus Tufnell's did the best job.

'Why give the work to Tufnell's? Because Bill's there. . .'

That's how he built up F.W. Tufnell Ltd Silversmiths – founded by my great-grandfather Frank Tufnell in the 1890s – into a company that served major hotels and jewellers across London.

Thank God Bill was so persuasive, or his son might have been shoved up to the front line, popped his head up and been killed. And I would never have been born. Fingers crossed, Johnny Fingers survived as well.

With victory in Europe secured, my dad, still a teenager, laid down his trumpet and returned home to continue his relationship with his future wife Sylvia and work under his father.

F.W.Tufnell Ltd was based at number 386 St John Street, five minutes' walk from the tube station at Angel, Islington. Twenty-odd people working in sweatshop conditions, five-and-a-half days a week: 8am to 6.30-7pm, half-day on Saturdays. Half-day on Christmas Eve. No sick pay. No paternity leave. Turn up, polish your pots and you get paid. If you don't, you won't. Proper hard work.

When Arsenal were playing at home on Saturday, they'd all clock off at lunchtime, take off their overalls and clean themselves up with freezing-cold water from a wobbly pipe and tap. Soap and Swarfega – which was invented a couple of years after the war – to scrub off the grease. No moisturiser.

Put on clean clothes: a collared shirt, cardigan, trousers, brogues and a flat cap – everyone wore the same thing, perhaps with the addition of a home-knitted red-and-white Arsenal scarf, or a rosette. Catch the bus from Upper Street to Highbury. Nip into the Empress of Prussia or the Woolpack pub for a pre-match pint or two, then go and watch the Arsenal.

Dad loved his sport. For him, it was Arsenal for football, Middlesex for cricket and anything to do with England.

Denis Compton, the original 'Brylcreem Boy', was his English cricket hero. Denis and his brother Leslie played football for Arsenal in the winter and cricket for Middlesex in summer, so they were Dad's ideal sportsmen.

He often used to see them on the bus up to Highbury on match days, sitting there with their boots and chatting with the fans.

'Alright, Denis, feeling fit, mate? Are we going to win today?'

When they got off, Denis and Leslie would walk to the ground to get ready for the game, while my dad and his mates would head to the pub.

My dad loved that. Sporting heroes were more accessible. They could take the bus with the fans and no one gave them any grief or mobbed them. Different world. Can you imagine Becks sitting on the 298 bus to Southgate? It would just be pandemonium.

Because of that accessibility, Dad spoke with great fondness about his sporting heroes, as if they were close friends: 'Oh, Denis was a good-looking bloke – when he walked out to bat at Lord's, everyone had their eyes on him.'

As a kid, him and his mates used to nip over the wall at Lord's to watch Denis play for Middlesex and England, sitting on the grass in the days when they let spectators sit just outside the boundary rope.

Even though he was an Arsenal fan, he would also gush about Manchester United's Duncan Edwards, team-mate of the legendary Sir Bobby Charlton. Sir Bobby has said that Edwards was 'the only player who ever made him feel inferior', so my dad obviously wasn't exaggerating. He went to Edwards' last ever league game, a thrilling 5-4 win for United over Arsenal at Highbury, before Edwards was tragically killed in the Munich air crash.

Towards the end of his life, Dad felt that football had turned into a business and he found that he'd get frustrated watching the games on television. 'Bloody prima donnas,' he'd say, when he saw players diving, cheating and trying to get opponents sent off. 'Why am I sitting here watching this?' – so in the end he'd turn off. He just couldn't relate to it.

He'd played Sunday League football and loved doing that, no matter what the weather. My dad always said he got colder watching me play cricket than he ever did playing football in T-shirt and shorts in midwinter.

When I was a kid, he showed me a pair of the old-fashioned hobnail boots he'd once worn: 'You used to take them off and have blood in your socks,' he said. 'And you never head those old leather balls on the laces – they would knock you out and leave dents in your forehead. Footballs now are like beach balls. . .'

They were naturally active, sporty people. Dad and Mum were also very good roller-skaters. They'd go to Ally Pally in the Forties and Fifties to compete in sprints and long-distance races. They competed in British championships. This was when roller skates had wooden wheels, so you had to be very fit and athletic. Rod Stewart's parents were in their roller-skating team – young Rod would sit there reading comics while his mum and dad skated. They knew a chap called Beadle, too, who went on to run the first big skateboard manufacturers in Britain, when skateboarding became a craze in the 1970s.

I was thrilled when a bloke contacted me out of the blue via Twitter in spring 2015, saying that he thought he had photos of my mum and dad during their roller-skating days. Sure enough, he had a couple of great photos – one of my mum lining up with a whole team of skaters and one of Dad in his best suit presenting a trophy. Massive trophy, it was too. He probably made it himself.

My dad loved sport for the pleasure of playing and watching the game, having a drink and a laugh with his mates afterwards; his attitude rubbed off on to me. Even though I became a professional cricketer and was naturally very competitive, I always maintained a club cricketer's approach to it. I wanted to enjoy my sport, too.

In his day, professional football wasn't about money or hype, it was about a few likely lads having a tear-up on a pitch. Everyone cheered, everyone had a Bovril at half-time and a drink before and after the match. Everyone wanted to enjoy their leisure time, perhaps because they didn't have much of it and worked hard between times. And my dad worked really hard, as I discovered when he started taking me to work with him in the mid-Seventies when I was ten years old. I loved being around the place and talking to all the old boys who worked there: Bob Day, Schwarzy, Little Harry, the Daly brothers. . .

I can still vividly remember the layout of 386 St John Street. It was a big Georgian building; you walked in the front door, and on the left side of a narrow hallway was my dad's office. This consisted of a couple of chairs, a desk with a thirty-year-old typewriter, a big old phone and a coffee cup that had never been properly washed up. Dust and dirt everywhere.

Past that was a landing with a sink and a table. This was where the silver was given a final buff with a cloth and carefully wrapped in tissue paper ready for dispatch.

Then you went down some wonky wooden stairs that had been there since about 1815, all worn away. My dad said there were more accidents from people falling down those stairs than there ever was actually doing the job, but if you made it down in one piece, that brought you into the polishing shop. Lined up on the right side, underneath small windows, were six lathes – three for grinding at the far end, three for polishing this end. Three men on the grinders spent all day grinding objects down to the bare metal ready for replating and the polishers would shine them up after replating.

On the left-hand side of the room, up a couple of rickety steps was a big room about forty-foot long. This was where the smithys and hammerers worked. It had all the tools my granddad, and great-granddad before that, had used – half a dozen vices, gas torches for soldering, etcetera.

Some more rickety steps on the lathe-side of the main room led down to the lower basement silver-plating shop. The easiest way to describe it is that it was like Doc Brown's laboratory in the *Back to the Future* film. Big electrified silver vats, lots of gauges, copper wires, needles on meters flickering, bubbling caustic soda, whirring noises and the odd spark.

Over the next few years, I learnt every stage of the production line, first by watching, then by Dad showing me and, finally, working there for real.

So, for example, a hotel would send us a consignment of EPNS (electroplated nickel silverware) to be fixed. Knives, forks, spoons, serving dishes, soup bowls and teapots that have been slung around the kitchen, dropped and bashed up.

First stage was for Schwarzy to clean them in bubbling vats of caustic soda in the plating shop, to get all the shit and grease off them, then they'd go up to the hammerers. Say you had a teapot full of dents, you'd hammer around the dents to make it flush again. Or perhaps you had got a serving dish where the decorative band had come away, you'd put the band in again, secure the bowl in the vice, heat it up with a gas torch and flux, get the silver solder and zip that round – zip, zip, zip.

Once an item was hammered back into its normal shape and any missing parts were soldered back on, it was allowed to cool and then given to the boys on the grinders to smooth all the hammer marks and get it down to nice fresh metal.

Then it was taken back down into the plating shop, where the magic happened. This was Schwarzy's domain. He wore rubber protective overalls, rubber wader boots, and rubber gauntlets (gloves) up to his elbows, which caused him to get boils on his hands and up his arms from wearing them all day.

First, he'd give the objects another dip in caustic soda. Then, once he had a load of stuff, they would be lowered into the silver vats. Electrodes were attached to both the items and a silver anode. Pull the lever and hey presto, by electrolysis, the silver coats the objects.

You'd vat all different things up in there – knives, forks, teapots, everything – and after lunch they'd all come out, the silver powder stuck to them. Then they'd go to Little Harry, the finisher. He'd get the rouge on with the soft, fluffy mop spinning fast on the lathe, which polished them up to bright silver. Beautifully finished, they were then wrapped up, ready to be sent back as good as new.

Making everything shiny was a very dirty job. The little windows were always black and the air was thick with chemical odours – caustic soda, flux and spirit. The grinders and polishers' overalls and exposed parts of their faces were blackened by the dust flying from whatever they were working on. They used to make hats out of newspaper every morning and tied ripped-up bits of cloth round their necks as makeshift necker-chiefs.

One time when I'm there, Little Harry gets his 'cravat' caught in the lathe and finds his head being pulled into the spinning polishing mop.

'Aaaarrrrggghh. . . Help! Help!'

Luckily, they always had knives and scissors next to them and the polisher next to him quickly picks up a pair of scissors and snips the cloth. Harry's head pings backwards and he's free. Fortunately for him, he was on the polisher and not the grinder otherwise he would have had his face sanded off. As it is his forehead is buffed to a gleaming sheen.

On another occasion, I'm down in the plating shop to help Schwarzy. We've had a consignment of thirty-odd big copper pans that need to be silver-plated, but only on the inside. To stop the silver attaching to the outside of the pan, as Schwarzy explains, you have to apply lacquer all the way around with a paintbrush.

'Okay, Phil. I'll leave you to it while I go for my lunch and when I get back, we'll plate them up.'

I open up a tin of lacquer. It's a translucent pinky-purple colour and overpoweringly pungent, but in quite a pleasant way. I crack on, taking care to make sure the exteriors are fully coated. Within ten minutes, I've got half a dozen pans finished and I'm making good progress, but starting to feel a bit woozy.

The next thing I know I find myself lying down on a chaise longue in a Roman palace, surrounded by beautiful women feeding me grapes while a eunuch wafts an ostrich feather over me to keep me cool. After that, things get even better.

Suddenly, a loud voice rudely breaks my reverie.

'Phil! Phil!'

'*Wargh!*'

From Roman maidens in veils, I'm rudely awakened to the sight of Schwarzy, in his *Texas Chainsaw Massacre* gear, standing at the door. It's not quite as erotic.

'Phil, what are you doing lying there?'

'Hey, man. . .'

'Everyone's been wondering where you got to. Oh God, you've only done half a dozen of the pans. Your dad will go mad.'

For the past hour, when I should have been lacquering, I've been collapsed on the floor tripping on the fumes.

'I did tell you to open a window, didn't I?' he says.

'No.'

The window down there is about the size of an A4 piece of paper, so I'm not sure it would have made much difference anyway.

Health and safety were not high on the list of priorities in those days. I always knew when Dad had someone from the council coming down to check the place over, because he'd be a bit edgy during the car journey to work. When we got there, I'd notice the toilet had been cleaned, which almost never happened. Then a bit later I'd see Dad talking to a fella on the landing above the polishing shop. They'd be chatting away and Dad would say, 'Anyway, lunch?' and shepherd the man out the front door before he could have a proper look around. Then he'd take him for lunch at one of the five-star hotels that we did the silver for and we wouldn't see him until the next time. It must have worked because we never got closed down.

Like his father before him, my dad believed in the personal touch. He always said to me, 'Whatever you do in life, son, squeeze the flesh. Shake people's hand. Don't do business over the phone – go and see people.'

That helped him to bring in business from all the major London hotels. All of the Savoy's silver went to Tufnell's, the Dorchester's too. He also used to do work for Garrard of Mayfair, the luxury jewellery house, and at that time the official Crown Jeweller to the royal family, responsible for maintaining and restoring the Crown Jewels ready for grand State occasions. He also worked for Mappin & Webb, whose master craftsman took over as Crown Jeweller in 2012. British Rail used to be a client when they had silver service in first class – the company used to do thousands of knives and forks for them.

As a wide-eyed kid, I used to love going on deliveries with my dad. We'd drive round the back of the Savoy and go in. If we were in a hurry, I'd stay in the car, but often I'd go in with him and sit in the kitchen while he had a chat with his mate.

It was mayhem in the kitchens of these big hotels and I could see why their silver needed sorting out so often. Up front, these hotels were swish, but behind the scenes it was low-paid pot washers and kitchen hands chucking things around.

Usually, someone would come and give us some food. At the Savoy we ate very well indeed. My dad would smoke a cigar and maybe have a nip of Scotch with his mate, talk about the football. Then we'd be off to the next place.

'Right, son, now we've got to drop off some stuff to old John at the Dorchester. . .'

Dad loved his work. His business was like Middlesex cricket team became for me. The people working for him were his mates as much as employees. Even though he was the boss, he was very hands-on. He was the best repairer and silversmith in the business; when something tricky came in, he had to do it himself.

'I got it wrong, son,' he used to tell me. 'I should be driving round in a Rolls-Royce, popping in to check everything is running smoothly, not doing it myself.'

But I think part of it was that he didn't want to let go. He loved getting his hands dirty:

'So long as my feet hit the floor, I put my overalls on and am hammering a bit of metal, I know everything's right in the world. If I haven't got any metal to hammer, something's wrong. When I know I'm working, I'm earning and looking after the family, I'm happy.'

That's why after my brother and I were born (in 1962 and 1966 respectively), he continued to work his nuts off.

We didn't see him much in the week, because he was out by 6.30am and not back home till half seven for tea. He stopped working on Saturday mornings though – the weekends were reserved for us.

By then the Tufnells had decamped to a four-bedroom detached house in leafy Hadley Wood, in the suburban north London borough of Enfield. Some of my fondest memories as a five- or six-year-old are of playing sport with Greg, Mum and Dad in the back garden – football in winter and cricket in summer. It wasn't a massive garden, but it was big enough at that age to have a decent kickabout in. My parents liked doing a bit of gardening, but they gave up the ghost with us around. Every time a little daffodil poked its head above ground in spring, a drilled shot or a sliding tackle would scythe it down. All our mates loved it, because they could come and trash our garden. Our mates' gardens were lovely – manicured grass, flower beds and water features – because their parents wouldn't let them play ball sports in them, so they loved coming over to trash our garden. Dad and my mum didn't mind – they would come out of the garden muddier than us. They got stuck in.

My mum could run up and bowl a cricket ball and hold a bat as good as anyone, too. Playing with Dad, Mum and my brother, all bowling overarm, fielding and throwing properly, was a good early introduction to the game for me.

And when I followed in Greg's footsteps playing for school and local teams, Dad would be driving us around every weekend. He'd often be the nominated parent to cart all the team's equipment around – be it a bag of footballs or cricket gear – in the boot of his Volvo Estate. He was a popular parent with our mates because he was always ferrying them about too and he was a cheeky, funny chap. He'd be standing on the sidelines cheering us on, always wearing his Russian fur hat to keep his bald head warm.

Mum and Dad's education had been interrupted by the war, and they were very keen that their children would get the best possible start in life, paying for us to attend Highgate Public School. Whereas my brother was a model all-round student – very good academically, good at sport, sensible head on his shoulders – it was clear from pre-prep school age that I was not the academic type. I was always getting into mischief. At junior school I started showing real potential as a cricketer though, and luckily there was a teacher there, Mr Kelland, who overlooked my disruptive behaviour in class and recommended me for a trial with Middlesex Cricket Club. At the age of nine, a year younger than everyone else in the team, I was playing for Middlesex Under-11s. People who saw me play as a pro will find it hard to believe but back then I was a good batsman, as well as being a left-arm fast bowler. It was only a couple of years later that the Middlesex youth coach Jack Robertson, a former county and Test player, suggested I bowl left-arm spin instead. Unusually for me, I took an adult's advice and immediately found I got a lot more wickets as a spinner. Dad was so proud that I was playing the county he supported, and he would always take an afternoon off work to watch me play.

However, by the age of thirteen my rebellious, self-destructive tendencies had really kicked in and cricket went on the back-burner. It was the era of punk and my attitude was made for it. I had five earrings in one ear, mohican, tartan bondage trousers. I started hanging out with a slightly older group of lads and girls and discovered the joys of drinking cheap cider, smoking fags, sniffing glue and riding motorbikes. Meanwhile my behaviour at school got worse and worse. I was so rude to an English teacher, he eventually lost the plot and kicked me. As he turned to walk away, I picked up my sports bag, swung it round and hit him on the head, knocking him out cold. It wasn't long after that that the headmaster decided that Highgate School might be better off without the younger Tufnell child and expelled me. I'd see out the rest of my schooldays at Southgate Comprehensive. My poor parents, who'd worked so hard to pay for me to go to private school – this was the thanks they got. Yes, I was the perfect teenage nightmare.

While my dad would let me get away with quite a lot, Mum was always the one to lay down the law.

She was tough and wouldn't suffer fools. Equally, though, she was a very caring and principled woman. She wouldn't see an injustice; anyone who was down, she'd give them a hand up.

One winter's day she took me shopping with her and we came across a bloke tied up naked to the shopping trolleys round the back of Sainsbury's. His 'mates' have all disappeared and he's left there shivering his nuts off.

'Can someone help me?'

He's got a couple of tattoos and looks a bit lively, so people are just walking past giving him a wide berth.

My mum goes straight over. 'Right you stand there, Phil. I'll go and get some scissors from the shop.'

She rushes off and then comes back to cut him free.

That's what she did. She did the right thing. She couldn't understand why people were just walking past.

The balance between the personalities of my mum and dad was just right. Their relationship worked. Even if I didn't appreciate it at the time, I couldn't have asked for more supportive parents or a more stable, happy home life. But a family tragedy was slowly unwinding.

Mum began to get ill when I was fourteen. At first, the change in her wasn't too noticeable — especially with me in the midst of my teen rebellion. She just lacked a little bit of her usual vim and vitality. I think her and Dad also covered up the extent of the illness so as not to worry Greg and me.

But over the next year or so she started going to the local hospital regularly for tests. Then she went in for what they told us was a routine operation, which proved to be anything but. Her blood wasn't clotting and she had to be moved to St Barts Hospital in central London. When she came home, her health seemed to improve for a while, but then took a turn for the worse again.

One Sunday lunchtime, after Greg and I come back from football, Dad explains the full reality of the situation: our mum has a terminal illness — leukaemia.

I can't process what he's saying. My mum is going to die? This strong woman? There's nothing anyone can do?

My mum came in and told us that she was going to fight the disease come what may and she fought hard for eighteen painful months, but it was an unwinnable battle. As her health deteriorated, she needed a wheelchair to move around and spent more and more time in hospital for blood transfusions. Dad's life became work and looking after her; my increasingly erratic behaviour was the least of his worries.

Mum got thinner and thinner, wasting away in front of our eyes until she was bedridden.

One Saturday afternoon in November 1982, I'm at home with her while Dad is at work. She calls me from her bedroom and I take her to the loo and back, but I can't lift her out of the wheelchair back onto her bed.

'It's alright, darling,' she says. 'Just leave me, leave me.'

I spend the rest of the afternoon in my room and later I turn on the telly. Football's on – Tottenham are playing. As evening draws in, I hear my dad return home. A bit later, I see lights flashing outside our house and look out the window to see Dad with Mum as she's being helped into an ambulance.

I don't see him again until the following lunchtime when I return to the house after playing football for my Sunday League team. He's a broken man: 'Your mum's dead now,' is all he can say.

My mum's death changed everything. She'd been the life and soul of our family and home. She was always inviting people round and hosting parties. The house was warm, friendly, with her around – all of a sudden, it went stone cold. I saw my dad shrink overnight. Dad was absolutely crushed and he never truly recovered.

His way of dealing with it was to stay at the workshop for longer and longer hours, often working through the weekend. He even made a bed up there and sometimes would stay overnight.

Dad wasn't the type who could easily share his emotions and feelings. Like Mum, he had that wartime spirit of getting on with things. That was passed on to me and Greg – when we got bumps and bruises playing football or cricket, they wouldn't mollycoddle us. They'd tell us not to cry, to dust ourselves off and get back in the game. We were not the sort of family to have deep conversations about our feelings at the best of times, so none of us had a clue how to do so in the worst time of all.

A couple of weeks after the funeral, Dad sits us down and says: 'Right boys, things have changed. Your mum's gone – things are going to get a bit harder. We're all men, we've got to man up. We've got to look after ourselves now – Mum isn't here to look after us anymore.'

By this time, I had left school, with a grand total of one O level, in Art, and was working full-time as a hammerer. When I started, I was on the polishing for a couple of weeks with Bob, then with old Schwarzy on the plating, but my dad pushed me towards being a hammerer because it wasn't as dirty, or as much hard work, but it required more skill and paid few extra quid.

I think Dad enjoyed having me around. Well, most of the time.

We're both at the soldering bench and he says to me: 'Clean all the lead solder off of these teapots.'

To do that you heat up the solder with a gas torch and wipe it with a hessian cloth – *schoom, schoom, schoom* – to smooth the surface.

I get my head down and stuck into the job with gusto. Meanwhile, Dad's sitting next to me, doing some very fine work on a candelabra. He's concentrating so hard, he doesn't notice that as I'm gaily swishing the cloth over these teapots, the molten debris is flying off in his direction, some of it landing on his overalls at thigh-level.

Over the next three or four minutes of intense work, unnoticed by either of us, the molten lead burns through his thick cotton overalls (perhaps not the safest thing to wear when soldering), then his suit trousers underneath, until it starts burning his skin.

Suddenly, I hear my dad shout: 'FAAAACKIN' 'ELLLLL, OW, OW, FACKINNNN' 'ELLLLLL!'

I look round and his overalls are pock-marked with holes and there's little flames and smoke billowing from them. Dad hastily rips off the overalls and scorched trousers, runs to the tap and slaps cold water on his sizzling legs.

'You silly bastard!'

All the other silversmiths have rushed in to see what's happening, to find my dad, wearing just his shirt, pants, socks and a pair of brogues, screaming abuse at me. They piss themselves laughing, but I'm a bit scared. I go down the other end of the workbench as far away as I can from him. It's the first time in my life I've seen him really angry, and the first time I've heard him swear. I probably only heard him swear a dozen times in his whole life.

Once he's doused his legs in cold water, he starts chasing me round the table, screaming: 'You silly ****ing sod, I'll kill you. . .'

It's only after ten minutes or so, after the cold press has been applied to his legs, that he calms down and starts to laugh about it: 'Next time you're up here, I'll ****ing do that to you,' he says.

His work, and the camaraderie among his mates there, kept him going after Mum died, but it took him a long while to start rebuilding a life for himself and to think about starting a new relationship. And when he did start dating again, he was always discreet about it.

When we finished work on a Friday, he'd say: 'Right, I've got things to do, son. I'll be back on Sunday night.'

He wouldn't say where he was going, but before he left he always popped over to the butcher's, where we parked the car, and bought two fillet steaks.

'That's for your dinners, boy.'

Then he'd drive me home and leave me with the run of the house all weekend.

I didn't really know how to cook fillet steak, so I'd just bung it under the grill. Maybe open a tin of baked beans to go with it. More cordon bleugh cooking than cordon bleu, the way I did it.

I think Dad felt guilty seeing other women after Mum, and leaving me to my own devices, but, in his mind, he was thinking, 'At least I'm giving him fillet steak – even though he's on his own, he's living well.'

I wasn't exactly slumming it, living off fillet steak, but after a year of eating it every weekend, it did lose its appeal a bit.

I was pretty directionless after Mum died. I hadn't played cricket for ages and was just hammering pots and pans for a few quid to go to the pub. I was more interested in motorbikes, chasing girls and getting up to no good than bowling spin.

Although I was a good silversmith, my dad could see I wasn't happy and he eventually persuaded me to give my cricket another go.

'You were always a lively boy, Phil, loving your sport and running around and now you're just doing what I'm doing,' he told me. 'Your eyes have gone dark.'

Despite hardly playing for three years, I found I could still bowl really well. Batting was a different matter – the difference in speed between fast bowlers aged thirteen and in their late teens, almost fully grown, is about 30mph and getting hit by that hard ball at 70–80mph was not my idea of fun.

I signed up for coaching at the MCC nets at Lord's and was recommended to take the trial for induction onto the Lord's groundstaff, the first step towards playing for Middlesex.

Dad gave me a half-day off work to go to the trial, but I was bunged up with flu on the day and bowled terribly. A lad called Keith Medlycott was chosen instead of me.

At that time, if something went against me, my normal reaction would be '**** it, I don't care,' but this knock-back had the opposite effect. I knew I was a good cricketer and I wasn't going to take no for an answer.

Over the next few months, I kept working hard at my game back at Southgate Cricket Club, although for reasons best known to myself I abandoned the left-arm spin which had first impressed the Middlesex coaches and went back to trying pace bowling, at which I was distinctly ordinary.

Seeing that I was applying myself to something properly for the first time in a long time, though, Dad took it upon himself to get me another chance at Middlesex. In early summer 1984, he phoned up Gordon Jenkins, who had known me since I played for Middlesex Under-11s and was now on the MCC coaching staff, and asked if they could meet for a chat.

Unlike Bill Tufnell with the sergeant major all those years before, it wasn't a case of making Gordon an offer he couldn't refuse, more just asking him for advice. He told Gordon I was getting into all sorts of trouble, but playing cricket was one thing that I cared about.

'Could you give my Phil another trial – he's good, but he needs a push. Try and sort him out.'

Luckily for me, though, the day they met it so happened that Middlesex's rivals, Surrey, had decided to sign Keith Medlycott so Middlesex now had a vacancy for a young left-arm spinner after all. Gordon knew I had talent and that I hadn't done myself justice at the trial, so he said for Dad to get me down there the following day and he would try to persuade head coach Don Wilson to give me another chance.

That conversation changed my life. I turned up at Lord's the next day, swiftly converted myself back from mediocre fast bowler to demon left-arm spinner and it was the start of an eighteen-and-a-half-year cricket career.

Dad was already in the process of making big changes in his life too. As much as he loved the craft of being a silversmith, after Mum died his heart went out of the business side of it. He was really only keeping it on for me, but he didn't really want to pass the company down another generation because he knew times had changed. A few of his old contacts had moved on to other jobs, new people came in and all they were concerned about was the bottom line – 'How much is it going to cost me to get ten teapots done? Tufnell's is £100, we can get it for £95.' But for that £95 quid you wouldn't get as much silver on it, the workmanship wouldn't be so good and they would need to be done again much sooner. They didn't see that; it became more about squeezing the margins than squeezing the flesh.

My dad liked to work on a handshake – pay me a reasonable amount and in return you'll get the best job. Cowboys came in and nicked the work and it all went downhill. Most hotels moved to stainless steel – only the absolute top-end hotels still used silver – so there was less and less to do.

Then there were more health and safety regulations, there was loads more red tape and he had to pay people for being sick. He was used to everyone clocking in, clocking out, totting up their hours, subtracting the tax and everyone lining up at the end of the week for their envelope. Name handwritten on the envelope, money inside. Simple.

He sold both the business – for next to nothing in the end – and the house in Hadley Wood and went to live in Gloucestershire with a new partner. My brother Greg had already moved out of our house, had a steady girlfriend and was on his way to a high-flying career as a retail executive (he went on to become the managing director of high-street clothing chain Burton, and then Mothercare), so Dad didn't have anything to worry about there. As for his wayward youngest son, he bought me a little studio flat in Barnet and I moved in just before I got my big break with Middlesex.

It was carnage in that flat. I didn't have a clue. I made a sofa out of glued-together pizza boxes. Never tidied up. Never had clean gear to play cricket. I just needed someone to show me what to do, how to live. That's probably why, when I met a girl called Alison Squires, who came round, cooked me Sunday lunch and put some washing in the machine, it wasn't long before I asked her to marry me. Much to my dad's dismay: 'Don't do it, son. I'm sure Alison is a nice girl, but you're only nineteen. You've got your whole life ahead of you, you prat.'

Naturally, I didn't listen and, of course, the marriage didn't last.

After a couple of years in Gloucestershire, Dad's own relationship ended and he decamped to La Manga, Spain. He bought a couple of properties to rent out, settled there and only returned to England – to Swaffham, Norfolk – towards the end of my cricket career.

When it came to my cricket, Dad was always there for me, but only when I called upon him. He was never critical, pushy or in my face about anything. His advice was: 'Go out there and enjoy every moment. It will be over in a flash.'

He was very proud of me playing for Middlesex and then going on to play for England, but never gushed about it to people unless someone asked. I think that was because he knew there would always be ups and downs, so he never got too high and he never got too low.

When I started playing professionally, I could have got him the best seat in the house, but he never asked for VIP treatment. He'd sometimes fly back from Spain, sneak in unannounced and sit at the back. Then a few days later, I'd phone him up to see how he was, tell him about the match and he'd say: 'I popped in and saw it. . .'

'Well, why didn't you say?'

'I just nipped in after lunch, and I didn't want to worry you.'

He just liked to get his own ticket, sit with one of his mates and enjoy seeing me play, without putting any pressure on me.

He was never worried about whether or not I was selected for an England tour, he was just delighted when it happened. If I did get selected, I'd phone him and say, 'Dad, I'm going to the West Indies for three months to play cricket for England.'

He'd say: 'Wow, that's great, son. Well done.'

I think I lived his dream for him and I think he would have been a little bit like I was. I played to win and played hard on the pitch, but I also went out and enjoyed myself. When I made headlines for doing stupid things or got into trouble off the pitch, he rarely commented on it (unless I'd done something *really* stupid). Usually he'd just phone up and ask if I was alright.

'Yeah, it's all a load of old bollocks, Dad.'

'Okay, well, just give us a shout if you ever need something.'

I think part of the reason he was never judgemental was because he was very anti-establishment himself. I think he quite liked it when I took a little poke at authority. His attitude was life's too short. Enjoy yourself. He'd often say to me: 'Well, you've always been a lively boy, son. It's best to have a bit of character. What's the point of just *being*? Have a bit of character.'

One time I rang him up after I nearly got slung off an England tour for coming in late.

'What have you done, boy?'

'Well I came in at half one and I was a bit pissed. . .'

'Really? Is that what you've done? In the First World War, your granddad used to pull young men still alive and on fire out of burning biplanes in no man's land. If you'd told my dad "They're having a go at me because I'm in the West Indies, having a great time and coming in half an hour late", he would have laughed. If that's all they've got to worry about, what a lovely life they've got.

'No one really cares, son,' he added. 'As long as you're alright.'

Although he took a back seat in my career generally, he was never slow to write a letter to a newspaper or to the bosses at the Test and County Cricket Board (later renamed the England and Wales Cricket Board, or ECB for short) in my defence.

Once he was watching an England game on telly. I hadn't been selected and he heard the legendary Australian commentator Richie Benaud say, 'Tufnell should be bowling here. He is England's best spin bowler but he's being made to stand in the corner because he came home late one night, or turned up not wearing a tie.' Dad sent Richie a letter thanking him for saying it.

Richie talked to me about it when I next saw him. 'I received a letter from your father and I agree with him. . . but perhaps put a tie on in future.'

Even though things became a bit disjointed after my mum died, I always knew that I could call Dad and he would be there for me. Whenever I had a problem – and I had a few in my turbulent personal life – I'd ring him up and he'd fly over to see me, help me get a plan together.

He eventually returned to live in England, in Swaffham, Norfolk. By then, my playing career was drawing to a close and my future was as uncertain as it had been at any time since I was a rebellious, angry, heartbroken sixteen-year-old.

DAWN OF A NEW ERA

1

Almost seventeen years after Dad and Gordon Jenkins engineered my second chance at Middlesex and I joined the groundstaff on sixty quid a week, I'm still with the club. I'm very proud to be a one-club man. Although we've had our moments, overall it's been a happy relationship and, by some distance, the longest relationship I've ever had. A productive one, too – I'm well on my way to taking a thousand first-class wickets.

On the other hand, my international career looks as if it's come to an end. Having played forty-one Test matches over a decade of being in and out of the side, the last time I was selected was for a tour of South Africa in the winter of 1999/2000. I'd bowled okay, but only taken six wickets in four Tests, so I was hardly setting the world alight. After that it was clear I wasn't in the plans of England coach Duncan Fletcher.

Fletcher was trying to instil a new, more professional philosophy into the England set-up. I probably didn't help my cause on that score when, a couple of months later, he turned up unannounced at a pre-season Middlesex Second XI game against the Army at the RAF ground in Uxbridge.

I'm only playing to turn my arm over and shake off the rust in preparation for the new season. As usual, I'm batting at number 11, so when our skipper wins the toss and chooses to bat, I have a few hours to kill before my services will be required (briefly, no doubt) out in the middle. I decamp to the bar upstairs for a bacon sandwich, fag and a lie-down on the sofa.

I'm watching some daytime telly when Fletch walks in to conduct a personal post-mortem of the South African tour. The conversation immediately turns to training, something Fletch is very big on and something I'm notoriously keen to avoid at the best of times. When I tell him I think I may be allergic to training, he's not impressed: 'Are you ****ing joking?'

I try to explain that the combination of heat and grass in hot countries like South Africa triggers an extreme physical reaction – hay fever, puffy eyes, eczema – and that's why I don't like to spend too much time rolling around on the outfield doing fielding practice before a day's play.

Fletch either doesn't fully grasp or care about the extent of my hay fever issues, because he departs without another word.

On ability, quite a few pundits feel that I should have played more for England over the years. Equally, though, I could have played a hell of a lot fewer games because of my off-pitch shenanigans.

My old-school approach to cricket just doesn't fly with the new regime. Following on from the example of Australia, who've spent the past decade battering us, Fletch wants to build a highly disciplined team filled with

'3-D cricketers' – players who are able to bat, bowl and field. If you're not good at one or two of those, you work your arse off to improve so you can make a contribution.

Following my three-year teenage sabbatical from the game, I'd made the decision to concentrate all my efforts into my bowling, while batting and fielding were an inconvenience to be undertaken when required. Team fielding practice has always been compulsory and in fairness I have improved on that score over the years to a decent standard, but I've always shirked batting practice – in a decade of playing international cricket, I've only batted in the nets twice, which must be some kind of record.

The new breed of player is expected to almost switch off from life because it's a distraction from all the training required to improve in all aspects of the game. I'm the opposite – I've never had time to be a 3-D cricketer. There aren't enough hours in the day, because I've had to go out boozing, chase women, recover from the hangover, get divorced, have my ex-girlfriend's dad attack me with a brick, etcetera. . . How on earth could I find time to also practise my batting and fielding?

Fletch is not the first person to try to introduce a more serious, all-round professional attitude to training. Graham Gooch, the first England captain I played under, who skippered the side in the early Nineties, was a fitness fanatic; but he had no chance, because he was dealing with the likes of Ian Botham, Mike Gatting, Allan Lamb and David Gower. Old boys who liked to play hard, on and off the pitch, and younger players like me – well, okay, me – who were always more likely to follow their example than run up and down the hotel stairs after training with Goochy. In the

Nineties, we didn't really have the players to beat Australia anyway, even if we'd all drunk smoothies and gone to bed early.

Of course, Fletch is on the right track in trying to turn all England cricketers into athletes and the team into a finely tuned machine. It's the way all sports are going. Look at rugby: you used to have the big, fat lads in the pack and the smaller quicker lads out in the backs. Soon wingers will all be sixteen-stone muscle men who can still run 100 metres in ten-and-a-half seconds. And the boys in the pack will be eighteen stone of solid muscle and mobile with it.

Fletch is approaching the task of bridging the chasm between us and Australia in a similar way to how the manager of a football club promoted from the First Division approaches their first season in the Premiership. Make sure everyone's fit, knows their job, get the defence right, don't concede silly goals and maybe nick the odd goal from a long ball. It can be effective, but it's a bit dull to watch.

The England teams I played with before often lost spectacularly. England's famous Barmy Army, who follow us wherever we play around the world, originated from those calamities. It was fans on tour Down Under saying, 'Okay, we're four-nil down, but we're still here and still singing.' The Barmies' attitude was to go to the match, have a laugh, enjoy the day and if someone makes a great hundred or does some great bowling, it was a nice bonus. They related to the characters in the team; we were like a load of them, playing the game. There were many dire moments, but rarely a dull one – when have you seen a dull collapse?

Anyhow, following the revelation of my fielding allergy, I'm not selected for England's next squad, or the one after that, and a year later it's absolutely clear that I'm not in Fletch's plans.

That's very disappointing, but by February 2001, my more immediate concern is finding myself homeless. I'm in the midst of my second divorce – well, third if you also include the acrimonious break-up of a common-law marriage. And I will include it, because, believe me, it was just as painful emotionally (and financially).

Having bought a big house in Essex for my wife Lisa (whom I married in 1994) and our daughter Poppy – using the proceeds of my benefit year, the professional cricketer's pension fund – she told me she wanted a divorce. If only I'd timed the ball as well when I batted.

While we're in the process of selling the house, Lisa is living there with Poppy and one day she tells me that she doesn't want me going back there at all in the meantime. I spend the next few hours driving round aimlessly, wondering: 'Where do I go now?'

I end up booking into a B&B for a couple of nights to work out my next move. With all my money tied up in a property I'm not allowed to visit, my options are limited. I'm not good living on my own at the best of times, so being holed up in a tiny flat by myself at a time when I'm feeling low is not likely to end well.

I phone up a few mates to ask if they have a spare room or even if I can kip on their sofa. Knowing what I'm like, some of my best friends, while very concerned for my welfare, seem rather reluctant to actually let me live with them. Thankfully my mate Joe comes to my rescue, inviting me to come and stay with his family: 'We've got a nice loft conversion – you can stop there for as long as you need to get your head together.'

Living with Joe gives me a base going into the new county cricket season, but mentally I'm all at sea. I want to find the love of my life and have a steady relationship, but it's just not happened for me. I've tried three times, but it's gone horribly wrong and I've got my fingers burnt. I take my share of responsibility for my part in these failed relationships – I was a bit lively, in my early twenties in particular – but it certainly wasn't *all* my fault that they collapsed. And I have changed.

Cricket as ever is the glue that's holding my generally turbulent life together, but coming up to my thirty-fifth birthday, the finishing line on my playing career is on the horizon. Spin bowlers normally last a bit longer than pace bowlers because there's less wear and tear on the body, and I reckon I might have another five years in me, but I'm much closer to the end than the beginning.

I can't escape the feeling that my entire life is in limbo. I'm just playing a bit of cricket, drinking too much and generally drifting about.

Then in June, on Friday the 13th, a ridiculously random encounter changes everything.

I'm playing in a six-a-side benefit game for the Yorkshire and England cricketer Darren Gough, down in Finchley. I'm fielding down on the boundary – well, I say, 'fielding', I've got a beer in one hand – when a fella wanders past talking on his mobile and hands it to me: 'Can you say hello to my mate, Phil?'

'Sure, no problem.'

So I start chatting to the stranger at the other end of the phone. Now, I've got a phone in one hand, a pint in the other, so if the ball comes my way I'll be struggling.

'Can you see the Braemar hospitality tent?' says the voice at the other end of the line. 'A girl I work with is in there. She's lovely. You should go and say hello.'

I look around and spot the 'Braemar Shipbrokers' company logo at the entrance to the marquee nearest me. If I'd been fielding at deep square leg fifty yards away, I probably wouldn't bother, but it's right there, so why not?

I stride off the field of play mid-match, with the bloke whose mobile I'm using following close behind. My new phone friend tells me the name of the woman I'm looking for is Dawn and she's 'blonde, five foot eight, five foot nine'.

'Is there a Dawn here?' I ask loudly on entering the tent.

Everyone turns round and looks in my direction, including an absolutely gorgeous blonde woman who looks mortally embarrassed. I thank Dawn's work-mate for the directions (I think I owe him more than that, really, for introducing me to her) and hand the mobile back to its owner.

'Hello, Dawn!'

'Oh my God, who are you?'

Do you believe in love at first sight? Well, that's me. I'm smitten. I sit down, she offers me one of her cigarettes and that's that for the rest of the afternoon. My team are left one short of fielders as I focus my efforts into getting to know all I can about Dawn.

She tells me that she has been working for a shipping company called Gotaas-Larsen for seven years, but has recently been seconded to another one called Tankers International. Before that she worked for a commercial estate agent in Mayfair and before that in life assurance. She started working in shipbroking as a PA but, as the staff had been trimmed, she's taken more and more responsibility. She is now the go-between who has to make sure everything is organised to get a fleet of ships and their cargo from A to B and on time. It's the sort of job where she gets called up in the middle of the night and as the single mum of a four-year-old daughter, Alana, from a previous long-term relationship, she's very busy.

Dawn isn't into cricket at all and she nearly didn't come to the match. She's been so busy and stressed, trying to juggle different jobs. In her mind, there was no point losing a day for silly cricket. By midweek, she'd pretty much decided not to go, but her client at Braemar kept on trying to persuade her, saying it would be a good afternoon out – free lunch, champagne, strawberries and cream. She kept saying no, then on the day, the client rang to ask her one last time.

'No, no, I can't,' she told him.

'I'm not going to ask you again. . .'

Then she changed her mind: 'Oh sod it, let's do it.' She had so much work, she was not going to finish it and was going to be just as stressed after the weekend no matter what, so she might as well enjoy an afternoon off.

I'm very pleased she had a change of heart. . . and that I wasn't fielding at deep square leg. Talk about *Sliding Doors*.

We just spend the entire afternoon laughing. I come away from the match feeling quite tipsy – we had a few glasses of champagne between us – and happier than I have been in months.

I pursue her by phone and text every day for the next two weeks, asking when I can next see her. Dawn's got so much on at home and with work, and I'm in the middle of the cricket season, that it's hard to get a date in the diary, but I finally batter her into submission.

Two weeks after our first chance meeting, we agree to meet at a pub in Knightsbridge for lunch.

I've come straight from training at Lord's and I've got my Middlesex blazer and tie on. While I'm waiting, a couple of cricket fans come over to ask for autographs and we're still having a chat when I notice Dawn looking round the pub. I catch her eye, she does a bit of a double take and comes over.

While it was love at first sight for me, Dawn tells me later that before the date she was genuinely worried whether she would recognise me. So my chiselled features obviously made a big impression then. . .

To apply a bit of ointment to my bruised ego, she explains that pretty much the whole day at the cricket match, I had been wearing a cap and sunglasses, and without them, she wasn't sure if she could pick me out of a crowded bar.

It's probably the one time I've ever been glad that Middlesex make us wear the club blazer and tie at Lord's, otherwise my date might have walked in the pub and straight out again.

We have a great afternoon. We both like a drink and a ciggy, and we share the same sense of humour. Everything just clicks. From feeling like I'll never fall in love again a couple of weeks before, I'm pretty sure I've met the woman of my dreams. I think Dawn will even remember what I look like next time we meet.

If I think that's miraculous, a month later I get a recall to the England

Test side. The reasons for this, though, are less romantic and it proves to be a short-lived affair.

England have been getting whupped by a wonderful Australian side most of the summer and, going into the fifth and final Test at the Oval, the Aussies have an unassailable 3-1 lead, which means they will retain the Ashes. On the plus side, England had won the previous Test at Headingley to end a run of ten successive Test match defeats, which gives the score a bit more respectability.

Fletch was heavily criticised for picking Glamorgan off-spinner Robert Croft ahead of me in the third Test, but to say he is reluctant to pick me for the game at the Oval is an understatement. Normally when a player is brought into a side, the team coach will talk them up, but Fletch tells the press, 'We're only picking Tufnell because no one else is fit.'

Oh, Fletch, you really know how to make a boy feel special. It's not so much a fine romance as, 'Really? Must I? Oh, go on then – you'll have to do.'

When I walk in for training before the match, there's a rather uneasy atmosphere between us.

''Ello, Fletch.'

'Oh, hello Tuffers.'

It might be my imagination, but as he walks away, I'm sure I hear him mutter under his breath: '****ing allergic to training.'

I've spent most of the Nineties playing in England teams that have been brutalised by the Aussies, but the Oval was the scene of my best ever display against them four years previously. In 1997, the situation going into that game was exactly the same – England were 3-1 down in the series and playing for pride, I hadn't been selected all summer but was brought back in for the final Test. Then I managed to take 11 wickets in the match to help us to a narrow victory by 19 runs.

This time, the experience is somewhat less pleasurable. Australia win the toss and choose to bat on a belting wicket. We then spend the best part of two days toiling in the field while Aussie's dynamite batting line-up fill their boots. Justin Langer and the Waugh brothers – Steve and Mark – all score centuries on their way to a massive total of 641 for 4 wickets declared. I also have a big century to my name. . . of runs scored off my bowling (174 runs off 39 overs of bowling to be precise, with one wicket to my name).

When I'm not bowling, I spend some time fielding at square leg supposedly 'on the one' (saving one run), but in reality almost hiding behind the square-leg umpire as Mark Waugh, Justin Langer and co. flick balls past me like Exocet missiles.

Nnnneeeeooooowwww!

The balls are far enough out of reach that I can't realistically be expected to catch them, which is lucky for me as they are fizzing past before I've even moved. Perhaps the old cat-like reflexes might be dwindling in my old age.

In reply, we score 432 all out – including a magnificent seven runs by me (not bad), batting in my customary position at number 11. As we're over 200 runs behind, Australia can make us bat again.

We're 40 for 1 at the start of the fifth day and a big crowd turn out to see if we can bat out the day and salvage a draw. Instead, legendary bowlers Glenn McGrath and Shane Warne rip through our batting line-up and by the time I womble out to the crease at half past three, we're still 25 runs behind their first innings' total and defeat is inevitable.

Batting at number 11 in this sort of situation is very futile. Many a time, I've found myself going out to bat in the second innings with two-and-a-half days left and still a few runs behind the opposition's first innings' score. In the dressing room, the batsmen will gee me up saying: 'Come on, Phil!' and part of me will think, 'Hang on, don't put it on me – you got us in this mess.' But another part of me is thinking, 'Yeah, come on, Phil. I can do this!' Then I'll walk out, remember my batting average is 4.5, look down the other end of the wicket and see that Devon Malcolm is my batting partner and reality bites. A few balls later, it's all over and while the batters are hiding away in the dressing room, I'm out there having to shake hands with the opposition.

One thing I have got going for me is that spectators always seem to enjoy watching me bat and today I'm given a standing ovation by the crowd on my way out from the pavilion. During my career, I've had the ability to empty almost as many bars at the back of the stands as Ian Botham did when he strode out to bat. The difference with Beefy was that they did so in anticipation of a thrilling innings, whereas they watched me more for the comedy value, safe in the knowledge that they would be able to return to their spots at the bar minutes later. For years to come, cricket fans will come up to me to talk about the pleasure they got from watching me bat badly as often as to remind me of my finest spells of bowling.

Today, if anything, the Australian players seem even more pleased to see me than the England fans. As I arrive at the batting crease, the cordon of slip fielders (of which there are many) greet me with a cheerful chorus of 'G'day, Tuffers!'

I can almost hear the tinnies being opened and bottles of champagne being uncorked in their dressing room as I take my guard at the wicket. They know the game is as good as won.

McGrath gives me his own traditional welcome, pinging down a bouncer which narrowly misses my head. Satisfied that he has softened me up, he then bowls his trademark delivery, pitching on off-stump, moving away a fraction to clip the outside edge of my bat. Shane Warne, standing at first slip, takes the catch and the match and series are over.

Our team, led by captain Nasser Hussain, have actually applied ourselves well over the five days and shown some character in the face of an onslaught, but, as has been the case for the past decade, the Aussies are just too good. They are setting the benchmark and it's pretty clear that old dogs who can't learn new tricks will not be required as Duncan Fletcher's England look to young 3-D players to try and bridge the gap. I've been in and out of the England side for ten years anyway and following Fletch's public show of reluctance to pick me for this Test, I'm pretty sure there won't be any more recalls for me.

My only notable success of the entire Test match was to sneak Dawn into the Conran Hotel, where the team was staying, one night.

Our relationship is going brilliantly. At a time when there is a lot of uncertainty in my life, it's great to have someone I can really talk to and share the burden with as well as have a great laugh together. I introduce Dawn to Dad, who likes her straightaway: 'She's a lovely, honest girl, son. She's good for you. That's a keeper.'

She is an absolute godsend and within a couple of months of us first meeting, she agrees to let me move in with her at her house in Sutton.

Mind you, she wouldn't have let me move in so soon if she'd fully understood my living arrangements at Joe's house. When we later go to visit Joe together and she sees his nice loft conversion she's taken aback: 'You told me you were living in an attic!'

The international chapter of my career may be ending, but I'm feeling much more positive about life in general and looking forward to playing for Middlesex for a few more years. I'm thinking 'five more years', stand down when I hit forty and then try to stay in the game in some other role. Cricket is all I really know – apart from silversmithing, and there's not much call for that these days.

I've been on a rolling three-year contract with the club for as long as I can remember. I've been Middlesex's top wicket-taker in the County Championship for the past decade and I'm still performing, so when I head to Lord's for my annual contract negotiation in autumn 2001, I'm expecting it to be a fairly routine affair, ending with me being given my usual one-year extension to my existing contract.

Instead, when I meet my club captain Angus Fraser and club secretary Vinny Codrington in the Middlesex Room, Gus informs me that from now on, anyone over thirty only gets a one-year contract. With no extensions.

I'm taken aback, because I've been performing on the pitch and he knows what I'm about. Then he really annoys me by bringing up the break-up of my second marriage and how my off-pitch behaviour has upset the team.

Now, big Gus and me are mates. We've sat together in the corner of the Lord's dressing room for years, known as the 'Bench of Knowledge', because that's where the other players would come to ask about cricket (Gus) or where we would be going out partying at the end of play (me). I've confided in him about my personal life and I think it's out of order for him to bring it up. I don't see how my marital status has affected the way the team is playing anyway.

Things go rapidly downhill thereafter, especially when they then tell me that all contracts will also be reviewed after three months. Keeping people on their toes is one thing, but taking away any job security is another. I'm not a trialist.

'You're no different from anyone else,' says Gus.

'I ****ing am. I've been here for sixteen years. I've trained next to your spotty arse.'

Gus and me end up having an epic stand-up shouting match across the circular table, while Vinny watches, mouth open in shock. This concludes with me grabbing the draft contract sitting on the table, chucking it up in the air, sending the sheets of paper floating off in different directions, before I storm out of the room, trying to slam the door on my way.

Unfortunately, it's one of those slow-closers, so the gentle click shut doesn't quite have the effect I'm looking for. Sod it. Perhaps annoyed by this impotent exit, I return half a minute later to continue my rant.

I find out later from Gus that, when I crashed back into the room, he was busy persuading Vinny not to fine me, telling him that such arguments are par for the course in the dressing room.

The upshot of all this sound and fury is that I don't get a one-year extension. I go into the following season feeling a little less valued by the club. Although I think I deserve a bit more faith after years of good service, I don't have any worries about proving myself every year, every three months or whatever. The ball is still coming out of my hand lovely and, while it's still early days for Dawn and me, a more settled home life can only help.

By spring 2002, Gus has decided to retire (I'm sure it wasn't dealing with me that finally persuaded him) to pursue a new career as a cricket journalist. A new young captain, Andrew Strauss, is installed. This marks the beginning of a new era for the club.

I've played in a couple of previous generations of Middlesex teams. From the mid-Eighties through to 1997, there were the teams led by Mike Gatting, featuring the likes of John Emburey, Neil Williams, Norman Cowans and Paul Downton, then the next wave of brilliant players such as Gus and the immensely gifted batsman Mark Ramprakash.

Gatt had been captain since 1983, taking over the job from Mike Brearley, another legendary skipper for club and country, who'd been at the helm at Middlesex since 1971. Those two oversaw the most successful periods in the club's history and it was a hard act to follow.

After Gatt's retirement, things were a bit less stable, with first Ramps having a go as captain for three seasons, Aussie Justin Langer coming in for a season, before Gus took the reins in 2001.

Gatt was the best captain I ever played under. He was a great man-manager. I didn't see it back at the time, but he helped me a lot and saved me on many occasions, even offering to put me up at his house after the aforementioned attack by my ex's dad. He was another father figure for me and, just like my own dad, Gatt was a proud Middlesex man. Between them they instilled that love of the club in me, too.

I never dreamt of playing for another club, despite receiving many offers to do so. One of the things that made it for me was having Lord's, the Home of Cricket, as my home ground. Why would I want to play somewhere else for the sake of an extra ten grand or so a year? I can remember Gatt saying that to me: 'This is the place to play.'

Gatt was tough, but cricket then was about how you performed on the pitch rather than in training – results on the pitch were more important than how much you could bench-press. We'd go out and have a good old celebration with Gatt too. I have fond memories of sunny mornings at Lord's, sat on the balcony, with Gatt doing the crossword, having a chat. He'd be padded up ready to bat at number 3 or 4, and when it was his turn, he'd just put his paper down – and perhaps a bacon sandwich if the wicket(s) had gone down early – pick up his bat and walk to the dressing-room door, answering a clue on his way.

'Thirteen across – "porpoise". . .'

More often than not, he'd then go out there and hit a big score for the team. He was a magnificent batsman.

That first era playing under Gatt I saw as my Middlesex side, because that was the team I battled to break into to play alongside the stars of the game. It was littered with international players and just getting in the side was an achievement in itself. Being a Middlesex first-team cricketer really seemed to count for something.

I always saw myself as a 'Middlesex and England player' in that order; England international players' bonds to their county were very strong.

But that is changed with the ECB's introduction in 2001 of central contracts, where top players selected for England sign a twelve-month holding deal, freezing their county salary which is replaced by an England central contract salary. It's all designed with the good intention of strengthening the international team, but an inevitable side effect is that county cricket becomes an afterthought for regulars in the England set-up, something you play in order to get a bit of match practice. In future we'll see stars like Andrew Strauss batting for Somerset just because he needs a game. That would have been unthinkable in the late Eighties.

As the new season approaches, I look around the dressing room. I can't help but notice that a lot of old familiar faces have disappeared. Embers returned to the club as the team coach in 2001 so he's around, but the old school is definitely shrinking. They're a nice bunch of young lads, but, naturally, the camaraderie is not the same as with people you grew up with.

I think, 'Well, I'm a senior member of the side now, I want to put something back.' I always played hard for the team, but now instead of having the extra incentive of being selected for England if I do well for Middlesex, it's more about bringing on the young kids, passing on my knowledge.

Not that I can teach them much about the fitness training aspect. In my early days, we'd go outside talking tactics, bowling a few in the nets, taking a few high catches, go in for lunch. Now we're in the gym for two hours, then go out and do some cricket practice after lunch.

I throw myself into this new fitness regime, if not totally wholeheartedly, and do get the benefits. I feel good, I'm keeping fit, but some old habits die hard.

Before the start of a day's play at Lord's, a bloke always comes in and asks the players for their drinks order, which is delivered at the end of play. When I started playing, the orders would be pint of bitter, pint of lager, gin and tonic, Scotch and soda. . . Now, it's all fruit smoothies, Gatorade and the like. Occasionally, an Um Bongo, whatever that is. When I stick my hand up and say, 'Er, can I have a pint of lager, please?', everyone looks at me in disbelief.

The primary goal for our season is clear. Two seasons previously, in an attempt to make it more competitive, the County Championship had been split into two divisions. Middlesex found itself in the Second Division, unthinkable for a club of such tradition and stature in the game. Promotion is priority.

Even higher priority for me is my relationship with Dawn. The divorce and break-up rate among cricketers is notoriously high because players spend so much time away from home during the season. That side of it isn't a problem for Dawn, though, because she's so busy with work and being a mum. She actually quite enjoys popping down to meet me every now and then, if Middlesex are playing down in Sussex or somewhere.

What she doesn't enjoy so much is me bringing my frustrations home with me. Although the team is doing well, I'm just not enjoying my cricket as much as usual and she has to put up with a lot of moaning.

Perhaps it's down to me missing my old team-mates, not having the carrot of playing for England, or maybe it's years of traipsing up and down the motorway to play that are now catching up with me. Maybe it's lingering bitterness that the club didn't feel I'm worthy of my usual contract extension that's dented my enthusiasm. Or having to do so many bloody press-ups. Probably a combination of all of the above and it all comes to the surface during a game against local rivals Essex at Southgate in July.

The pitch is slow, the ball isn't spinning and their opening batsman Darren Robinson and skipper Ronnie Irani are piling up the runs. I don't look like bowling anyone out and Ronnie is also throwing in a few comments to wind me up. It's the sort of day I've had many times before where you just have to stick in there and fight for your wickets, but I've got no fight in me. Well, not the right kind of fight.

After dispatching another of my deliveries with ease, Darren is running to the bowler's end. On his way down, I give him a mouthful of abuse and then as he turns to run back, I kick him in the leg: 'You ****.'

Instead of playing hard to win, I've just given in to frustration and petulantly booted poor old Darren. My thinking was: 'I'm better than you – can't you just get out? Why do I have to go through the grind of actually doing what I need to do to get you out?' It was totally out of order and a sign that, while I can still bowl a ball, maybe that competitive edge you need to be a top professional player, that I've always had, is not quite there anymore.

Luckily for me, neither the umpire standing a few feet away nor the square-leg umpire have seen what I've done and even though Darren is clutching his leg, he doesn't let on what's happened. Ronnie and Essex coach Graham Gooch saw the incident alright though and at teatime they come to our dressing room to see me. I can only apologise profusely. I've chatted to a few former team-mates before about how you know when to retire. They've all said that you just know. One described it as a 'lightbulb moment'. The lightbulb is flickering in my head, as I sit there feeling disconsolate.

With promotion still to be earned, though, I put the incident behind me and put in some good performances. By September, when we rock up at the County Ground in Derby, we just need to win our last match of the season to secure promotion.

And on the third day of a scheduled four-day match, I produce a match-winning bowling display, taking five wickets for 35 runs off 23 overs in Derby's second innings, to help us to victory.

As we're celebrating in the dressing room afterwards, Embers says to me: 'See, I told those supporters they were wrong. . .'

'What's that?'

Embers explains that he'd been walking around the boundary on the first day when a couple of Middlesex supporters had accosted him. They'd asked him why I had been selected to play on a greenish wicket that was more suited to seam bowling than my spin.

In theory, their logic is correct. But for many years, whenever I've turned up for Middlesex matches, it's never even an issue that I might be left out of the team. Whether we're playing on green top, dustbowl or whatever, I'm always in the eleven. Always.

'Really, they said that?'

'I told them you play your best team,' Embers says. 'I know what you can do.'

I'm genuinely taken aback and I feel a bit slighted, like, thanks very much. I've been at Middlesex for eighteen years taking loads of wickets and helping the club to win loads of matches and, now, it's 'Why did you pick Tuffers?' Instead of being first on the teamsheet, from now on will I be one of the first on the list for the chop? The feeling that my club don't value me as highly as they once did is one thing, but now the Middlesex supporters feel I'm dispensable too.

Attitudes have changed towards me. Even though I can still perform and bowl people out, maybe I'm just taking up room in the side. Why am I here playing in Derby, when people think I shouldn't be?

It's a strange feeling. All season we've been working to get back in the top flight. Now we've achieved that aim, instead of sitting here thinking, 'Yeah, we've done it – next year we're going to get together and smash it in the First Division', I'm wondering whether this has been my last hurrah for Middlesex. Am I just going to be driving round the country next year trying to hold onto my place in the team, waiting for my next tri-monthly contract review? What am I trying to prove?

Oh well, on the plus side, it's a lovely sunny afternoon and we've won promotion. I get showered and changed and head upstairs to Derby's club bar, looking forward to a long celebratory drinking session with the boys. Embers is there doing his usual bit of having a drink with the opposition, but I'm the only Middlesex player in the bar. I wait a bit, but after a while it becomes clear that the rest of my team-mates aren't coming. Turns out that they've all got in their cars and hit the motorway back home.

On the two occasions I'd won the Championship with Middlesex in 1990 and 1993, a hotel was booked and we'd spend the whole evening celebrating, stay overnight and drive home the next day. This time, instead of my usual celebratory alcohol intake, I end up sitting there having a pint of shandy with a couple of the Derby lads who say, 'Well done, well bowled mate', then get in my car and go home too.

The whole season came down to this game, we won it and yet there's no celebration. It's such an anticlimax and I go into the off-season with plenty to think about.

A couple of weeks later, my agent Mike Martin calls me up and says the producers of *Celebrity Big Brother* want me to be in the next series. There had been a couple of series of *Big Brother* which were a massive success and the first celebrity version the previous February, which had been done as a one-off as a charity special for Comic Relief, won by comedian Jack Dee, had also been a ratings success.

The second celebrity series is scheduled for late November, so the timing is good. I'm a bit baffled as to why they are asking me – I'm a cricketer, not a celebrity – but the money on offer is tempting.

If it was down to me, I'd probably have done it for the money, but when I ask Dawn for her opinion, she says: 'Hmm, I don't think that would suit you.'

She had watched the show and seen how it works, manipulating people to turn against each other, while everything you do and every conversation you have is recorded. She points out that I'm still going through a bad divorce, I'm having a few wobbles about my cricket career and future – I may say or do something I later regret?

Again, it's really good to be able to talk things through with Dawn. Not that she wants to slap me into shape and tell me what to do, but I've noticed almost from the day we met that she has a great instinct for what will suit me and what might not. After some discussion, I totally agree with her that I should let this one pass. The last thing I want to do right now is have a meltdown on *Big Brother*.

It's not long before another celebrity reality show offer comes in, though – to appear in ITV's *I'm a Celebrity. . . Get Me Out of Here!* This time, I'm a bit doubtful, so I'm quite surprised by Dawn's reaction when I tell her. 'Go for it,' she says.

She reckons that it's a very different set-up to *Big Brother*. Whereas *Big Bro* is more divisive, judging by the first series of *I'm a Celebrity. . .* (which was won by poptabulous DJ Tony Blackburn, who befriended logs in the Australian jungle) this is more of a team game. Also, as much as Australians have been a cricketing enemy over the years, I love the country and spending some time in the jungle round a campfire, doing the odd challenge, could be therapeutic and fun.

The problem is the show is happening in springtime, towards the end of pre-season training. It may cut into the start of the season. Missing a bit of pre-season doesn't bother me, as I'm no fan of all that dashing about. Spin bowling doesn't require that much physical fitness and it never takes me very long to get into my bowling groove. Middlesex might not agree with that assessment, however, and missing a match for a reality TV show is probably a non-starter. Sure enough, when I ask the head honchos for permission to do it, the answer is no.

I'm a bit disappointed, but can't really argue – I am under contract after all, albeit one that is getting shorter by the day – so we have to go back to the production company and say I can't do it.

During the off-season, I have a few odd jobs to keep me ticking over, including some cricket commentary for the BBC on the World Cup in South Africa, which I really enjoy (more in Chapter 4).

There's also time for the odd jolly. In February, I'm invited for a weekend in Dublin with VIP tickets for the sold-out Six Nations Championship match between Ireland and England at Croke Park.

It's a corporate do and I'm in a group of half a dozen people. When we arrive at the hotel, they're serving Guinness in the lobby, while outside there seems to be a Guinness stall every few steps. In the middle of one street, they're doing this thing where you have to stand on a podium holding two pints of Guinness and they spin you round while you try not to spill it. That's good fun. By the end of the first night we're all absolutely smashed on the black stuff.

The next morning we opt for the hair of the dog method of dealing with our monstrous hangovers and head down to the pub. Pint of Bloody Mary, please. With celery.

We're sitting there having an all-Irish breakfast and a chat when a guy comes up and asks if we've got spare tickets. Two of the lads end up selling their priceless tickets to him for a very huge price – they get about two grand each for them. I nearly crumble, but think that it might be rather rude to sell mine as I've been invited as a guest and haven't paid for it.

So we leave the two ticket-sellers there and the rest of us go to watch the match. Ireland win and it's not the greatest game as it happens and we're all wishing we'd cashed in earlier and stayed in the pub. When we go back there afterwards to meet the other guys, we open the doors to find the mother of all parties in full swing. I'm looking round for our two mates and spy the dynamic duo moonwalking behind the bar and making cocktails like Tom Cruise. With four grand in their pocket, the drinks are on them. They've got the whole pub in the palms of their hands. And so another big night out in Dublin begins.

Come March 2003, it's back to the grind of pre-season training and this year it really feels like a grind. One lunchtime in the pavilion at Merchant Taylors' School in Northwood, I have a moment of clarity. We've been out practising all morning in rainy, cold weather when no one should be playing cricket. After slapping a bit of ham between two dull slices of bread, I'm lying on a table nibbling at my sandwich, contemplating a few more weeks of this rather than going to Australia. More Sunblest sandwiches rather than sun-kissed in Oz.

'What the **** am I doing here?' I say to my team-mate David Nash, who's sitting nearby. 'I could be going to the jungle and I've turned it down for this?'

All the warning signs of the past year are flashing at once – do I really want this any more? Not playing the game, but everything else that goes with it – the training, the endless travel during the season, the days when nothing goes right but you need the willpower to stick in there and keep going.

I've always been in cricket for the love of the game, the competition and the camaraderie. For me, after Mum died, cricket saved me. My team-mates at Middlesex were like a second family to me and without having that focus – of trying to play cricket at the top level – in my life, I'm not sure what would have happened to me. Now, with my England career over, most of my old mates retired and my competitive edge blunted, perhaps I'm just prolonging my career to nick a few quid.

Dad must have felt the same when he sold his business all those years ago. A lot of his pals had drifted out of the trade and the game had changed. As much as he loved the art of silversmithing, and was still one of the best at what he did, the demand for his services had fallen. It wasn't quite the life he loved anymore and with Mum gone and his two boys grown up, the incentive to carry on wasn't there.

Ducking for cover at square leg under fire from the Aussies, kicking an innocent batsman, the Derbyshire anticlimax and now pre-season misery. . . the lightbulb is blazing brightly.

I miss the next couple of training sessions while I think things through, prompting a phone call from Andrew Strauss, who, understandably, is a bit miffed that his most experienced bowler is going missing with the start of a new season back in the top division fast approaching. By the end of our conversation, after nearly nineteen years with the club, I'm effectively an ex-Middlesex player, an ex-cricketer.

I call up Mike to tell him I've decided to retire. He doesn't try to change my mind – I think he knew this was coming. I ask him if *I'm a Celebrity* is still a possibility.

He says he'll check with the production company, but not to get my hopes up because the series is starting in a couple of weeks' time.

He calls me back half an hour later: 'They've still got a spot.'

'Great, I'm in.'

With no fanfare at all, no waving to the crowd, my cricket career is over. I've pulled the plug.

Just a fortnight later, I'm with Dawn drinking champagne in the first-class cabin of a plane bound for Australia.

ITV are paying me the equivalent of about a year's salary at Middlesex for being on the show, which is great, but it's still a massive gamble. The money will give me breathing space while I work out what to do next, but there's no master plan for the future.

With my one O level, companies are not likely to be queuing up to offer me executive roles when I return. It feels right, though, and despite the uncertainty about the future after doing the show, Dawn is right behind my decision. She's seen how dissatisfied I've been the past few months. She could tell I was searching for something new, but at the time I didn't know what. I still don't know to be honest, but I feel lighter and more excited than I have for months.

I think Dawn is quite relieved too, because, as much as she's put up with my grumbling and been supportive, I don't think she really wants to be a professional cricketer's wife. She's looking at a change of career too, having recently accepted redundancy from the shipping company and begun retraining to be a fitness instructor.

In many ways, the timing of when we met, with me playing just one more season, has been perfect. I think the prospect of two weeks in the five-star Palazzo Versace hotel on Australia's Gold Coast is softening the blow of potentially having an unemployed boyfriend.

If I was single, I might have chosen to go into the jungle anyway, but I would have felt insecure knowing that I was coming back to nothing – no cricket career, no partner, a very uncertain future. It's always good to have a mate in my corner and in Dawn I think I've found my soulmate.

A couple of months short of my thirty-seventh birthday, my cricket career is over, I'm with my new girlfriend who I hope is going to become more than that and we're going on an adventure together. It feels like the start of a new chapter.

THE CELEBRITY JUNGLE

2

The flight to Australia is long, but luxurious. We spend the first half of it enjoying the first-class service, meeting fellow contestants and members of the huge production crew, who are slumming it in club class. Then, after the fuelling stop in Kuala Lumpur, we flatten our seats and kip most of the rest of the way. It's so comfortable, it seems a bit of a shame to get off.

The journey brings back memories of flying Down Under on my first England tour back in 1990. As the wheels hit the tarmac in Brisbane, there's that same feeling of excitement of the unknown, wonder at what might be round the corner. . . and of being absolutely smashed. The only difference is that I've spent the flight sitting next to Dawn rather than Wayne Larkins, and she's a lot better looking.

From the airport we are transferred to the Versace hotel where we spend a couple of days to acclimatise. Then it's 'Bye, Dawn' and me and the rest of my future camp-mates are flown by helicopter to Springbrook National Park, near Murwillumbah, and deposited in a clearing at the edge of subtropical rainforest. (I'm a nervous flier in a plane, let alone a helicopter which seems even less safe, but at least we aren't forced to skydive out of it as contestants do in future series.)

Then we have a bit of a trek before reaching camp, our home for at least the next week before the public start voting people out and up to fifteen days for the three who reach the final.

Our ten campers are John Fashanu (ex-footballer), Wayne Sleep (ballet dancer and choreographer), Chris Bisson (actor), Catalina Guirado (model), Linda Barker (TV interior designer), Danniella Westbrook (actor), Antony Worrall Thompson (TV chef), Siân Lloyd (ITV weather forecaster), Toyah Willcox (Eighties' pop star) and me.

As Dawn predicted, the atmosphere between us all is generally pretty cordial in the camp. The Bushtucker Trials and other little challenges are geared to earning meals and treats for the whole group, so we're all supportive of each other. We're all in this together, although Fash is in it more than the rest of us during the first week because the evil British public vote for him to do most of the trials.

Despite being hard as nails physically, Fash has got every phobia under the sun – spiders, snakes, rats. . . wildlife in general. . . oh, and heights – just walking across the rope bridge above a gorge to get to where the trials are held is a huge ordeal for him. Of course, the viewers keep voting for the poor bloke to confront his fears because it's funny to watch him suffer.

Fash is a great believer in positive thinking and does really well to get through them day after day. 'You've got to think the public are voting for you because they want to see you,' he says. 'They're not voting because they don't want to see you.' Which is a *very* positive way to think about it.

Every star he picks up in the trial equates to 'a meal' for the camp, but the producers' definition of what constitutes a meal is certainly not a roast beef dinner followed by treacle sponge with custard. Luckily, we have a professional chef in Antony, aka 'Wozza', with us in the camp, who makes the best of meagre rations.

Because we're surviving on basic rations of a couple of little bowls of rice a day and a few beans, plus anything extra Fash can earn for dinner, food becomes something of an obsession. A lot of conversations around the campfire revolve around the home comfort foods we're missing – 'Ooh, roast potatoes' . . . 'Ahh, a bacon sandwich'. There's also the odd silly argument over someone nicking a bit of salt or eating too much rice and, one day, Catalina gets the hump with Antony because she doesn't like him butchering a chicken for our dinner in front of her in camp – although I'm not too sure where else she expects him to do it.

The lack of food is particularly tough for someone like big Fash, who still looks as fit and strong as he was when he played football. He's absolutely starving and he knows lack of food can make him irritable. To keep himself calm, he does thousands of sit-ups, practises his martial arts moves on a tree and says 'Focus' a lot. Indeed, he says 'Focus' so much, at first I thought he was angling for an endorsement deal with Ford. Maybe I'll start saying 'Ferrari', 'Rolex'. . .

Any extra food is welcome, but sometimes opinion is divided on what constitutes food. Like the day when Antony finds a crayfish sitting on a rock in the lake and brings it back to camp.

'Oh, that is a big 'un,' I say. 'Shall I get the pot on? We've got to eat it, haven't we?'

'We mustn't eat it!' replies Wayne, horrified at the idea.

'Let's see what we've got for dinner tonight,' replies Linda. 'If our dinner tonight is rubbish, we're eating that.'

'No, you're not,' says Wayne.

Toyah chimes in: 'No, Linda – you don't want to eat him, do you?'

'If our dinner's rubbish, we're going to eat it.'

There is a clear split in the camp. Wayne's opinion is that this experience is about seeing these creatures in the wild and leaving them there. I'm more of the hunter-gatherer opinion, but I'm not going to argue about it. Colin the crayfish, as I christen him, is placed in a pot of freshwater while the group discuss his fate.

I go for a wander and a bit later, I'm back in the camp, wondering what has happened to Colin.

'Where is he?' I say.

'In the pot,' says Wozza, lifting the lid on a steaming saucepan.

'Oh, too late. . .' Not sure who made the decision to cook Colin in the end, but he is very tasty.

It's my birthday while I'm in the camp and the producers send a note in saying that they will provide a bottle of alcohol-free wine and two bottles of wine as a present. The catch is that if we take them, we will lose three of the ten meals Catalina has earned in the latest trial. We have three minutes to decide as a group whether or not to take the booze. In the end, though, the general consensus is that it's my day so I should do what I want and they'd back me, so I'm sent off to the Bush Telegraph hut – the show's version of *Big Brother*'s diary room – to give our decision.

I quite fancy a fruity Shiraz to toast my birthday, but everyone's starving and I know there's a couple of teetotallers among us who would much prefer the food. After sitting in front of the camera for a few minutes mulling it over, I plump for the meals and, judging by the reaction when I get back into camp, it's a popular decision.

Two evenings later, though, things come to a head over the food shortages. With nine of us left in the camp and having had just four meals (and a meal is a couple of forkfuls) shared between us since the night before, our little food parcel for dinner doesn't arrive. We all stagger up to the hut and huddle in front of the camera to threaten a mass walkout.

'This is a ****ing joke,' says Antony. 'What if we all walk out tomorrow? You're ****ing screwed.'

A disembodied voice from the production team assures us that food is on its way.

'Unless you want some serious problems, you better sort the bloody food out, *mate*,' adds Linda with some venom.

Antony starts asking to speak to his agent and everyone is getting very agitated.

When we get back to the camp, the food basket is lowered down and Antony is unimpressed.

'Nine sausages and two mangetout each and no potatoes does not constitute a meal in my opinion,' says Antony, who promptly packs it all back up and leads us back to the hut.

'We haven't even got a kiwi for a bit of fruit,' he says.

'And nuts without a nutcracker, what's that about?' adds Siân.

'It's taking the piss,' concludes Antony. 'Anyway we're leaving the food and unless you send something immediately. . .'

The woman behind the microphone cuts in: 'Antony, Antony, just to let you know that the calorific value of the portions are all worked out. . .'

Before she can finish the sentence, there's a chorus of '**** the calorific values!' from disgruntled campers.

'At the end of the day, we've all got out clauses,' continues our rebel leader. 'We've only got to say "We're celebrities, get us out" and we'll all go together. You're not going to split us. We're united and we'll go together. So sort it.'

Looking around at other faces, I don't think I'm alone in thinking that maybe this is all getting a bit out of hand. I'm pretty sure I haven't got an out clause. No one dares to divide the united front now, though, because Antony's on a mission. He takes off his shirt and hangs it over the camera in front of us and I stick my hat over another one in the top corner of the room.

'Come on, let's take our mikes off,' says Danniella.

We exit the hut and troop across the rope bridge in pitch darkness to the treehouse where Ant and Dec normally present the show. The production team are there waiting, ready for an emergency summit meeting. A couple of security guards are with them, big ex-military fellas, whose intimidating presence immediately makes us a little less brave and a little more polite than we were talking to an anonymous voice from the Bush Telegraph. Well, most of us except Wozza.

I look at Fash and say, 'I don't fancy our chances here. . .'

'We're prepared to put up with no food but rice and beans all day, but you have given us a very inadequate meal,' Linda begins.

'It's not a main course, it's a starter,' adds Wayne.

'There's nothing different about the food tonight – we vary the food every night. . .' begins the producer but can't finish her sentence as Wozza wades in.

'That's nonsense. When Cat got ten points, we got masses of meat, enough to make a stew the next day.'

Another production team member standing next to me chips in, saying, 'We measure everything out. . .' and immediately regrets it as Wozza marches up to him, smacking his hands together: 'Well, you're ****ing useless at measuring things out. I'm a chef. I know perfectly well that that amount of rice is more than that amount of rice we got today. . . Please don't insult my intelligence.'

In the end, after all the furious debate, Antony and the rest of us meekly accept the producer's offer to swap the food parcel. A couple of people chance their arm by asking, 'Can we have a bar of chocolate as well?', as the security boys usher us back across the bridge to wait for it.

The new parcel seems a bit more substantial, so the producers probably also thought, '**** the calorific values' and lumped a few extra bits in just to shut us up.

It's all quite embarrassing and comical in retrospect – I mean, arguing over a lack of mangetout and kiwi fruit – but everyone was feeling just so tired and weak at the time.

Generally, though, as I'm not a big eater normally, I'm quite content in the camp. I spend a lot of time just sitting on a log or in an inflatable Union Jack armchair Chris brought in with him for us, having a chat. There's not much else to do other than go to get water or gather logs for the fire.

The camp is really small and the atmosphere reminds me of a cricket dressing room, so I find that I slot into the lifestyle quite easily. When you had a rainy day at the cricket and were stuck inside for hours, out of boredom, you'd come up with things to do to pass the time and keep people amused.

The most enjoyable moments are when we're just messing about.

One day, they send a little Kwik Cricket set into the camp and we have a game, during which the noted spin bowler Toyah Willcox bowls me out.

Another time, Fash teaches me a few of his Wing Chun self-defence moves. He gets me to go for him with a knife and shows me how he'd break my arm and puncture my lung with his knee.

'It's not about aggression,' he says, 'but using the other person's aggression against themselves.'

I show him my own interpretation of Wing Chun arm movements, which end up looking more like Rod Hull operating Emu. Then Fash shows me how it should be done with a blinding whirl of arms.

'Yeah, that's good, good. . .' I say.

'It's always about protection,' continues Fash earnestly and just as he looks away I whack him with an imaginary cricket bat.

Fash is an absolute fitness freak. One day, just to make things a bit harder for himself, he spends all day carrying round a rucksack full of rocks. So when he comes back to camp carrying logs for the fire, he's also carrying rocks on his back. We all think he's lost his mind.

Big Fash and little Wayne form a nice friendship and the massive height difference between them makes them quite a comical-looking pair. One day I return to the camp after a little stroll to find that Wayne has hurt his ankle. He claims he did it practising his ballet moves, but eyewitnesses tell us he was jumping up and down on his hammock bed like it's a trampoline and went straight through the cloth.

He has to go and see the camp medic and it turns out it's a ligament strain, so we make him a little crutch to hobble around on and let him have the Union Jack armchair for the day. Someone makes him a Julius Caesar-style crown and he sits there like a little emperor with his foot up over the fire, milking it all afternoon. It's hilarious.

In the evening, nature calls, and Fash has to give him a piggyback up to the toilet. While he's doing his business, Fash comes back down to the camp. As he's telling me how he's going to pretend to snore and be asleep if Wayne asks him to take him to the loo during the night, we hear a cry:

'Faaaa-aaaaassssshhh! Faaaaaa-aaaaassssh! I'm rrrreadddd-y.'

Fash dutifully goes off to bring his little mate back down again on his back. Maybe all that carrying rocks was worthwhile training after all.

Another night, a couple of bottles of wine are sent into the camp and having hardly eaten, it doesn't take much to make me very tipsy. My daily ration of ten cigarettes has run out and after I make an unsuccessful bid for more at the Bush Telegraph, fellow smoker Wozza and me try to persuade one of the TV cameramen to give us one of his fags. They are stationed in huts all around the camp and we make a beeline for the hut up the slope from where we sleep.

Our make-it-up-as-you-go-along plan consists of me begging 'Gissa fag', offering to give him £500 when I get out and then us trying to kick down the door – to which the cameraman responds by barking like a dog to scare us off.

Who will win the show is completely out of our hands – it's all on a public vote. There's no real sense of competition – well, early on, at least, although as we go into the second week and people start getting voted off, I sense there's a few people who really want to win. Team spirit usually conquers all, though, and if a couple of people fall out, I always try to smooth things over and help to bring the group back together.

During my cricket career, it always pissed me off when people said I wasn't a team player. Maybe it was because I was this supposed 'maverick' figure, but I always played for the team first and foremost. I got selected for eight England tours, which I don't think would have happened if I'd been selfish. When, on the odd occasion, I did fall out of line, I always said sorry. It's quite nice that cricket fans who watch the show can get some sense of how I was in the cricket dressing room. I try to give everyone a helping hand or a hug if they're struggling a bit, missing their family or whatever.

Danniella is the only one who withdraws from the show rather than being voted off. She's had a tough time personally in recent times and has never been apart from her young children before. She's missing them and her husband really badly and, after once wanting to leave and being talked out of it by the show's resident psychologist, she decides to go. The final straw comes when she goes to the dunny – which is just a hut and a wooden box with a hole. As she goes to sit down, a couple of rats jump out and she comes running out, screaming. She's petrified of rats and tells us she won't be able to go to the loo again. In the first week, the rice and beans diet meant that a few of us didn't manage to do a number two at all so we didn't need to brave the makeshift toilet too often, but by this time we're all a bit more 'freed up', so lasting the final week without using the dunny could be a problem.

She's a nice girl and very popular within the group, so we're sad to lose her, but she's been getting so upset, it's the right decision.

I don't have any such worries. I'm missing Dawn, but I'm sure she is enjoying herself at the Versace and she has a friend in Australia she's going to visit while we're in the country. Mind you, it becomes a bit of a running joke in the camp how much I talk about 'my Dawnie' and how much I love her.

One night, sitting round the campfire, Linda asks me how long we've been together.

'Two years.'

'Is she there forever?'

'Yeah, she's there forever. . . I just want some "ever".'

'You've got it though.'

'Hope so.'

'But you know it.'

'Well, yeah I do know it. I've been wrong before. But I'm not wrong on this one. . . not wrong on this one.'

I end up getting emotional and having to put my hat over my face.

'Sorry. . .'

Otherwise, I think I'm coping quite well with camp life. When the viewers start voting for who they want to stay in the camp in the second week, I'm not finding myself in the bottom two so I assume they are enjoying watching me in there too.

Gradually, ten is whittled down to six as first we lose Siân on day eight, then Danniella walks on day nine (so there is no eviction that day), before Chris and then Catalina are voted off.

After Fash bore the brunt in week one, it's down to the campers to decide who does the trials in week two and I stick my hand up to do a couple. One is called the Jungle Slide, which sees me attached to a bungee rope and scrambling up a muddy slope to grab a star. Once you've got the star, the rope twangs you back to the bottom of the slope to start again.

The first run, I go for it, but by the time I start my second foray, I realise that I'm already out of puff. I've burnt up the fifty calories' worth of food I've eaten all day and got zero energy. I get halfway up the slope before being twanged sideways down the slope into an eel-infested swamp.

I grit my teeth and keep going and manage to get four out of a possible six stars, but I'm absolutely zonked. After a week or so of not getting enough nutrition, your body does kind of shut down to preserve the little energy you've got. I have a great ability to look like shit even when I feel fine, but that trial really knocks me back for a couple of days. I'm really sleepy from lack of food, can't be bothered to shave, can't be bothered to wash – standards really start to slip.

Just at the right time, the producers send in letters from friends and family for us to read out to each other. Everyone else's letter is about missing them, how everyone back home is supporting them. Dawn's message is more along the lines of: 'Carry on being yourself, but stop going to sleep all the time, stop swearing so much and have a shave.' Just like being back at home.

It really makes me laugh and gives me a second wind. Reading between the lines, it's her way of egging me on to cheer up a little bit. We've all been getting very lethargic and she knows that when I get like that, I *really* do get like that. I'm so glad she didn't send me the standard tear-jerking sort of letter.

As I'm told later by Dawn, the letter nearly didn't happen. She was asked to write a letter to me, but when she spoke to some of the other friends and relatives staying out there, they hadn't been asked. Then the producers told her that they were having trouble getting hold of Fash's wife via his agent and he might not get one, so she asked for a guarantee that everyone would get a letter, because she felt it would be a killer for someone to be sat there while everyone else gets a letter from a loved one and they don't.

They eventually make that assurance and on the night, I read out one for Fash from his wife, so I assume they managed to contact her.

I'm so glad we did get the letters, because the next morning, I get my razor out and have a shave and jump in the pool. Immediately I feel refreshed and ready for the last few days.

Toyah and Antony are the next two people to be voted off, leaving just Wayne, Linda, Fash and me in the camp. I've still not found myself in the bottom two so I must be doing something right, although I'm not sure what that something is.

However, again, unbeknown to me, the way I'm being portrayed to the outside world is changing. Watching the daily programmes, Dawn has got the impression that the producers have favourites they're pushing towards the final. I've been among them in the first week or so, where the edited bits of footage all seem to show me in a good light and the bookies install me as one of the favourites to win. But perhaps to shake things up a bit in the second week, the new angle of the coverage is that I might be cracking up in there.

On the companion show, *I'm a Celebrity. . . Get Me Out of Here! NOW!*, hosted by Mark Durden-Smith and the first series' runner-up Tara Palmer-Tomkinson, Mark says that I've visited the show's psychologist Sandra Scott a few times, implying that I'm struggling, when the producers know perfectly well I've just been asking for more cigarettes! Visits to the psychologist are supposed to be kept private anyway, so Dawn is not happy about that and tells them so.

Meanwhile, on *This Morning* back in the UK, their celebrity psychiatrist Raj Persaud has been hinting that perhaps, for my own good, people shouldn't vote to keep me in.

They show one piece of footage of me in the Bush Telegraph one night where I'm wibbling on about missing alcohol and fags:

'I think I might be an alcoholic. . .' I begin, with a laugh. 'I think I might have a lychee Martini. . . or a pint of lager. . . pint of lager might be nice. . . Cold pint of lager might be nice. . . I don't really like the wine. . . I like red wine. . . What's the point of not having a fag? You're going to die – well, you're going to die anyway. . . You ain't got any fags have ya? No one's got any fags. . . I think I'm turning into a ****ing raving lunatic, y'know. . .'

Now I can see why people watching this rambling diatribe might think that I'm in the throes of a mental breakdown, but it's actually just me feeling tired, hungry and talking nonsense.

Anyway, whether all these shenanigans were factors or not, with just one day to go, I'm voted in the bottom two for the first time. It's me or Wayne for the chop and unfortunately for Wayne, he gets the heave-ho, leaving me in the final with Fash and Linda.

Because of the time difference, the evictions always take place at about 7am, so we have a full day ahead of us and to win ourselves a nice banquet in the evening, all three of us have to do Bushtucker Trials. We can each win five stars and the more stars we get the bigger the feast.

Linda is tasked with moving five eels from one tank to another. Fash has to walk across a big, rotating log above a swamp and try to grab stars hanging down above his head without falling off. When it's my turn, I meet Ant and Dec in a clearing near the camp to do the Bushtucker Bonanza.

A table is laid for me with ten plates, each covered with wooden cloches, and a wooden goblet of water. One by one, a bushtucker 'delicacy' is revealed alongside one of my favourite dishes from back home to tempt me to fail the task.

First course is a beetle larva, delightfully served inside the dried dung it was found in in the wild.

'That's disgusting,' I say, cracking open the dung shell. 'Oh, I can't eat that, mate. I can't eat that. . . hold on, hold on. . .'

'Or Phil, there's that or the shepherd's pie,' says Dec, lifting the cover from the other plate.

I poke the larva around the plate, contemplating my fate. And it moves.

'That's disgusting, man. . .'

I pick up the larva and turn to Ant, who's leaning casually on the back of my chair: '*That* is edible?'

'So they tell me,' he shrugs.

I sit there psyching myself up for about another minute, holding this thing between my thumb and forefinger, not able to look at it, before swallowing it down whole with a glug of water.

Next up are green ants running about on the plate. Knowing there's likely to be worse to come, I quickly pick up a handful and chug them down without waiting to see the alternative option.

Meanwhile, a waiter — well, a big Aussie bloke from the production crew, all dressed up in the full penguin gear — is pouring a frothy pint of lager. He deliberately wafts it right in front of my face, before passing it to Dec, who takes a sip: 'Oh, lovely, that is,' he says, putting it down next to me. 'Just leave that there because you might want it later.'

He's laughing, and I'm laughing, thinking, 'You little bastard.'

The third course on the tasting menu is pupa of a large moth — or a big plate of chips and ketchup. The pupa looks absolutely horrid and I really have to steel myself to take it down.

'Awwwww, auuughhhh! Oh my God. Oh. My. Godddd. Arrrggggggh! ****ing ****!'

I pick it up, shove it in my mouth and slurp it down with a big gulp of water, but it almost repeats on me.

'That's it, swig the water down – go on,' says Dec, as he moves swiftly out of projectile vomiting range.

The camp doc comes over and hands me a bucket as I'm bent over double.

'Phil, Phil – couple of deep breaths. . .'

After taking a couple of minutes to recover, I ignore a steak with mushrooms and onions in favour of a handful of mealworms.

Just one to go and Ant lifts off the plate cover to reveal my dessert: two big fat witchetty grubs.

'You only have to eat one,' he says. Oh good. That's alright then. They're both wriggling about and seem very friendly with each other.

'Look, they're ****ing getting it on on the plate. . .'

'It'd be awful to split them up now,' laughs Ant.

'Apparently, the way to eat them is to grab the head and bite the body off,' advises Dec. 'Swallow the body. I don't know if that's any help. . .'

'If I do that, that's done, yeah?'

'Yeah that constitutes eating it, you don't have to eat the head.'

With no further ado, I pick it up, bite into it and witchetty-grub guts explode in my mouth and up my nose.

I swallow it with the help of a goblet full of water. It's hideous, but I manage to keep it down and as a reward to myself I down what's left of the pint of lager in one and depart the jungle dinner party stage left.

Between us, we get fourteen out of fifteen stars – Linda only missed out on one because she dropped an eel – so we have a hearty last supper in the evening. It's lovely to have some proper grub at last, but we're all full up within a few bites and retire to our camp beds holding our stomachs.

We're all up bright and early the next day and it's about quarter to seven when Ant and Dec rock up into the camp to announce the final results. They are accompanied by all the previous evictees, all looking suitably clean and fresh after spending a night or five back at the Versace.

Linda is announced in third place and she heads over the rope bridge with Ant and Dec to the treehouse for her interview. This leaves me and Fash battling to be crowned King of the Jungle – although, 'battling' is probably overstating it as we're just sitting round a campfire having a cup of tea with the rest of the contestants.

I can't wait to see Dawn, who by this point is feeling nervous and excited, on her own in a jeep near the treehouse. Linda's husband Chris was with her, but he's been ushered down to be reunited with Linda. About half an hour later, when Ant and Dec descend back into the camp to announce the winner, someone from the production crew fetches her to watch it all on a screen in a tented area next to the treehouse.

Dec gives it the big build-up: 'The British public have decided and the winner. . . and King of the Jungle. . . is. . .'

The pause is so ridiculously long all of us burst out laughing, before Ant shouts: 'Phil!'

It's hugs and slaps on the back all round. Meanwhile, up at the treehouse, everyone's congratulating Dawn.

'What do you mean?' she says, totally confused. In all the noise and hubbub around her, she thought she heard 'Fash'.

While ITV break for adverts, Ant, Dec and the rest of them dash across the bridge and I wait to be called.

As I make my own way into the treehouse a few minutes later, doffing my hat to applause from the people gathered around, I'm looking round for Dawn. I spot her, but she ducks down to hide when I catch her eye. Maybe I'm not supposed to see her yet?

Ant and Dec direct me to sit down on a wooden 'throne' with vines, flowers and a snake twisting around the back of it. . . hang on, a snake?

'It's rubber, don't worry. . .'

After the experiences of the past couple of weeks, you can't be too careful.

'I can't believe it – I only turned up for a bit of kip for two weeks,' I tell the boys.

'The British public have enjoyed watching you,' says Dec. 'And someone else who's enjoyed watching you, has been your girl, Dawnie. Let's get her in.'

She runs in and we have a hug.

'I've missed you so much, baby.'

'Come over, Dawn, come and join us,' says Dec. 'How bad does he smell?' he asks. 'Tell us, be honest.'

'I didn't really notice actually, I'm so overwhelmed to see him,' she says turning to me. 'Congratulations – you deserve it.'

Dawn has never been on TV and never wanted to be. She blushes and is a bit nervous, but speaks very well. (She tells me later, that she got transfixed by Dec's long eyelashes – he has really long eyelashes – and had to keep telling herself not to keep looking at them in case it looked like she fancied him.) It's the first time I've been in the spotlight on TV outside of cricket, so it's all a bit whoosh for me, too.

Tara Palmer-Tomkinson presents me with a crown of ferns and wooden sceptre, to officially anoint me as King of the Jungle.

Dec asks: 'So you've got no regrets?'

'No, no regrets at all. I went in there real happy and I've come out happy too.'

'Phil, the time has come for you to go back to your life of luxury. You're a celebrity – get yourself out of here!'

Ah yes, back to our luxurious terraced house in Sutton with walls so thin you can hear the people next door go for a wee.

Fireworks go off, flutes of champagne are distributed and Dawn and I walk off into an explosion of camera flashes from the assembled press photographers. I'm surprised by the amount of them there.

After a bath back at the Versace, an ill-advised McDonald's meal which my stomach swiftly rejects, doing an exclusive interview and photos with Dawn for one of the tabloids and a wrap party that evening, the next day we fly home. As part of the newspaper deal, Dawn and I aren't allowed to speak to any other reporters and we are told to avoid being photographed together until the article is published.

So when we emerge through the arrivals gate at Heathrow, we're walking well apart. If I thought there were a lot of photographers the day before, this is another level. There's a mob of paparazzi the like of which I've never seen before in all my days touring with the England cricket team.

When I speak to Mike, he tells me that nearly thirteen million people watched the final show.

'Bloody hell, really?' This is a lot bigger than I imagined.

And because I won, my chosen charity, the Leukaemia Research Fund, will receive the lion's share of the income from the phone vote, amounting to around £400,000. Fantastic.

Two cars are waiting, one to take Dawn home and another to whisk me off to a TV studio for *The Jonathan Ross Show*.

Mike meets me in the dressing room and reels off a long list of offers he's received for me to do personal appearances, endorsements, advertisements and the like. I'd been worried about what I was going to do after the show, but unemployment doesn't look like it's going to be an issue for a while at least.

We're both dancing round for joy, like that scene in *Only Fools and Horses* when Del Boy and Rodney finally become millionaires. I'm a guest on Jonathan's show because they won the bid to have me on ahead of other chat shows. People bidding for me to be on a sofa and have a chat with them about witchetty grubs? I can't believe it – I've been sitting in the jungle scratching my arse for two weeks and all this has been going on.

The show itself passes in something of a jet-lagged blur – we mostly talk about cigarettes and my £500 offer to buy one from a cameraman – and a car is laid on to take me home afterwards. When I get there, Dawn is already asleep. After a surreal, manic 48 hours, everything is quiet. I plonk myself down on the sofa in the living room for a few minutes, trying to process what has happened.

The next morning, Dawn is up early, doing chores. She's done a load of washing the day before and gives me a big pile of clothes to take to the ironing lady down the road.

After dropping off the washing, I pop to the newsagent to pick up a couple of things, only to discover my name plastered across the front page of every tabloid. It's really hitting me now how big this show was. What I hadn't bargained for is the angle some of papers are going with which, to my astonishment, is a supposed flirtation between me and Linda Barker in the camp.

One of the papers has a photo of us all coming through the arrivals gate at Heathrow and there's me and Dawn walking a distance apart. Linda happens to be walking next to me and in the photo it looks like she's looking over at Dawn and Dawn is staring back at her, po-faced. God knows how many frames they had to sort through to find that split-second image, but it makes it look like Dawn's got the hump with me, when the reality is we've been told to walk out separately. And we've just been on a plane for nigh on 24 hours, albeit in the first-class cabin, so we were feeling a bit spaced out.

I had a good laugh with Linda in the camp as I did with all my campmates, but the idea of some sort of blossoming romance is news to me, and, no doubt, to Linda and her husband. Dawn is as baffled as me by the newspaper coverage. She watched all the shows while we were out in Oz and she would certainly have told me if she'd had a problem with anything I'd done in the camp.

It's all very odd and the next day I have another weird experience walking up to Sutton High Street to do some shopping and get a McDonald's. As I'm wombling along, I become aware of a growing group of people following me. There's a few cries of 'Hello, Tuffers'. 'It's the King of the Jungle!', 'Well done, mate', that sort of thing and I'm waving and saying hello. More and more people keep tagging along, people of all ages, male and female. By the time I reach McDonald's, there's about 200 people trailing me and they all cram in after me. Everyone's really friendly, asking for autographs and to take photos, but the crush inside the restaurant is getting rather dangerous for all concerned and eventually the manager has to call the police to help me get out and disperse the crowd.

Blimey, so this is what it's like to be famous.

A couple of evenings later, Dawn and I are at home together watching Graham Norton's chat show. They show a clip of our final chat with Ant and Dec on *I'm a Celebrity* when I'm saying to Dawn: 'I missed you so much.'

Dawn just replies, deadpan: 'I noticed.'

They cut back to Graham: 'Ooh, look at Dawn's face – just wait till she gets him home.'

'That's not how I meant it!' Dawn says. 'It was a joke about how often you kept talking about me in there. I wasn't trying to be cutting. I was just so nervous and embarrassed to be on camera, the main thought going through my head was: "Don't faint, don't faint."'

I know Graham was only making a throwaway joke, but a narrative seems to be building in the media that there's some problem between Dawn and me.

The weekend after our return to Britain, Dawn heads off to Edinburgh for a friend's hen weekend. As she's waiting for the flight back at the airport, she's reading a Sunday newspaper and comes across a picture of us: Dawn standing at the front door with a stern look on her face and me carrying a big pile of clothes and the headline news is that she's chucked me out of the house.

She wracks her brain to work out what the hell this is all about and then realises the photo was taken the morning after *The Jonathan Ross Show*.

Dawn's most upset because in the photo she's got her hair scraped back and because she's wearing a coat she loves – the most expensive she's ever owned – and, in her own words, she looks 'like Arthur Daley'.

The girls with her are saying, 'What's that coat all about?' – for some reason it doesn't photograph well.

It's quite comical and we have a laugh about it. There we were just going about our daily chores, happy as Larry. All of a sudden, it's 'Dawn throws Phil out!' We're like, 'Whaaat?'

We've been as happy as ever since returning from Australia, but you can walk around with a big smile on your face all day long and if a paparazzo with a long lens reels off enough photos, there is bound to be one where you don't look full of the joys of spring.

After me being filmed 24/7 in the Queensland jungle for a fortnight, we've both been thrust into this celebrity jungle where our every move is scrutinised and often the totally wrong conclusion is being reached. It's an eye-opener for both of us, especially Dawn, about the weird world of celebrity.

We're beginning to realise why Hollywood celebrities get so paranoid and don't leave their houses without consulting their stylist and making sure every hair is in place first. We had no concept of any of this stuff before. We're just normal people going about our business and suddenly people are taking pictures and making up stories about us.

Thankfully, not all the press coverage is delving into our private life – there is plenty of nice stuff written as well. A reporter from the sports section of the BBC website gets hold of my dad for his thoughts on my jungle adventure and I can always rely on my dad for a positive review.

'I thought he was absolutely marvellous on the show,' he says. 'He was absolutely as he is in reality. . . Phil played in his first organised cricket game when he was four. I can still see him with his bat, and pads bigger than he was. We always hoped he'd be a cricketer, but this kind of celebrity was never on the agenda.'

Typically, though, Dad can't resist getting in a dig about the England cricket selectors while he's at it: 'What you see is what you get with Phil. There is no pretence at all. That is part of the reason why he hasn't got twice as many England caps. . . When I was watching that Bushtucker Trial, which was pretty horrendous, it made me smile. He has put up with so much from the England selectors in the last fifteen years, eating a few measly worms and bugs isn't that much different really.'

Haha – nice one, Dad.

The main focus of the article is whether I might un-retire and return to cricket. Dad says that he thinks I would still like to be playing – 'There's no blacker day for a sportsman than when you hang up your boots' – but he doesn't know 'whether I will or not'.

Middlesex club secretary Vinny Codrington – last seen by me mouth agape in shock while Gus and I had a stand-up row in front of him – is also quoted in the piece and seems open to the idea of a Tufnell come-back: 'We would never say never because players of his quality don't grow on trees. If he wants to come back it would be up to the coach and captain to decide. If the boys decided we needed experience towards the end of the season to avoid relegation or push for the Championship, then I'm sure we would consider him on a match-by-match basis.'

Unfortunately, I don't see this article at the time and Dad doesn't mention it. As the cricket season goes on, I do miss playing, but I assume that Middlesex wouldn't want me back and they never approach me to do so. And, anyway, a three-month contract review had me storming out of the Middlesex Room, what would I do if I had a match-by-match clause? Thanks, but no thanks.

I do receive a couple of offers to play four-day cricket for other coun-ties. As a diehard Middlesex boy, though, I don't want to play for anyone else and the reality is I've got too much on to go back to professional cricket.

For the first few months after *I'm a Celebrity* my feet hardly touch the ground. Almost every day – weekdays and weekends – I'm getting picked up first thing in the morning and pinging about from one place to another – doing TV shows, making personal appearances, etcetera, and finishing up with an after-dinner speaking engagement in the evenings before getting dropped off at home at midnight. Repeat to fade.

People sending cars for me to get around is a great luxury. All I have to do is be up on time, and not worry about driving or catching the tube or train. If I've had a heavy night the night before, I can have a kip in the back of the car.

Dawn and I both know I need to make hay while the sun shines – who knows how long I will be in demand as a 'celebrity' – so it's worth putting the hours in and, in fairness, a lot of the stuff is so much fun it can hardly be termed work.

For instance, one of the first endorsements I get is to be an ambassador for Foster's lager. It's basically my dream job and somewhat dangerous, because, no matter the time of morning or night when I turn up to carry out my ambassadorial duties for them, there's always ice-cold lager on tap for me.

Cricket got me into a few nice events, but this is a different level. Foster's are sponsoring the British Grand Prix and the next thing I know, they're flying me into Silverstone by helicopter. I'm dropped in and taken to this amazing hospitality tent where they sit me down for lunch on a table with Dannii Minogue, former girlfriend of Jacques Villeneuve, and various other glamorous people. I'm looking round and every few seconds doing a double take: 'Hold on, that's the Prince of Monaco. . .?'

After lunch, five Foster's pitgirls make a beeline for me. They take me to visit the pitlane to meet the drivers and I get to have a wander round the cars on the grid before the race begins.

I watch the first two laps from down there and think, 'Oh, it's a bit noisy,' so head back to the hospitality tent to watch what proves to be a memorable race for the wrong reasons unfold on screen, before heading back to watch the last couple of laps live. After eleven laps, a defrocked Roman Catholic priest called Cornelius Horan runs on the track forcing cars coming round Becketts Corner to swerve to avoid hitting him. Ironically, he's wearing a kilt.

It's a blinding day, although I can take or, preferably, leave the helicopter part of the jet-set lifestyle due to my fear of flying. My agent Mike seems to have ignored the memo on that, because soon after, Barratt Homes helicopter me in to open one of their new estates in Battersea. There are loads of grannies there to wave me in and then wave me out again after cutting the ribbon. It's a different kind of glamour to the Grand Prix.

Following my Pied Piper experience in Sutton High Street, I notice that I'm getting recognised much more than I ever have before. My 'fans', or whatever you want to call them, used to consist of lads down the pub and people who were interested in cricket. Since the jungle, it's the whole spectrum from little kids to old dears, including many who know nothing about my cricket career.

Even in the cricket environment that I'm used to, the level of attention on me increases dramatically for a while. For instance, a couple of weeks after returning from Oz, I'm walking into Lord's with Mike and my mate Peter 'Reggie' Hayter, the journalist, to watch England play Zimbabwe. Cricket at Lord's is normally a sedate affair – I might get the odd auto-graph request or shout of 'Alright, Tuffers', when I'm walking round the ground. This time, Reg, me and Mike are having a chat when we hear a cry of 'It's Phil!' and we all turn at once to see a big group of school-children coming towards us from fifty-odd yards away.

At first, I'm thinking, 'Alright, say hello, sign a few autographs,' but within seconds the group has turned into a mob, screaming my name.

'Tufffferrrrrrrs!'

We start walking a bit more briskly, then break into a trot as an ever-growing, ever-more-frenzied throng of people chase me round Lord's. As I glance back, I even spot a couple of elderly Lord's members in their egg-and-bacon ties among them waving their walking sticks at me.

Reggie's running alongside me, blowing out of his arse, keys and mobile phone rattling in his pockets. He looks across at me: 'Why am I bloody running?', but he keeps going anyway.

I'm running, Reggie's running, Mike's running. Everyone's running.

We duck into one of the champagne hospitality tents for a breather, then sneak out the back way, only to be spotted again.

'Tufffferrrrrrrs!'

And so begins another sprint pursued by screaming schoolkids, before diving past a startled attendant and through the doorway opposite the pavilion entrance. On reaching the sanctuary of a room overlooking a real tennis court, we all burst out laughing between wheezes.

'What is going on?. . . And where are we?'

The response I get from people on the street continues to be really positive, but a couple of the newspapers seem to have a different agenda. In June, one of the tabloids runs a story claiming I started a fight in one of the hospitality boxes during the Royal Ascot race meeting.

This is what actually happened. I was there as a guest of BBC Radio 5 Live and late in the afternoon I'm invited into one of the hospitality boxes. Vinnie Jones is in there too, and everyone's a bit pissed. A few minutes later, I'm standing on the balcony with Vinnie holding a glass of champagne and a vol-au-vent, when I hear a commotion inside. I turn

LEFT: My dad Alan and mum Sylvia on their wedding day - they were made for each other.

BELOW: Mum gets her skates on ready for another race at the Ally Pally. Rod Stewart's mum and dad were in the same team as my parents.

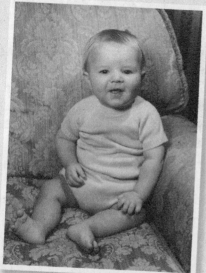

LEFT: Here comes trouble... In 1966, Philip Clive Roderick Tufnell was born.

LEFT: Batting practice in our back garden. Those roses in the background wouldn't have lasted long with our sports-mad family around.

BELOW: Butter wouldn't melt... An angelic-looking Highgate public schoolboy, a couple of years before I was expelled.

LEFT: With my big brother Greg, all dressed up and ready to go to Highgate junior school. Greg was the model student. Me? Not so much.

BELOW: I used to play a bit of cricket, you know... Having a bowl for England versus Australia in Adelaide, 1995.

ABOVE: Spinner with attitude: you might detect a hint of youthful rebelliousness in this portrait.

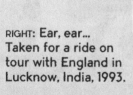

RIGHT: Ear, ear... Taken for a ride on tour with England in Lucknow, India, 1993.

FAR LEFT: Enjoying the best of matches against Australia at The Oval in August 1997.

LEFT: Taking 11 wickets for 93 runs in one match is thirsty work...

BELOW LEFT: The Aussie batsmen made me suffer plenty during my career, so it was nice to get one over on the likes of Mark Waugh for a change.

ABOVE: Hopping around at the crease against the Aussies at The Oval in 2001.

LEFT: More classic Tufnell strokeplay - clean bowled in Cape Town, January 2000, in my penultimate Test match.

Yum, a handful of mealworms...
Facing the 'Bushtucker Bonanza' Trial.

Messing around in the jungle. Despite the lack of food,
alcohol and cigarettes, I enjoyed my time in the camp.

'You've just got to swing over that gorge and hit the stars with a stick, Tuffers...' Ant and Dec gleefully reveal another Bushtucker Trial.

King of the Jungle! I had no idea then of the consequences – both good and bad – of my new-found 'celebrity' status.

LEFT: After turning down the chance to be a Playboy TV presenter, my first major gig after *I'm a Celebrity* was as a team 'captain' on *They Think It's All Over*.

BELOW: Gurning for glory – my regular right-hand man Jonathan Ross did most of the talking and I just tried to keep up.

around to see three or four blokes rolling around clumping each other. I stay out on the balcony watching it all unfold. Champagne flutes, sandwiches and smoked salmon are flying everywhere. By the time everyone has calmed down, the box is absolutely destroyed.

It's a bit annoying to be blamed for all that, but far more concerning to me are the continuing attempts by journalists to pry into my relationship with Dawn.

Our neighbours tell us about people knocking on their door asking questions about us.

'You must be happy for Phil and Dawn. . . oh, what are they like?'

'They're very nice. . .'

'Ever heard them rowing?'

All they have to say is, 'Well, I'm sure they do row like any couple. . .' and that turns into something else on the printed page.

To start with, we're left wondering why people are picking holes in our relationship when there's nothing to pick holes in. We're ploughing through all of this – telling ourselves, 'We're good with it, we're good with it. . .', but as time passes, the pressure grows on our relationship and cracks begin to appear.

Part of the problem is that my work diary is booked solid week after week so I'm away a lot and we hardly see each other. Dawn isn't invited to all the dos I go to and even if she is, when she's got Alana to look after, she's not going to be coming to Ritzy's in Northampton on a Tuesday night.

After coming back from Australia, she went back to do the final module of her course to become a fitness instructor and from just being Dawn, she found herself being labelled as 'Phil Tufnell's girlfriend', which she found very weird.

When she does come to a function with me, people can be very dismissive of her to the point of rudeness, almost like she's invisible.

It'd be, 'Phil, Phil over here. . .'

'Hello, this is my girlfriend Dawn. . .'

'Yeah, yeah. . . anyway, Phil, tell us about the jungle. . .'

Or she'll come back to the dinner table after nipping to the bathroom, only to find someone has sat down in her seat talking to me. Even once they've realised they are in her seat, they don't move to let her sit down. That happens more often than you'd think it would.

She's used to people being positive about her and nice to her. If people were ever rude to her before, she would say something, but she finds herself biting her tongue because she doesn't want to cause me a problem.

Understandably, she starts to feel sidelined, that my life is always taking precedence and she's losing herself a bit. Where does she fit in to all this?

The first time we have a night out together, just the two of us, after the jungle, is two months later, 13 July, on the second anniversary of when we met. We go to the Bluebird restaurant on the King's Road and as we arrive, a group of women spot me and come over.

One asks Dawn politely: 'It's our hen night – do you mind if we have our picture taken with Phil?'

Dawn says: 'No, not a problem.'

'Oh, it must get on your nerves people asking for photos – you must get it all the time.'

'Well, I don't mind you getting a photo, but it is our anniversary tonight. . .' replies Dawn.

'Tough,' retorts another girl sharply and plonks herself down on my lap for the group photo.

I don't want this stranger sitting on me and she's being so rude to Dawn.

Dawn makes light of the situation, saying: 'Well, you go and get the stag and I'll sit on his lap, shall I?' But it's another example of people being rude to her.

This isn't the first time women in particular have been quite bitchy towards Dawn. I do the photo, but I feel bad afterwards that I haven't said anything to this girl. I have no problem signing autographs and doing pictures with people, but why should I have my picture taken with you and your friends if you are going to be rude to my girlfriend?

The penny drops that while the work I'm getting post-jungle is all well and good, Dawn is the most important person in my life and I need to look after her. If we're out together and someone is being rude, don't just let it go just to avoid making a scene or because someone's paying me a few quid to be at their event.

I also need to get things a bit more structured to make time for her and Alana, rather than dashing up and down the country to do every last job offered to me. I'm not prepared to sacrifice my relationship with Dawn for the sake of a quick buck. So I'll pick and choose the things to be involved in. That's easier said than done in the short term, though, because my diary is booked up for the entire summer and they are work commitments I can't really get out of.

Four days after our anniversary, I turn up to film an ITV show called *With A Little Help From My Friends*. The concept of the show is to get a celebrity to build a facility for a charity – in my case a cricket pavilion for the London Community Cricket Association, which I became president of back in 2000. It's a great charity (more on that later) but imagine my surprise when I rock up on the first day to discover that Linda Barker is the presenter and, among the old schoolfriends they've roped in to help with the project, is one of my ex-girlfriends. I'm looking round half-expecting my ex-wives and Duncan Fletcher to walk round the corner next. Unbelievable.

Dawn knows the whole Linda Barker thing after the jungle was a farce, but how am I going to tell her an ex-girlfriend is part of our building crew? Stupidly, I don't, thinking it's the last thing we need right now. Of course, a few days later there's a bullshit article in the press making out that we've rekindled our romance. And, unsurprisingly, when she sees the story, Dawn is furious that I haven't told her.

Over the next few weeks, the pressures on our relationship continue to come from all angles and gradually take their toll.

In theory my divorce had been finalised before the jungle, but I have to go back to court on the basis that I've earned more money. An interview with my ex-wife appears in a tabloid where she rants about what I'm supposedly like.

When I appear on a panel show with Jonathan Ross, he makes a joke about Dawn chucking me out. He really catches me on the hop and all I can say is 'Thanks mate'. He also asks me if I'd 'like to give Jordan one?' Dawn wants to kill him for that, but when she next sees him, she kills him with kindness instead.

Of course, it was just Jonathan being Jonathan, messing about, but it adds more weight to the public impression that my relationship with Dawn is breaking up at a time when things are awkward between us.

We are arguing more and more – on the phone mostly because I'm still running all over the place – and *The Mirror* newspaper in particular seems to print almost daily updates on our relationship status. Whereas back in May, there was no truth in what the papers were writing about us, now they are on the right track. They seem to know a lot of detail about what's happening and our arguments and it's making us both feel very paranoid. Who's telling them this stuff?

It's horrible to be in a situation where our relationship has become a story and all the media people involved seem to be interested in is it ending with a break-up. They've got snippets of facts and are distorting them to fit that narrative. Because there are elements of truth to the things written, over time Dawn begins to believe that it might all be true.

The arguments and intolerable pressure on us both come to a head one night in late September when I go out, get drunk with some mates and don't return home till the morning, by which time Dawn has chucked all my clothes out the window. She's had enough.

We spend the next two weeks apart and they are two of the worst weeks of my life.

It seems like my reputation as this boozing, womanising bad boy of cricket has preceded me into this celebrity world I've stumbled into and it's easiest to pin me down as that person and nothing else. I'm trying to break out of this image people have of me, but it's like people aren't going to let me do that without a fight. Pulling an all-nighter without calling Dawn to let her know where I was is just the sort of irresponsible behaviour that got me that reputation in the first place. When she met me, knowing that I'd been married a couple of times before, she could have thought, 'What kind of bloke are you?' but she didn't. Now she is really starting to wonder.

If I had really wanted to continue with the partying lifestyle, what a position to be in after winning *I'm a Celebrity*. The world has opened up to me and I could be out there going mental; in my teens and twenties that is exactly what I would have done. But the reality is that even though I had a lot of fun during my cricket career, there was often a lot of pain behind my behaviour. I rarely had any peace of mind or feeling of being settled and contented. I was always chasing the next buzz.

If I had been single, I would have been an absolute liability these past few crazy months and I've been so thankful to have Dawn there to keep me grounded. She enjoys a party as much as me and it isn't like she's stopped me going to these functions night after night, but she knows when I need to slow down. I can go out, have a drink, a dance and a laugh, but none of that is as important to me as being with her and having the settled home life I've been searching for all these years. There's nothing worse than being the oldest swinger in town and it would be a bit sad if I was still behaving like a *Loaded* lad in my late thirties.

It's taken a while, but, contrary to popular opinion, I think I've grown up a bit. I know I want to be with Dawn, but it looks like it might be over and certain sections of the media are chiselling away at the cracks.

Journalists doorstep Dawn, slipping notes through the letterbox: 'Can we talk to you? Call this number. . .' Newspapers are offering fortunes to her for an exclusive and meanwhile writers and photographers are tracking both of us and writing stories about what one or other of us is supposedly doing and who we're seeing.

In the end, ironically, it's their snooping that brings us back together.

One story describes how a tall man was seen leaving Dawn's house by the back way. The man was in fact Freddie, a very good friend of both of ours – and he's actually quite short. He'd come over to see if Dawn was alright but she'd spotted press photographers outside and suggested he left via the back garden gate.

Meanwhile Dawn was told I was staying at a house with another woman. It took a while for Dawn to realise that the woman in question lives upstairs from our mutual friends Jen and James where I was actually staying. Someone had obviously followed me to that address and put two and two together and made five. Apart from the fact that I was with Jen and James, the girl upstairs is highly surprised to discover that I am her new lover as she is a lesbian.

We eventually agree to meet up at a hotel in Wimbledon and spend a couple of days together to talk everything through. We haven't had a chance to stop for six months so it's great to just have a bit of quiet time to take a breather, step back and analyse the situation. Those two tall tales (well, short in Freddie's case) have really brought home to both of us how the truth is being skewed and we are allowing people who don't know or care about us to dictate our lives. We had a really strong relationship before all of this *I'm a Celebrity* madness and despite everything that's happened, we still love each other and want to be together.

We decide to draw a line under it all, because it's breaking up something that is really good for no reason. It's been tough, really tough, and we've had to cope with the sort of intrusion into our private lives that most people will never experience and we've withstood the onslaught. Whatever happens between us in future, we aren't going to let ex-wives, ex-boyfriends, newspapers, ex-associates and the negative side of things get in the way. We're a team and our relationship is the most important thing. This is what we want. All the rest is just noise.

It's a huge turning point in our relationship and in my life. Over the next few months, I trim my work schedule to make sure I'm not away weekend after weekend and we spend much more time together. Instead of feeling imprisoned by my new-found celebrity, we enjoy the fringe benefits and make it work for us. Our communication improves and the trust returns until we're back to how we were before I ever ate a witchetty grub. In fact, we're stronger than ever as a couple.

In April 2004, Dawn joins me on a 'Tuffers on Tour' trip organised by Paragon for England fans to watch the last two Tests of the West Indies versus England series. The tour starts in Barbados for the third Test in Bridgetown and finishes in Antigua where the final match is played.

The England team under the leadership of my old mate Fletch and led by captain Michael Vaughan are climbing back towards the pinnacle of world cricket and dominate the series, going into the final Test with an unassailable 3-0 lead. However, in the drawn game at Antigua Recreation Ground, the West Indian captain and legendary batsman Brian Lara rises above the mediocrity of his team-mates to score a world-record innings of 400 not out.

Lara's innings brings back memories for me because I was one of the bowlers who served it up when he set the previous world record of 375 back in 1994, also in the final Test on the same ground. That time, we were down 3-1 in a five-match series against a strong Windies side, so the series was already lost, but we'd just beaten them in Barbados so we came into the game with a bit more confidence. Things were looking good when we had them two wickets down for just twelve runs on the first morning. But Lara had come in at number three and he just made it look ridiculously easy – everything was hitting the middle of his bat from ball one.

It was an amazing innings. He never played any huge, risky shots – he hit 45 fours in total, no sixes – but every time I looked up at the scoreboard he seemed to have added another ten or twenty runs to his total. It was brilliantly skilful batting. As hard as we tried, all of our bowlers were powerless to stop this genius at work. The whole thing had an air of inevitability about it.

He'd scored about sixty runs by the time I was summoned to bowl. At the end of my first over, skipper Mike Atherton toddles over to have a word with me. Usually, the captain will give you a bit of encouragement about how you might get the batsman out, but instead he says: 'Brian's batting well today, he might break the record.'

I'm thinking 'He's still got three hundred-odd to go, you overeducated twat – what do you know?'

By the end of the first day, Brian had scored 164, 320 by the end of the second day, in sight of fellow West Indian Sir Garry Sobers' record of 365. Athers studied history at Cambridge University, but it seemed he could also predict the future.

There was always a great atmosphere at the Antigua Rec. It's a rickety little ground, but it was packed with 10,000-odd people and they were bouncing along to Calypso tunes played by a DJ between each ball. He turned the music up every time a boundary was scored, but as Brian approached the record, there didn't seem to be any breaks in the music at all. I think the DJ just left it on and went off to enjoy the party.

When Brian drew level with Sobers' record score, our fast bowler Chris Lewis was bowling. I'm fielding nearby and Lewie looks at me as if to say, 'What do I bowl here?'

'Make him do something to earn the runs,' I tell him. 'Don't just let him have it easy.'

Chris follows my advice and bowls him a bouncer, which Lara effortlessly swats away for four runs.

After that it's just carnage for about twenty minutes. There's a mass pitch invasion, people doing cartwheels in celebration and mobbing Brian. Sir Garry Sobers comes on the pitch to congratulate him. I just sit down in the sunshine watching the whole spectacle while people try to sell me chicken feet and corn soup (which I decline as we were halfway through a session) and enjoying, in an odd way, being a small part of history.

That day, we did eventually get him out for 375. His innings had lasted for 12 hours and 46 minutes. If you added up every innings I had in 42 Test matches, I don't think I spent anywhere near that at the crease.

Ten years on, it's a privilege to see the master reclaim the record (Australian Matthew Hayden had scored 380 a few months before) in a shade under 13 hours of batting and it's a whole lot easier to watch this time, with a cold beer in my hand, from the other side of the boundary.

I'd also bowled against Brian in Antigua on our 1998 tour and that time he 'failed', just scoring the 89 runs. So over three Lara innings at the Antigua Rec – one watching and two bowling against him (although I might as well have been a spectator for all the success I had bowling to him), I've watched him bat for nearly 28 hours, score 864 runs and get out twice, giving him a respectable average of 432 over the three innings.

After a great trip, when we get to Antigua airport, we discover the plane back home to England is overbooked. Dawn needs to get back for Alana, and luckily, Warren Rumsey, whose travel company organised the tour with Paragon, manages to get her a seat.

A couple of days before, Dawn and I were looking at engagement rings at a shop in St. John's, the capital city of Antigua. I think it was more out of curiosity on Dawn's side in case we did decide to get married some time in the future. But I've made up my mind already, so with time to kill, I seize the chance to go back to the jewellery store and buy the ring she liked best.

The next available flight is an overnighter and I arrive back to our house in Sutton about half seven on a weekday morning.

I've decided now's the time. I knock on the door and Dawn opens it:

'I've got something to say.'

'Well, if you've got something to say, you better get down on one knee.'

'Oh, you know what I'm going to say!'

She always knows what I'm going to do before I do it.

Just as my left knee touches the ground, our next-door neighbour comes out of his door on his way to work. Our front doors are right next to each other. As I turn my head to see him, I catch sight of another neighbour over the road also coming out of their house, looking across.

I'm thinking: 'Oh no – why didn't I wait till I got inside?' and start to get up again.

'No, no. . . stay there,' says Dawn, smiling at my discomfort.

So I grit my teeth, get back down on one knee, hold out the ring: 'Will you marry me?'

'Yes.'

As we embrace the neighbours give us a little round of applause.

We decide to book our wedding for summer 2005 and, once news of our engagement gets out, various celebrity magazines – OK!, HELLO! and the like – make offers to cover it. They are talking substantial sums of money, enough to make us sit down and think about it. I talk to a couple of people who've sold exclusives to their wedding and they say that it's a bit weird because they invite celebrities who you might not know that well to give the whole occasion an added sprinkle of stardust. It's a bit like being on a day-long photo shoot, because the magazines want to get plenty of photos to fill a few pages for their money.

In the end it's not a difficult decision to make. After all we've been through to get to this point, we want our wedding day to be ours and ours alone, no stress. The last thing we want is it to turn into another working day. A couple of years on from the jungle, it's not as if the work is slowing down, so much so that we're struggling to find ten days when I'm free.

To make sure it really is our day, we decide to get married in Mauritius and then set up a marquee in the garden of our new house in Kingswood, Surrey, and throw a big party for 185 friends and family when we get back.

Knowing how bad I am with dates, Dawn wants to schedule the wedding for 13 July, exactly four years to the day that we met, so I only have one anniversary date to remember in future. In the end, some work commitments booked months in advance that I can't get out of mean that we can't actually do that day, so we go for 7 July instead. By moving the wedding forward a few days we'll have more time to relax.

When we fly out to Mauritius about five days before, all the stresses of the past two years seem to melt away. We've got a beautiful chalet on the beach and it's orchids and champagne all the way.

Two nights before the wedding, we have a big night out and wake up with raking hangovers. We have to be down at the local registry office for 9.30am to do the marriage declaration, which makes it all legal in the UK. After nibbling at breakfast, we jump in a cab to town.

When we arrive, we join the back of a massive queue of tourist couples that has already formed. A few of them look like they're coming off a merry night out, too, and it's roasting hot in the building. We're standing there, shuffling forward every couple of minutes, both feeling more and more queasy. Then, suddenly, before I have time to dash to the toilet, my stomach does a cartwheel and I throw up, which makes me really popular.

'Oh God, I'm so sorry. . .'

Thankfully, a man with a mop and bucket soon arrives to clean up the crime scene.

When we finally reach the front of the queue, we are ushered into a little room where we hand over our passports to be checked and then we each make the legal declaration. Being a leftie, I hold up the wrong hand to start with doing mine, but eventually we get through it and head back to the resort to lie on the sun-loungers and recover from the previous night's exertions.

Later on, we're thrilled to hear news from back home that London's bid to host the 2012 Olympics has been successful.

The weather for our wedding day is fantastic and the beach setting for the ceremony is like paradise. My mate has arranged for a little band to come down and a gay couple we've met out there have agreed to be our witnesses.

Dawn gets transported down to the beach in a golf cart looking gorgeous in her sarong with a white bikini underneath which has 'Just married' written on the back. (In the same shop she got it from there was also a black one with 'Just divorced' on it. Hopefully, that won't ever be needed.)

It's a really simple, small ceremony, just what we want and need – an oasis of calm after a couple of years of madness and final confirmation of what we feel for each other. We've made it through all the craziness and what anyone else thinks about us from now on doesn't matter.

Afterwards, we nip back to our room to freshen up, but flick the telly on to discover the horrifying headlines about a series of suicide bomb attacks across London.

We immediately try to get hold of all our family and friends back home to make sure they are okay. For a while the phone lines are jammed so we can't get through to anyone. It's unlikely that someone we know will have been a victim, but many of the people we know are Londoners who live and work there so we were very concerned until we eventually got through and speak to them.

There's a table set up for us on the beach, but the next couple of hours are a bit weird as we get calls back from people we've left messages for. Thankfully everyone we know is okay, but there are mixed emotions thinking about all the innocent people who've been injured and killed back home. To go from the huge high of winning the Olympics bid to this atrocity the following day is awful for any Londoner.

It's our wedding though, and once we know our nearest and dearest are alright, we enjoy our day. Everything might not be right in the world, but on a beach in Mauritius, I've married my perfect woman and I can't wait to spend the rest of my life with her. It's the best thing I've ever done.

WHO AM I?

Following our summit meeting at that Wimbledon hotel in autumn 2003, as well as structuring my work schedule so I get to spend more time at home with Dawn, if I have to go away for work, I look out for the chance to take Dawn with me. There's no better opportunity than when I do a stint as the presenter of ITV breakfast show *GMTV*'s competitions to win holidays. It's the sort of thing I would never have been considered for if I hadn't 'done the jungle' and it's an absolutely plum job. It involves the terrible hardship of being sent to various exotic locations, being put up in a fantastic hotel for four or five days and filming a few minutes'- worth of footage of me trying out the facilities that the competition winner will enjoy. The item as shown on TV usually ends with me wandering along a white, sandy beach and asking the notoriously simple multiple-choice question that people must answer.

'What colour is red? Is it a) yellow; b) green; or c) red.'

Okay, not that, but a similar level of simplicity.

I pay for Dawn to come with me and we have some amazing experiences together. We get to swim in the stunning Blue Lagoon in Portland, Jamaica. 'The Blue Hole' – as it used to be rather less romantically called before the Brooke Shields' movie *The Blue Lagoon* was filmed there – is surrounded by lush greenery and it's about 200 feet deep. When you dive underwater, you feel like you're suspended in space. It has a mixture of cold freshwater from the underground streams and warm saltwater from the Caribbean Sea, so you get these refreshing changes of temperature as you swim around in it. Absolute paradise.

We also get to swim with dolphins in the Bahamas. I know swimming with dolphins is on a lot of people's bucket lists, but I actually find it a bit weird.

They are trained to come up and dance with you. They can also lift you out of the water; you put on a lifejacket and sort of lie on the water with your legs straight, then two dolphins come up behind you, put their noses under the soles of your feet and power you along and up out of the water.

The director is very keen that I do this and that they get a shot of me saying something to camera while I'm being propelled by dolphin power. Dawn has a go and she comes soaring out of the water, arms wide like Kate Winslet in *Titanic*. When it's my turn it doesn't go so well.

I assume the starting position, but one of my dolphins just keeps circling me, more like Jaws than a friendly dolphin. He's not up for it at all. His trainer says that he's sulking because he's done too much work today. To be honest, I don't blame the poor dolphin. When he was born,

I doubt the height of his ambition was to push an ex-cricketer along by his feet while he yells: 'What colour is red?'

The director asks: 'Can we get a new dolphin please?'

'No, it's too late in the day – they're all tired.'

Instead, my fatigued dolphin agrees to come and have a dance with me while I'm delivering my line. Dolphins have big old mouths and sharp teeth on them. I'm thinking this bloke's going to bite my head off. He's already had a long day, he doesn't want to push me and now he's got his gob a few inches from my nose. I've never seen an unhappy-looking dolphin, but he was the closest.

The only time these *GMTV* jaunts ever threaten to turn into work is in Tenerife, when they want me to enter a medieval jousting tournament. I'm always up for doing something active – stick me on a surfboard and I'll have a go at that – but I haven't ever ridden a horse, so riding and jousting at the same time may be a challenge.

'Oh don't worry, one of the riders will show you how to do it,' says the director.

'Alright then. . .'

But when we get there, we see it's a proper, full-on, choreographed tournament. We watch a couple of the jousters in action and they're in full armour on these ginormous horses, galloping at full pelt and jabbing each other with eight-foot-long lances, then jumping off and having a sword fight.

'I don't think I can do that. I'll die.'

'Hmm, yeah – you might do, actually,' agrees the director, 'we'll have to have a rethink. . .'

In the end, the plan is for me to dress up like Henry VIII, sit down at a table in front of a feast and read out the question, which I think is much better.

I get into costume and while the producers are waiting for the right moment to film the link, Dawn and I have a great time getting stuck into the local vino collapso, a surprisingly agreeable mixture of red wine and Tango, and a large chicken.

By the time I have to do my little bit to camera, I've got a plateful of chicken bones, chicken grease all over my face and am half-pissed on the red wine-Tango cocktail. Being the consummate new TV professional, I still manage to nail my line – after about the twentieth take: 'Whaaah, cull-urrr izzzz rrrred?'

Maybe Dawn and I enjoyed those *GMTV* trips a little bit too much, but they were great fun while they lasted.

After *I'm a Celebrity*, I get offered all sorts of work, but as with the coverage in certain sections of the media of my relationship with Dawn, quite a lot of it pigeonholes me as the lad I was a few years before. To start with, I say yes to pretty much everything, perhaps because I'm so grateful to be in demand when, before the jungle, I didn't really have a clue what I'd do afterwards. Again, though, it's good to have Dawn there to guide me and stop me doing things I might regret.

For instance, soon after the show, I'm asked to officially present the cheque from the *I'm a Celebrity* phone vote to Leukaemia Research Fund. Someone has the bright idea that I should hand over the cheque while naked – except for some strategically placed cricket balls to cover my modesty.

What? No one wants to see that.

That's my first reaction, but I'm delighted to have helped raise so much money from winning the show and sort of go: 'Well, if that's what they want, maybe I'll do it. . .'

But Dawn is like: 'Hang on, that's so unnecessary.'

It's not that she's bothered about me baring all for a laugh, but not in this context. I already have a personal connection to the charity because of my mum, so to strip off doesn't feel right. Once she spells it out to me and to the organisers, everyone agrees and I hand over the big cheque fully clothed.

As time goes on, I start picking and choosing a bit more, thinking more long term about making a career in the media – both sport and enter-tainment – instead of turning up at the opening of an envelope and going '*Wahaaaaay*', like Tuffers circa 1995.

Reality TV is a relatively new thing, but already it's clear that winners have their time in the spotlight and it doesn't last forever. Doing *I'm a Celebrity* has opened doors for me to try things beyond cricket that otherwise would never have been possible, but ultimately I need to find a new career path.

Judging beauty contests, for instance, is not really the sort of thing I want to be doing anymore. It's not exactly a case of reinventing myself, but I no longer want to be the playboy/womaniser that people expect me to be. I can still be a good lad, have fun, but not be that. As Dawn puts it: 'Be careful not to overplay your hand – don't become a caricature of yourself.' I want a proper career after cricket to show there's a bit more about me.

My resolve to lose the playboy image is tested to the maximum when

I'm offered £150,000 to be a presenter on Playboy TV for six months. Turning down money to judge a beauty contest is one thing, but a six-figure sum is hard to ignore. Again, sitting down and discussing the possibility with Dawn helps me to see the bigger picture.

I'm getting chances to do non-cricket shows on mainstream terrestrial television. I've also been doing bits and pieces of cricket-related media for three or four years now – newspaper columns, some radio and TV commentary – and it's something I'd like to do more of. You can count on the fingers of no hands those people who've had a successful career in soft porn, light entertainment and cricket. If I'd been asked when I was a teenager, I might have kissed the Linda Lusardi poster on my bedroom wall and said, 'Thank you very much – where do I sign?' But not now.

In the end, it's an easy decision to politely decline, because there are plenty of other options coming in, via my agent Mike Martin, to take me more in the direction I want to go.

I've been working with Mike since 1998 when he began preparation for my benefit season the following year. He organised 53 events in '99, with help from my brother Greg, including a launch dinner for 1,100 people at a Hilton Hotel in London. If I'm not mistaken, that was the first time I'd ever put on a proper dinner suit and black tie. To fit in with my nickname of 'Cat' – which was more about my ability to take cat-naps at any time of day than my less-than-feline reflexes as a fielder – I also came out wearing a giant Sylvester the Cat head.

That was also the first time I'd ever stood up and talked in front of an audience. I was absolutely bricking it as I was sitting there waiting to be introduced. I had a few notes on people to thank, but otherwise I did the rest off the cuff and it went quite well. People laughed along, there was a great buzz and it gave me the confidence to get into after-dinner speaking.

You get your benefit ten years after becoming a capped player for your county, and the goodwill I felt towards me at that launch event and throughout the year was lovely. That was the first time I actually realised the level of support I had from other people – and what I'd meant to them – during my career. I'd been playing for years, making the odd back-page headline (and one or two unfortunate front-page ones), playing for Middlesex, playing for England, bumping into Middlesex members and them saying 'Hello, Phil – well bowled'. I didn't really understand that people were supporting me not just as a cricketer, but as a person, and they were interested in what I was up to.

I'd ring up people I've never met before, telling them about an event and asking them if they wanted to sponsor it or buy a table, and more often than not the response was so lovely: 'Oh, Phil it's you – yes, love to. Love watching you play. . . you always make me laugh with your antics. . .'

I was really touched that people were willing to put their hands in their pockets and support me. It made me think that I must have done something during my career, whether it was the entertainment value of my best bowling spells – or my terrible batting.

The year went so well, and I got on well with Mike, that it was a natural progression for him to become my agent. I'd never had an agent before, but having my benefit was probably the first time I'd even considered that my cricket career might one day come to an end. It still felt a long way off, but I was looking to dip my toe into the media side of cricket and Mike took that on. My only advice to him was, 'If in doubt, whatever someone offers, ask for double!'

Then in 2001, Greg approached Mike with the idea of setting up a company offering event management and agent services to other sports-people. They both invested fifty-fifty and Paragon Sports Management was born, with me on board as a director and shareholder to help promote the company. That's all been developing nicely and it's been good to have Mike there, since it's all gone crazy for me after the jungle. There were other people lining up to be my agent, making all sorts of promises about what they could do for me, but it was good to be able to stick with someone I knew and trusted to handle my affairs.

Since popping my cherry as an after-dinner speaker at my benefit launch, I'd done a few gigs here and there and that experience really helps me after the jungle when the number of bookings goes through the roof. By this time, I've settled into a format that I'm comfortable with.

The standard night will begin with a meet and greet with the guests, having a beer and a chat and taking photos with them. Then we'll sit down for dinner and ideally I'll be on my feet by about half past nine, quarter to ten.

Rather than just stand up on my own and do a prepared talk, I normally do a Q&A with the compère or comedian they've booked for the night, then open it up to questions from the floor. I think that this gets the best out of me because I'm better when I'm talking off the cuff and reacting to things people ask me, rather than working to some sort of script. It also means that every night is a bit different and I can go off at tangents depending on whatever direction the conversation heads in.

The one thing I have to be wary about is alcohol consumption, because the moment I arrive a glass of fizz or pint of beer is usually thrust in my hand (not that I ever complain about that). Then if the wine is particularly free-flowing during dinner, there's a danger of being rather too merry.

If I go in cold, I'm not so good, but if you have too many, you can lose your sharpness and wit. They used to tell me on *They Think It's All Over*: 'You're two pints of Guinness and a couple of vodka Red Bulls' – that's when I'm ticking, bright, breezy and moving, but not slurring. Half a lager over that and while you might think you're hysterical, you're really not. That's the only thing I have to guard against.

There have been a couple of times when I've got it wrong and not through any great fault of my own, but when my slot to talk was severely delayed for some reason or other. The latest I've had to speak was half eleven and I can vaguely remember staggering up to the stage thinking I'm alright, but then opening my mouth and hearing myself speaking like the *Fast Show* character Rowley Birkin QC: 'Now, led me tell you about the tiiiime, I bowled at Brii-an La-rah. He was a verrr-y, verrry good player. . . who was I talking about? Ah yes – Larrrra. . . By jingo, what a plaayer. . .'

Another embarrassing moment at a dinner function occurs when I'm not actually booked to be a speaker, but am called upon to help out as an auctioneer. It doesn't go well.

That's during Ant and Dec's 2006 *All*Star Cup*, a Ryder Cup-style celebrity golf match played at Celtic Manor in Newport. I represent Team

Europe in the second series, which is screened on ITV, alongside the likes of Chris Evans, Jodie Kidd, Ian Wright, Ross Kemp, Damian Lewis, Ruud Gullit and 78-year-old Bruce Forsyth. The USA team had among them Olympic superstar Michael Johnson, *Dallas* legend Patrick Duffy, shock rocker Alice Cooper, meaty rocker Meat Loaf and actor Jane Seymour playing for her adopted country. Each team of eleven is captained by a pro – in our case, eight-time European Order of Merit winner Colin Montgomerie, while surprise 2004 Open Championship winner Todd Hamilton skippered the Yanks.

Chris Evans, who played in the first series, encouraged me to play – he said it was a great laugh and you also get some great freebies from the sponsors. Indeed, when I get down there, we're all kitted out with a brand-new set of clubs, golf bag, sunglasses and watches – top-notch gear. So when we all march out to play our practice rounds we do look the part. The problem for the huge crowds that turn out for the event – something like 25,000 people, the sort of numbers you'd get for a major golf tournament – is that while we might be dressed like pros, we don't play like them.

I'm an eighteen-handicapper and only play about ten times a year. When you're playing a shot and you've got people eight- or ten-deep around the tee and lining the fairways, it's quite nerve-wracking and between us we take out seven or eight people with wild shots. Ross Kemp viciously shanks one and hits someone on the head, Bradley Walsh snap-hooks off the tee and smashes another innocent spectator. I'll be standing over a shot off a tight lie with a three-iron and there are families with young children standing a few yards to my right who don't seem to realise they are in the firing line. I'm telling them: 'You've got to give me a bit of room here, otherwise someone is going to get hurt.' It's not like standing next to Tiger Woods as he arrows the ball out of the rough through a tiny gap in the branches and onto the green.

It is great fun though, especially when I do manage to hit a half-decent shot, which lands near the flag and get a big round of applause, just like at a pro tournament.

Unfortunately that doesn't happen when our captain Monty turns up to watch our group during the practice round. He's walking round to assess our form before deciding who to select for the opening round of matches. Only eight can play which means three will be left on the subs bench.

I've been playing quite well and am keen to impress and force my way into the starting line-up. As he arrives, I'm facing a little wedge to the green off a downhill, fluffy lie. The crowd is hushed, I can feel Monty's steely gaze on me as I address the ball. Right, just take the club back nice and smoothly, keep my head still and follow through. That's all I have to do. . .

Instead, I get a bit anxious at the top of my backswing, lurch forwards and top the ball, sending it scuttling straight over the other side of the green. The crowd piss themselves and I'm like: 'Can you stop laughing? Stop laughing, alright?' and toddle off to the back of the green to play the shot back. Do the same thing again, skulling it straight back across the green.

When I finally get on the green, I six-putt. There's a couple of claps from people who feel sorry for me as I finally pick the ball out of the hole and I look up just in time to see Monty striding away to look for better players.

Unsurprisingly, I end up on the subs bench and exercising my drinking elbow with Chris Evans for the next two days. So by the time we have a charity auction after dinner one night, I'm well oiled. The auction isn't going particularly well, so someone has the bright idea of getting everyone from each team up to sell an item.

When it's my turn, I have it in my mind to do a Jonny Gould. If you've never seen Jonny in action, he's a legendary auctioneer on the after-dinner circuit. He's helped raise over £35 million in charity auctions and his schtick is playing one bidder off against another with tongue-in-cheek insults. He knows how to 'read a room'. He might get two rich blokes for the City bidding against each other for an item and when one raises, he'll go to the other: 'Come on, sir, he's trying to humiliate you. Are your balls big enough to take him on, sir?'

But instead of doing it with wit and charm, I go in a bit too aggressive.

I'm like, 'Right then, you bunch of ****s, put your hands in your pockets you tight bastards.'

Someone puts their hand up for a hundred quid and I'm like, 'We've got some wanker here who's bid a ton. Who else? Come on, you bunch of tossers.'

It's just a tirade of abuse and I'll never forget Ant and Dec's little faces, sitting there at the front table going, 'No, no. . .' as I reel off a load of obscenities in an attempt to whip up an atmosphere, but only succeeding in horrifying the entire audience. It's just so wrong.

On the plus side – and no thanks to me – Team Europe do win the match, with 'The Golf-father', Bruce Forsyth, sinking the winning putt.

My first big opportunity to be a regular in a television series comes just a few months after the jungle when I begin a stint as captain on BBC One's *They Think It's All Over* in September 2003. Despite the show's name being borrowed from Kenneth Wolstenholme's iconic commentary on Geoff Hurst's goal in the 1966 World Cup final, it's more of a comedy panel game than a sports quiz. Jokes and the banter between the regulars and the guests is a lot more important than getting the questions right.

I'm nominally the 'captain' of one team and David Seaman is the captain of the other. We're both new boys, taking over from Gary Lineker and David Gower who'd been in those seats since the show began eight years before.

While I sit in the middle of three people each week, Jonathan Ross is always sitting to my right, but he's much more than a right-hand man – he's the one that drives all the chat. Rory McGrath does the same for David Seaman on the other team, while host Nick Hancock is just as quick-witted, so we try to follow in their slipstream.

It's a very popular show and quite daunting for me. It's the first time I've worked with seasoned TV entertainers and the first few episodes I'm really struggling to keep up. It's one thing being a cheeky chappie and coming out with the odd one-liner in a cricket dressing room – or even in edited highlights from a whole day in the jungle camp – but another thing being funny on demand in a half-hour show. I'm sitting next to someone who's on his way to being a legend of British broadcasting and feeling well out of my depth.

Where am I?

It takes me a while to get used to the format and relax into it. You can't go into a show like that with no back-up, so we go in a few hours before filming and get a heads-up about the subjects that are going to come up, which gives us a chance to have a bit of a brainstorm in the green room over a beer. Also, I learn that it doesn't matter if a joke falls flat because each show is recorded over ninety minutes and the fat can be trimmed off in the edit.

I can always rely on Jonathan, too. He has his own little team of writers so he goes into each show loaded with plenty of material and has an ability to improvise and talk about any subject at length anyway. There's a guest on each team every show and Jonathan will usually do a mini-interview with them which is basically an excuse to reel off a few gags. I'll just be sitting there, smiling along and dropping in the odd comment if something pops in my head. Most of the time I don't really have to do anything much.

For instance, when we have the chef Ainsley Harriott on our team and the conversation turns to Delia Smith.

'Phil, she's your favourite cook, isn't she?' says Jonathan.

'Very much so. . .'

'He even bought her book, *Cooking with Ease*. . . he was a bit disappointed when he found out it was a different sort of Es.'

And then he turns to Ainsley: 'I've got an idea for a new show – *Can't Cook, **** Off*.'

He's a great person to have on my team – you just wind him up like a toy car and watch him go.

Jonathan knows naff-all about sport — apart from a little bit about tennis which he likes playing — but the format of the show means that doesn't matter and actually adds to the humour. For rounds like 'The Name Game', where Jonathan would have to give me and our guest clues to the name of a sportsperson, he usually won't have a Scooby who it is so he'll have to be more creative in his clues. For instance, one time he's trying to describe a well-known Indian Test cricketer to me and former political spin-doctor Alastair Campbell:

'This is a Sikh name, I believe. Something you would do for your supper. You would. . .'

'Singh'

'First name is. . .'

'Vijay?'

'No, no, no, no. . .'

'Where do you keep your yacht?

'In Cowes,' offers Alastair.

'In your back garden,' I say, probably thinking of the old days of *Bullseye* when people would win a boat to take back to their council house.

'No. . .'

'Nets, alcove. . . harbour. Oh, Harbour Singh. . . Harbhajan Singh!'

One of the most popular rounds was 'Feel the Sportsman', when Jonathan and me were blindfolded and had to identify a mystery sporting guest or team. One time we're feeling around in front of us and it's clearly two or three people.

'Oh my good God! Is that a gun?'

'I can feel a gun.'

'I've got a gun here. . .'

'Is it Charlie's Angels?'

'I know what that is. . .' says Jonathan.

Just as I cry out: 'Arggghh, argh argh. . . I've been shot up the arse.'

Almost simultaneously, Jonathan yelps: 'Owww. . . not my suit – it's a Vivienne Westwood suit!'

The mystery 'sportsmen' are the paintball champions of the world; I can tell you now that getting paintballed from short range really stings.

'Are you alright?' asks Jonathan as we go back to our seats.

'Yeah, I'm alright. . .' I reply before turning to the audience: 'Has anyone got a rubber ring I can sit on?'

I do three series of the show over the next year or so, during which time Ian Wright takes over from David Seaman in the opposite captain's chair, and it's a really valuable experience. Nick, Jonathan, Rory and the production team are all fantastic to work with and I learn a lot from them about thinking on my feet. I come away feeling more confident that I can hold my own on a light-entertainment show and I can see that the jungle really is opening doors for me for longer-term options outside cricket.

Ironically, another door the jungle opens is the chance to go back to the jungle, as a roving reporter on the companion show for the next two series of *I'm a Celebrity. . . Get Me Out of Here! NOW!* in January and October 2004. It's a lovely experience. My job is just to potter around, interviewing the families and friends of the contestants and some of the many people who work behind the scenes. It's not very pressurised – just ask questions, be enthusiastic – and between times stay in a nice apartment, which is definitely preferable to eating rice and beans and sleeping in a hammock.

Far more challenging is my first ever presenting role, which lands in my lap in summer 2004. It's a really big one – co-presenting a new primetime Saturday-night show on ITV1, called *Simply the Best*.

The concept of the show originated from France many years ago, where it was called *Intervilles* (*Inter-cities*) and then England took on the idea with the iconic *It's a Knockout*, which ran on and off across five decades from 1966, the year I was born. Growing up, I enjoyed watching the bizarre team games like obstacle-course relays in big foam fat suits. The last series of *It's a Knockout* aired in 2001 on Channel 5 and ITV have decided it's time to bring wacky competitive family fun back to Saturday nights.

They are throwing a lot of money at the show – it's one of the biggest they've invested in in years. The whole series is filmed over a month in St Helier, Jersey, and they build a temporary 1,500-seater 'Simply the Best Arena' – a mini-amphitheatre – by the seaside just for the purpose. It includes a stage where each week a couple of big-name pop acts will sing their latest singles as a breaker between the games. They also hire the cheerleaders from American football team the Scottish Claymores to add to the all-singing-and-dancing atmosphere. As for the game format, they don't stray too far from the winning *It's a Knockout* formula – teams from different cities competing against other in madcap games wearing silly costumes is the order of the day and the Arthur Ellis role as referee is taken by recently retired Premier League ref Paul Durkin.

Auditions are held in Birmingham, Belfast, Manchester, London, Leeds,

Edinburgh, Newcastle, Brighton & Hove, Portsmouth, Glasgow, Sheffield and Bristol to find extremely physically fit men and women to represent their city. Each city has a team of six (plus four standbys) plus two guest celebrity competitors.

Each week, two cities face off and the winner of the grand final at the end of the series gets a cheque for £50,000 to benefit a local charity.

I'm co-hosting with Kirsty Gallacher, a very experienced presenter, which gives me some reassurance that at least one of us knows what they're doing. But it's not like *They Think It's All Over* where I can hide behind Jonathan and co. – this time I'm supposed to be fronting the show alongside Kirsty and I have to do my share.

We have a week of rehearsals beforehand and I'm learning everything from scratch. It's the first time I've ever used an autocue and that is very tricky for me because I have mild dyslexia. Instead I decide to memorise as many of my lines as possible in advance and use the autocue more as a fallback option if I forget something. Then I've got the added complication of a director giving me instructions via an earpiece, which is also new to me and really quite distracting when you're trying to interview someone.

'So Dave, what do you do back home?'

While he's answering, the director's in my ear and I'm not really listening to the fella's answer.

'Oh right, yeah and what sports do you play?'

'Er, I've just told you, I play cricket. . .'

Two conversations going on at once.

I can't help thinking that perhaps I should have been sent on some sort of training course before being thrown in at the deep end, but the production crew seem happy enough with what I'm doing. They just keep telling me to go for it and 'Be yourself'. That makes me laugh because my dad has always said 'Be yourself, son and show a bit of character'. Well, Dad, it seems that unlike the many cricket captains, coaches and officials I upset over the years by being myself, the TV people actually want me to do that, so maybe I've finally found my niche.

By the day of the first show, however, I'd gladly swap my character for a year's TV presenter's training. As the clock ticks down towards the show my gratitude at being handed this huge opportunity is being overtaken by a fear of absolutely tanking. The show is not going out live, but it's being recorded 'as live' and you can't have too many glitches.

I'm sitting in a little camper van outside the arena, watching the spectators flood past on their way to their seats, holding 'Simply the Best' flags and wearing giant foam hands. Then as the stage manager calls 'Ten minutes', I'm just thinking '****' and my mind is going blank.

What seems like a minute later, I'm waiting with Kirsty and the stage manager behind the massive steel doors that open up for us to walk into the arena.

'Here we go, Tuffers. . .'

'Five, four, three, two, one – GO!'

The doors swing open, the crowd cheer, the pyrotechnics begin, cheerleaders dance and then, like I've been told, I just have to go for it and be myself, which initially mainly seems to consist of jumping up and down, waving and cries of 'Waaahhh! Hello everyone! Whoooo'.

Thankfully, after Kirsty welcomes the viewers and spectators, I get my opening lines out smoothly enough:

'We're here every week through the summer finding out which UK city is simply the best. So you reckon your hometown is the business. We're going to settle the arguments right here. . .'

It's a bit like bowling your first over in a Test match – just get through that without getting smashed around the field and then you can settle down and play your game. Once the show is underway, there's no time for self-doubt or worrying about making mistakes, you just have to do it, because the time seems to pass so quickly.

Some games work better than others. There's one called 'Air Kick' where a person from each team sit in two human catapults. At the other end of the arena are two catchers – again one from each team, holding little fishing nets and wearing flippers and snorkels to make it harder for them to run around. The catapults are activated in turn, launching the person inside twenty feet in the air. While airborne, they have to chuck their ball towards their team's catcher who has to catch it in the net while the other team's catcher tries to do the same and steal the point. The problem is the nets are not much bigger than the ball and when the other team's catcher is grappling with you it's really difficult to make a catch. Consequently, there are some rather drab, low-scoring 1-0 and 0-0 scorelines as balls fly everywhere but into the nets.

My favourites are the more surreal games, like one where two players from each team are dressed up like giant electrical plugs. They can't see where they're going and after being spun around for thirty seconds until they're really dizzy, they have to find their way across the arena and plug their heads into a socket. Their team-mates can scream directions, but they're going all over the place. There's one guy who's walking round with his arms outstretched in front of him and keeps on walking straight towards the cheerleaders, which makes me suspect he actually can see where he's going. I have to keep diverting him back towards the sockets.

One of the toughest physical challenges is a game called 'The Human Runway' – actually, tough is an understatement – it's bloody dangerous. Each team takes it in turns to run across a runway carrying two buckets of water and if they manage to get to the other end with any water still in their bucket, deposit it in a container. The catch is that the 'runway' is basically just a canvas, which has been lightly oiled to make it slippery and people from the other team are underneath kicking as hard as they can to try and make the runner fall off either side of the runway into the pool.

This is where I make my biggest creative contribution to the show, dreaming up my own catchphrase: 'Don't fall in the pool!' I think it's positively Bruce Forsythian and feel sure it is going to catch on with the spectators in the arena and the millions of viewers at home. My hope is that when I introduce the item, I'll always sign off with '. . . and the idea of this game is. . . DON'T FALL IN THE POOL!' and it will get to the stage where I won't even have to say the words because the spectators will be shouting them for me, just like Brucey on *Play Your Cards Right*.

Instead, every week I'm met with a wall of indifference. Tumbleweed doesn't do justice to the apathetic silence. I keep persevering and the stage manager does his best to rouse the crowds, waving his arms like a football manager urging his team to dig deep in the last minute of extra time, but they just aren't having it.

The reality is for the contestant that if you do fall over – and most do – you're actually better off falling straight in the pool than on the runway where you're liable to be brutally kicked in the head or genitals. Quite a few of the competitors go home nursing injuries from that game. No wonder the producers brought out so many standbys to Jersey.

We're on the island from late June through July and aside from presenting the shows, my other role is being a kind of tour rep, hosting a new group of people every four or five days. The day the competitors and celebrity guests arrive, everyone's excited, so we'll have a few drinks together in the hotel bar. The next day, we do the rehearsal and then the day after is the show itself. After the show, everyone's on a high and we have a big night out. The next day, I wave goodbye to them and the next batch fly in.

There is a real buzz after completing a show, not dissimilar to the feeling after winning a cricket match. Add in a sense of relief that I've got through it and I'm very happy to join the teams in big nights of celebration.

That cycle is repeated eight times as we record all the episodes – welcome drinks, panic about the show, do the show, celebrate, do it all again – and by the end of the series, I'm rinsed out.

Unfortunately, despite everyone's best efforts, the show doesn't get the level of viewing figures it needs to in a prime Saturday-evening slot. Perhaps it is a bit too long – to start with it is screened for a whopping two hours including advertising breaks. For the later episodes it gets trimmed back to ninety minutes, which does make it a bit more pacey, but arguably it might have benefited from having another fifteen minutes lopped off.

Another problem is the variable weather – while the outdoor arena looks great in the sunshine, we have a few days where it's rainy and grey and that doesn't look very good on the telly. Although we have some big-name pop stars like Lionel Richie, Anastacia and McFly on the show, maybe the transition – from people having the living daylights kicked out of them on The Human Runway to someone like Katie Melua singing a romantic ballad on the stage nearby – is a bit odd.

Anyhow, for whatever reason, the show just doesn't quite catch on with the public as hoped. Personally, though, it is a great experience. For all the nerves and stress about co-presenting such a high-profile show, I've got through it without any disasters and proved – to myself as much as anyone – that I can do it. At the time, I can only really go on the feedback I have from the producers and they seem very happy with my efforts. I don't often like to watch myself on television and it's only many years later – for the purpose of writing this book – that I'm persuaded to watch a couple of episodes and actually I'm pleasantly surprised. Apart from my tendency to, when in doubt, nervously dance around and wave my arms about, my links generally are quite smooth and natural. While many competitors fell in the pool in the making of that show – and my catchphrase sank without trace – I didn't drown as a presenter. Maybe the producers' advice to be myself wasn't so simplistic after all?

On that matter, since the jungle I've found myself a few times sitting up late at night having a heart-to-heart with Dawn, asking her, 'Well, what is my personality? Who am I?' I won I'm a Celebrity on the basis of my personality, but that was not a conscious thing on my part. If my job now is to be myself, I better know who I am.

When people tell you to be yourself, the danger is that you become very self-conscious and end up presenting what you think people's perception of you is. From the experience of doing *They Think It's All Over* and now *Simply The Best*, I'm starting to realise that the key is being as natural as possible on camera. With TV they want people who can be a bit off-the-wall on a show and that's not something I try to do, it's just how I am normally.

I think the fact that I played most of my cricket career in a slightly less serious era for the sport is helping me. Don't get me wrong, we played hard to win – I was hugely competitive on the pitch – but we enjoyed life around it. I'm not saying I'm some big entertainer, but some of the characteristics that held me back towards the end of my cricket career as it became more professional, seem to be making me more employable in the new career that's opening up for me. There's no point going on a light-entertainment show and not smiling and mucking about a bit.

Woody Allen once said 'Eighty per cent of success is showing up' and I'm finding that even if the job is something as daunting as presenting a TV show, so long as I get myself there, I've got half a chance. Always turn up – that's my new motto!

I've always been reasonably good at that, to be fair. In years of touring with England, I only missed the bus to training twice – which is an amazing record considering the state I was in sometimes. I've got no excuse now I'm working in a industry where, for the majority of jobs, they also send a car to pick you up.

It does help if you've had a good night's sleep before turning up, mind, especially when you're appearing as a guest on a morning show. I've got that wrong a couple of times when I've been invited on Sky's *Soccer AM* programme. That's a 5.30am pick-up on a Saturday morning. One Friday, I'd gone out to a mate's house for dinner. The evening stretches into the early hours ending with a couple of whisky nightcaps and me coming home and falling asleep on the sofa. The next thing I know the driver is banging on the door.

I've got a couple of hours at the studio to wake up, but I'm still not totally with it when I'm being asked questions on the sofa.

That's where another thing I've learnt about being on chat shows comes in handy: you don't actually have to answer the questions they've asked you. If I don't really know much about what they're asking, I just talk about something I do know about.

'So, Phil, what do you think about the formation Wenger's got Arsenal playing right now?'

'Well, you know, when I was a kid, I used to go up to Highbury with my dad and we didn't worry about things like that. Which reminds me of the time when. . .'

As long as you talk with enough conviction and passion, people forget the question you were asked and don't seem to pick me up on the fact that I've gone off on a massive tangent.

As I approach my fortieth birthday in April 2006, everything seems to be coming together. Three years on from retiring from playing cricket and becoming a reality TV celebrity, I'm carving out a new career path for myself in the media, both in cricket (more of that later) and light entertainment. I'm learning all the time and feeling more comfortable in the different roles. Being more selective in the things I take on has given me more direction. I have a better handle on who I am, where I'm going professionally and couldn't be happier in my personal life. Since we got married, the public perception of Dawn and I has definitely changed a lot. It's like, 'Oh, she's not just another of Tuffers' birds, they do love each other'.

I still feel young in my outlook, too, but turning forty is a landmark and I do wonder if it means I am getting old. I'm thinking I should probably have a big party, but instead Dawn organises a surprise trip just for us; it proves to be the perfect way to ease into my forties.

She doesn't tell me where we're going until we get to the airport and then reveals we're going to Venice, which I'm thrilled about because I've always wanted to go to Italy. Things can get a bit fractious when we're flying because of my phobia, so even though it's a short journey Dawn's got business-class flights so we can indulge in our usual pre-flight ritual of drinking Bloody Marys in the lounge, which helps to take the edge off.

When we arrive in Venice we hop into one of the speedboat taxis. The taxi 'drivers' are wearing slacks, boaters, Prada sunglasses and perhaps a pink Lacoste jumper thrown over their shoulders – I'm not looking quite so sophisticated in my Union Jack shorts and vest. As a rule the boats have classical music wafting gently from the onboard speakers. Our guy is the exception, pumping out house music all the way to our hotel, which makes me feel more like I'm twenty than forty.

During the holiday, we go to St Mark's Square to visit the famous

Doge's Palace, but when we see the queue, we think, 'Sod that – let's just get a photo outside it and go for a coffee.'

We take a look at the many café options around the square and Dawn chooses one with a string quartet playing.

A waiter comes over to seat us and I decide to give my dad a call.

'Dad,' I say, 'I'm sitting with Dawn in a café in St Mark's Square in the sunshine.'

'Well, that's lovely, boy. I love Venice. . . But watch out – that will be the most expensive cup of coffee you'll ever have.'

'Haha – yeah, righto, Dad.'

When I get off the phone, I'm telling Dawn about Dad's warning just as a waiter arrives with the menu. I glance down at the beverages section.

'****ing hell! Dad was right, look at the prices here!'

'Oh, come on, Phil, it's going to be our most expensive coffee ever wherever we go – at least here the band's included.'

So we stay there and place our order. Just as we're settling in, the music tinkling in the background stops. When we look round, the string quartet are packing up.

'Excuse me, where are they going?' asks Dawn.

'Oh, it is their lunch hour, madam.'

The bill for our unexpectedly quiet coffee break comes to fifty-odd euros for two coffees and my ham sandwich, including a massive cover charge, presumably for the live music we haven't heard. Despite it being a ridiculous rip-off, we have to laugh because my dad was bang on.

We have another memorable experience when we visit the island of

Murano, famous for its handmade glassware. Before we came out to Venice, a couple of friends had warned Dawn not to go on a tour of the Murano glass factory because they said we'd be bullied into buying something. However, another mate said: 'Go along with it – they ply you with champagne while you look around and you don't have to buy anything. . . well, we did end up buying something, but it's quite nice.'

We decide to risk it for the free champers, but at the start of the day we make a pact not to buy anything.

We're given a tour of the workshop and they show us how they blow the glass, how everything is shaped and finished and the level of craftsmanship is fantastic. At the end, the guide comes over to us: 'So, you wanna buy something for the beautiful lay-deee?'

No sign of any champagne yet, so we want to keep our options open.

'Well, we're thinking about it.'

That's all he needs to know. Within seconds, we are whisked out from the workshop onto a jetty. At the end are two golden thrones – like they had at Posh and Becks' wedding – and three white stone Roman plinths placed in front.

We are directed to sit down, our former tour guide claps his hands and a handful of minions spring into action, bringing out flutes of champagne and a succession of gorgeous glassware items.

'What colour would you like?' 'What form do you like best?'

They place each item on these stone plinths, against the backdrop of Venice.

It's a lovely warm day, there's a clear blue sky, the sea is sparkling, gondolas are passing by with people singing onboard and our glasses are being topped up constantly – they know exactly what they're doing and eventually our defences weaken.

A couple of bottles of champagne later, we're half-cut and walking out having made three very expensive purchases which will be shipped over to us.

When the package arrives at our house a couple of weeks later, we open it up and they are very nice, but they don't look quite as nice as they did, glistening on those plinths at the end of a pier in Venice, with the Italian maestro clapping his hands. It's like drinking rum punch in the Caribbean, then trying to recreate the magic in The White Hart on a cold Wednesday evening back home – it doesn't quite have the same allure.

We do love them, though, especially the glass sculpture of a couple embracing, which now sits on the window ledge in our living room as a reminder of a romantic Venetian afternoon.

TALKING CRICKET (AND PENGUINS)

4

After the jungle, for all the opportunities to spread my wings beyond the sport, cricket remains my first love and I'm really keen to stay involved in one way or another. Since Mike became my agent, he's got me gigs as a cricket columnist for various newspapers, including the *Evening Standard*, *Daily Telegraph*, *Sunday People*, *The Sun*, *Racing Post* and *Daily Mail* plus *The Cricketer* magazine. (Back in 2001, I also did a column for lads' mag *Loaded* for six months, but that was not so much about the technical aspects of cricket. . .) I've also done some radio, from the occasional phone interview for BBC Radio 5 Live, to studio analysis and 'colour commentary' for Sky. The Sky work includes some winter nightshifts commentating on Test matches from a cubicle in their Isleworth studio.

One of my first jobs for Sky is covering an overnight one-dayer from the other side of the world, working with experienced presenter Matt

Lorenzo. We have to be in the studio at three o'clock on a Sunday morning for the start of play and he gives me a bit of advice on how to make sure I'm fully awake for our shift.

'Go out on Saturday lunchtime,' he tells me. 'Have a few drinks till five or six, go home a bit tipsy and sleepy, get your head down and you'll wake up fresh as a daisy.'

'Good idea, I'll do that.' I follow his advice – well, apart from one important detail.

I get home at midnight, crash out and the next thing I know my alarm rings and the car is waiting outside to take me to the studio. Matt shakes his head when he sees my slightly discombobulated state.

'I got it slightly wrong, Matt. . .'

I order a full English breakfast, do the opening links and then promptly fall asleep.

Matt is watching the game with my head resting on his shoulder, drooling on his suit, thinking: 'This isn't going to work; you've got to watch the game.'

Sky Sports News are due to come to us at the break between innings for a report and with an over to go, I'm still fast asleep, so he gives me a nudge.

'Uh, what? What's happened?' I ask him.

He gives me a potted summary: 'Well, three wickets down, so-and-so was caught Healy, bowled McGrath' etcetera.

Soon we're on air and Matt tentatively hands over to me for my opinions on the morning's play. Afterwards, Matt is looking at me agog: 'Well, how did you do that? That was spot on and you didn't even watch it!'

Apparently, I more than got away with it; I absolutely nailed it. After my two-hour snooze, I'm refreshed enough to actually watch the rest of the day's play.

I learn from my mistake and in future I go to bed early.

Another nice guy I work with is Simon Lazenby, the future lead presenter of Formula 1 for Sky. He has an MG car and one night he's running late for our shift, so he hurriedly parks it in the first space he can find. When we come out the following morning, after an eight-hour shift, we discover that it's been snowing and our little corner of Hounslow Borough is covered in a blanket of snow. There, on the corner of the road, is Simon's car, now the only one parked there. We come out just in time to see a succession of cars coming down the hill, trying to turn left, but skidding on the sheet-ice surface straight across the road into his car. Someone just nudges into the side of it, others plough into it. He rushes over to move it and finds a stack of notes pinned under the windscreen wipers from other drivers who've accidentally been playing bumper cars with his beloved (and now very dented) MG, while we've been talking cricket on the radio for insomniacs.

I serve my apprenticeship on the graveyard shifts to open the door to slightly more glamorous gigs, the first of which I get when the BBC invite me to join the *Test Match Special* (*TMS*) radio team out in South Africa for the World Cup in early 2003. I have to say, going up Table Mountain and sampling the fantastic wines from vineyards around Cape Town sure beats the rubbery scrambled egg and fatty old bacon they used to bring us in polystyrene containers at half six in the morning in Isleworth.

When I first start commentating, I think listeners and even some of my co-commentators are pleasantly surprised that I am capable of intelligent analysis of the game. You don't take a thousand first-class wickets bowling spin without having some idea what you're doing, but, as I've found in the world of celebrity, my 'bad boy of cricket' reputation precedes me.

When I was playing, I doubt many people would have pegged me as a potential commentator on *TMS*. In some ways, I don't blame people for that. People have the impression that I didn't train that hard – which is true when it came to the physical aspects of cricket – but I did spend a lot of time thinking about the game. I used to do some of my best preparation in bed the night before a day's play (no, not doing *that*. . .). I'd lie there tucked in under the covers with my arms by my side like a penguin on its back, thinking about the batsmen I'd be bowling against the next day; where they like to hit the ball, their strengths and weaknesses and where to place the fielders to trap them. When you're a spin bowler, you sometimes find yourself playing on a flat wicket where the ball doesn't spin, which means you're basically bowling balls thirty or forty miles an hour slower than the pace bowlers that don't deviate off the pitch. In that scenario, at international level against top-class batsmen, you need to have lots of back-up plans or your bowling is liable to be flayed to all corners of the ground.

That's where my 'penguining' helped me, and also my reputation as a maverick. If anything, I used to cultivate that image of myself as volatile and unpredictable and use it to my advantage. If I didn't know what I was doing, how on earth would batsmen know either?

My supposed maverick tendencies could have worked for or against me when it comes to my ambition to be a commentator. People could either have said we don't want this chap to be involved because he's a bit lively, or, he's worth the risk because he has a bit of character.

Thankfully, I've got an England career – albeit a spluttery, stop-start one – under my belt. I know what it's like to play at the top level and I've had an eventful time with media attention on back pages and front pages at times, so I've got a 'name'.

Like my dad used to say about me, cricket fans are always saying to me, 'When you played, you were a character', which I never quite understand. Does getting pissed and getting thrown out of nightclubs make you a character? But I take encouragement from the example of John McEnroe, who was as anti-establishment as they come during his career and yet went on to become one of the best commentators in any sport. He's a tennis genius and while I certainly don't put myself in that bracket of ability as a sportsman, I have a similar non-conformist streak in me.

However, there are a lot of knowledgeable ex-players out there and only so many slots available working for the BBC, Sky or for other channels that win the rights to broadcast cricket every now and then. It's a very competitive field to get into, so when I get the call at the start of 2005 to become a regular colour commentator on the *TMS* team, I'm absolutely thrilled. When I tell my dad, he is too, and also highly amused that I, of all people, have joined a Great British institution.

'Look at you, son, part of the Establishment at last. . .'

So begins ten years and counting of doing the absolute dream job for a cricket lover like me. To give you an idea of what it's like, let me take you through a typical day at my old stomping ground Lord's (with a few *Test Match Special*-style diversions along the way).

I'm dropped off at the ground about quarter to ten in the morning. I dress pretty smartly – old habits die hard after years of having to wear the Middlesex blazer – and on the first day of the match, I always wear a suit with my official *Test Match Special* tie. Spectators with their sunhats and picnic hampers are already gathering outside the ground, looking forward to the day's play. I say hello to the people at the gates, most of whom I've known for years. A few passers-by wave and hail me: 'Alright, Tuffers. Be listening to you today – good luck. Can I have a quick selfie?'

I buy myself a bacon sarnie from one of the concession stands inside the ground and head to the Lord's Media Centre. The centre won the prestigious Stirling Prize for Architecture when it opened in 1999. A striking all-aluminium construction, it is a wide, rounded oblong shape and has a huge front window that is perfect for viewing the game. It has been described as a 'futuristic pod' but is better known to regulars as 'Cherie Blair's smile'; when people pull the blinds down at the top level on sunny days, it even looks like it's got a top row of teeth.

I enter through the big section for the written press, say hello to a few people, then go up the stairs to the TV and radio commentary boxes, where there's lots of hustle and bustle. You can spot the ex-players because they're hobbling about due to old injuries. I'll see old team-mates like Mike Atherton rubbing his bad back, or Ian 'Beefy' Botham staggering up the stairs.

'Knees still playing up, Beefy?'

'Too right, Tuffers – all those bloody overs they had me bowling up the hill into the wind.'

Go into the commentary box, which has capacity for about ten. People are popping in and out all day long. At this time, producer Adam Mountford and his sidekick Henry Moeran are already at the back, tapping away on their laptops, getting things set up for us. Our main man, BBC cricket correspondent Jonathan 'Aggers' Agnew, is up front on his iPad, with the South African stats man Andrew Samson to his left, updating his own database of facts and figures. Other lead commentators such as Ed Smith will be floating around, as will my fellow colour boys like Michael Vaughan and Geoff Boycott. More colourful than any of us, though, is invariably our inimitable lead commentator, Henry 'Blowers' Blofeld, wearing some outlandish combination – purple moccasins, stripy socks, lime-green trousers, pink shirt and stripy blazer topped off with a Panama hat.

We catch up on what we've all been up to, chatting about current cricket affairs and things we might discuss on air later. It's a throwback to the camaraderie I enjoyed in the dressing room as a player.

Adam sticks the commentary rota for the day up on the wall. Aggers and the other lead commentators will normally do twenty minutes in the hotseat before handing over to the next man, while the colour guys each do one half-hour shift per session. Just as captains rotate their bowlers out on the field, this helps to keep things fresh and bubbling throughout the day.

We go on air at 10.30am, so, before the start of play, one of the lead guys will be assigned to hold the fort from 10.25 in the commentary box and introduce the show, while two of us will head out to do a pitch report.

If I'm one of the people on pitch duty, Henry Moeran takes us down and we get hooked up with the roving microphones so we can move around while we talk on air.

The players are out there warming up, so I'll say hello to a couple of the England boys – 'Allo, Cookie – well played the other day' – and perhaps a slightly less enthusiastic nod to the opposition players: 'Alright. . .'

If things haven't been going so well for the England team the atmosphere can be a bit more tense, in which case, you keep your head down and let them get on with it.

We'll take a look at the pitch, palm it to see if it's a bit damp or if there's any grass on it and generally pretend to know what we're doing. Have a chat with the groundsman to get the lowdown on how he expects it to play today. If it's me and my mate Vaughanie out there, we'll be messing about a bit.

It's lovely to be back out there seeing all the final preparations for the game, feeling the whole atmosphere building, with spectators taking their seats amid the hum of excited conversations. It's just like when I played, but without the stress of actually having to play, or to deal with my terrible allergy to fielding practice. Mind you, you do have to keep an eye out because there's a few cricket balls zinging about – I've had a few whistle past my earhole. One or two, I'm sure, on purpose.

About twenty-five to, we're on air, setting the day up – talking about the game situation, the pitch and how we think both teams are going to approach the task ahead of them. When an invited guest rings the bell to signal the start of play at five to eleven, the players make their way down the steps from the pavilion onto the pitch, while we wander back towards the Nursery End boundary and hand back to the studio.

Go back up, grab a cup of coffee and either sit in the back of the commentary box or next door with the BBC's technical team. Watch the opening overs, scan the newspapers and wait for my turn to commentate. Maybe go for a stroll and chat to a couple of other old pals I bump into, always keeping an eye on the game on one of the many screens around the place.

By this time a cake mountain is already forming at the back of the commentary box. *TMS* and homemade cakes have become synonymous and every match people from all round the UK very kindly send us an array of delicious cakes which the security guys bring up throughout the morning. We also get sent loads of pork pies, Scotch eggs and cheeses. I tend to start with savoury and progress to the sweet treats later in the day. Borrow a Leatherman knife from one of the production crew next door and hand it back to him with bits of pork pie stuck to it.

We all put on a few pounds doing a Test match, but despite loosening our belts, after two or three days we can still accumulate a sizeable cake surplus. At Trent Bridge once, we had so many cakes, we sliced them up and put them out on a little trestle table outside in the main stand for the spectators. Whoosh – they were gone in a flash.

There's always a letter attached to the food gifts and while we can't thank everyone live on air, we make a point of doing so to those who send in ones that we particularly enjoy. We get some amazing creations

– such as cupcakes with impressive likenesses of the faces of the commentary team iced on top. The rudest one we ever receive is during an Ashes series – a beautifully decorated cake depicting a Lion, um, 'mounting' a kangaroo. Aggers has to be very delicate in how he describes it on air. 'The kangaroo is in a similar position to Australia in this game,' he says.

When it's my turn to commentate, I stick my headphones on – which include 'Tuffers Muffers', an elasticated breathable cotton covering a lady made for me after I said on air that my ears were sweating from contact with the plastic headphones – and sit alongside whoever's on lead duties at the time. I've got the best seat in the house and I'm talking to my mate, so I try to keep the commentary as natural as I would if I was sitting in the pub or in the Compton Stand watching it with them. The idea is to both inform and entertain, and what's lovely is that we can meander away from just describing the play every now and then.

If a couple of batsmen are slowly building a partnership without looking remotely troubled by the bowlers, you're still looking to point out subtle changes in the game – maybe the captain is adjusting his field placings, trying to set traps – but there is space to let the conversation drift as you do when you're a spectator.

'What did you do for dinner last night, Blowers?'

'I had a lovely lobster in my room.'

'Oh, did you eat it or watch telly with it?'

I have a vision of a lobster sitting on the couch, drinking claret and watching telly with Blowers.

England fast bowler Stuart Broad once came up to me, with a smile on his face: 'I was listening to you on the radio the other day for twenty minutes and you never mentioned cricket. Loved it.'

Of course, when there's a good spell of bowling, the ball is swinging or spinning, then you're right back on the game. If three wickets fall in ten balls or a batter is flaying the ball to all corners of the ground, you're not going to be talking about where you've been on holiday or pigeons, although Blowers will always make time if a particularly good-looking pigeon lands on the commentary box.

As the game hots up, the coach in me comes out and I do sometimes wish I was out there playing, especially if the ball's spinning. I get right into the field placings and working out what I'd do: 'I wouldn't have a short leg in there, I'd move him to the offside, bowl slightly wider of off stump. . .' We have a great vantage point, so it's actually easier for us to see the whole shape of the game than for the captain out on the pitch.

Listeners pick up on what we're saying and with social media now they can send us their own thoughts immediately. Adam monitors all the tweets and emails coming in and forwards any that catch his eye onto the screen in front of the commentators on duty. Whether the messages are on the state of the game or the reason for the traffic jam of buses that Blowers has noted outside the ground, viewers comments can often trigger a whole new chain of thought.

In that little cubicle, it's sometimes easy to forget how many people are listening to us and how far afield they are. We receive messages from people listening via the BBC World Service from every part of the globe. We had one once from an English scientist working in Antarctica. He's up there counting penguins or something in minus forty-five degrees and listening to the cricket on his headphones while he works: 'Come on England – loving your work, guys.' A lot of people say that when they are listening to *TMS*, they know summer has arrived, wherever they are in the world.

My recurring mistake when I first start commentating for *TMS* – and I still occasionally do it by accident years later – is referring to England as 'we'.

'Oh, *we* haven't done too well this morning. . .'

Aggers or whoever's next to me will give me the nod and I'll have to quickly backtrack: 'Other teams are available. . .'

It's difficult to keep a lid on my patriotism, especially when England are battling against our old enemy Australia. My most spectacular breach of the BBC public broadcaster's code of conduct occurs during the final Test at the Oval of the 2005 Ashes series. As England head towards our first series win since 1987, the long-suffering ex-England players in the commentary box are losing all semblance of neutrality, but I take it to the next level, joining in the crowd chants of 'They're coming home, they're comin' home, Ashes comin' home!'

In each series, we always have guest commentators from the team England are playing to give their views and add balance, and the Aussie boys are a good bunch who can give as good as they get, so I was permitted that lapse.

Sometimes my fellow commentators will do their best to throw me off my stride, just for a laugh. Aggers, for instance, lives in the Vale of Belvoir (pronounced 'beaver') in Leicestershire and he knows that, being a teenage schoolkid at heart, I can't hear the word 'beaver' without cracking up. At the start of play, he'll be discussing the weather outlook for the day and drop something in, like: 'Woke up this morning and it was very damp in the Belvoir.' He knows exactly what he's doing and sometimes he has me on the floor laughing. I just can't deal with it.

Another time, when I'm opening the day's commentary with Ed Smith, Ed accidentally almost floors me for a different reason. As the players are running out and he's introducing the play I'm opening a Fox's Glacier Mint and momentarily lose track of what he's saying. When I tune back in the first thing I hear him say is '. . .up your arse'.

I'm thinking, 'Whoah! You can't say that on the BBC in daytime. Ed's flipped before a ball's been bowled.'

I look round at Adam and then back at Ed gesticulating wildly and mouthing at him 'What? What are you saying?'

Ed is looking at me totally confused and then finally twigs onto my concern that he may have introduced anal sex into a *Test Match Special* commentary at eleven o'clock in the morning.

'Oh, no, no, Phil – no problem, it's in quotations. I'm only quoting Keith Miller. . .'

Keith Miller was a flamboyant Australian cricketer of the postwar era. Widely regarded as Australia's greatest ever all-rounder, Miller looked like a matinee idol and was known for his aggressive, carefree style. Even though he was an Aussie, he was my dad's ultimate childhood cricket hero – ahead, even, of Denis Compton. Dad used to bunk over the fence at the Oval and Lord's to watch him play when he was touring England with the Aussies. Previously, Miller had fought in the Second World War as a Royal Australian Air Force fighter pilot and he famously said: 'Pressure is a Messerschmitt up your arse, playing cricket is not.' So it all becomes clear. Phew.

Before his cricket-playing career, Ed studied history at Cambridge University and graduated with a double first, and he is among a number of very well-educated people in the *TMS* team. With my single O level pass, I could be forgiven for feeling a little inferior academically, but that changes in 2011 when Middlesex University award me an honorary doctorate. They give these honorary degrees 'to people who have made an outstanding contribution to their profession or the community' and I'm in lofty company. At the same ceremony, degrees are also given to Shami Chakrabarti for her achievements in law and human rights, writer and commentator Will Hutton for his achievements in business and Lynne Franks for her work in business and media.

My dad comes along to the ceremony and is very proud to see me receive my certificate, wearing a gown and mortar board on my head: 'I knew you'd get another qualification one day, son.'

My only disappointment is the discovery that my doctorate does not entitle me to prescribe medication.

A few weeks later, the subject of honorary doctorates comes up in the *TMS* commentary box and I proudly proclaim that I have belatedly joined the club. The legendary Indian batsman Sunil Gavaskar happens to be with us.

'Have you got a doctorate, Sunny?'

'I think I have five now. . .'

He has to count them up. Oh, okay then.

One of the great things about being a *TMS* commentator, is that if

England take a couple of wickets or one of our batsmen hits a few boundaries during my half hour in the hotseat, I get the credit for their good play. As I put down Tuffers' Muffers, the incoming colour commentator says: 'Well bowled/batted, Tuffers.' It's a whole lot easier than actually doing it out on the pitch.

We're very well looked after at the Test grounds, to the extent that there is even a woman who comes round and gives us neck massages. One time, I have one just before lunch and it's so relaxing I fall asleep, only to be rudely awoken by a phone call from someone at the Lord's shop. I'm supposed to be doing a book signing and there's a big queue of people wondering where I am, so I have to open my now very relaxed shoulders and run down there as quick as I can.

Normally at lunchtime, I'll pop down to the buffet in the press canteen, have a break and a chat. Meanwhile, Aggers is doing his 'View from the Boundary' interview with a celebrity guest who the production guys have lined up – usually planned in advance, but sometimes we just discover someone interesting has come to watch the cricket today and the production guys go and nab them to see if they fancy coming for a chat. *TMS* is such an institution that almost without fail, people are honoured to be asked. If it's someone I'm really interested in, I'll pop back and either listen in from the back of the commentary box or next door. We've had all sorts of people in – from Russell Crowe to Lily Allen, Stephen Fry to Alice Cooper, Daniel Radcliffe to the pop group Keane (who play a song for us).

In the afternoon, we continue in the same vein: rotating strike between different commentators, trying to keep the conversation and analysis sharp, fuelled by the action on the pitch and more slices of cake.

If the weather's nice, we'll open the window – the BBC commentary box is the only one in the Lord's Media Centre with a window that opens – and it's just a glorious way to spend time. Watching cricket in the sunshine at the Home of Cricket is hard to beat, but I have to say England versus India at the Ageas Bowl, Southampton, in summer 2014 might just edge it. Initially, we placed our commentary box in one of the rooms in the new hotel at the ground, but we have wonderful weather for all five days so the BBC commentary operation decamps outside onto the balcony. We're positioned right behind the bowler's arm, with a perfect view of the game and we spend five days under parasols in sunglasses, shorts and T-shirts, eating 99 Flake ice creams. And England win. Best five days' 'work' you could ever hope for.

The worst day you can have on *TMS* is when it's pouring with rain. If it's going to rain all day, the producers may look to take us off air, but when it's doubtful, we can often be filling time for hours. Then it's all hands to the pump and we're all called in. That's when you have to work your contacts, pulling in a couple of press guys or ex-players to join the discussion and keep a twenty-minute, half-hour turnover of guests so the conversation stays bright and breezy.

We'd all much rather be talking about action on the pitch, but even then we're still enjoying ourselves, talking cricket with our friends. You might think, 'Crikey, a couple of hours to fill here,' but there's always something to discuss. That's where the skill of Aggers comes in, because he knows how to drive the conversation, pick up on the issues of the day, whereas my role is more reactive, answering questions. I know a lot of listeners actually really enjoy the periods when there isn't play, because we can talk in depth about the major topics of the day in cricket. That's the delight of *TMS* – even when nothing is happening, there's still something happening.

I can get so wrapped up in a Test match. Most spectators only get to come to a day or two, so what a privilege to be able to watch the whole match unfold. A lot of people might come on the first day, but they want to follow the rest of the match and that's where *TMS* comes in.

Sometimes, after a day's play, I'll also be doing the *Tuffers and Vaughan Cricket Show* on BBC Radio 5 Live in the evening, where Michael Vaughan and me will review the key incidents, the good, the bad and the controversial, with Mark Chapman.

Normally, Vaughanie is much more likely to say something controversial than me, but on a show in June 2015, we do a phone interview with young England cricketer Alex Hales where I surprise everyone with a very tough question.

'Next year, Halesy, would you be happy to miss an England game to go and play in the IPL [Indian Premier League]?' I say, out of the blue.

The issue is a hot potato because players can make a lot of money playing Twenty20 cricket in the IPL and Alex is momentarily rendered speechless. 'Wow. . . now that is putting me on the spot. . .' he replies, and laughs nervously.

'Goodness me, Tuffers!' exclaims Chappers. 'Where's that come from?'

'Have you been to a journalism school this week?' says Vaughanie.

'Sorry. . .' I say.

Saying you'll play in the IPL over England leaves a player open to accusations of greed and that he is lacking national pride, but actually my question leads to an interesting little debate where Vaughanie, a former England skipper himself, says that he thinks Alex should play in the IPL. 'I never thought I'd say this, but it's not an Ashes year next year. Yes, Test match cricket is important but if you look further ahead to the World Cup in 2019, getting our players playing in different formats around the world is [also important]. Even if it means missing one Test match in May I actually wouldn't be that concerned. . . I don't expect you to answer that Alex, but I'll answer it for you.'

Chappers rounds off the conversation, saying: 'Well, Alex, listen, thanks for talking to us this evening. That's the first time Tuffers has ever come out with anything that difficult for any guest to answer in the four or five years of doing this show. Well done for dealing with it.'

Everyone's laughing.

'I just came out with a question, that's all,' I say.

'Oh, I've just had the editor of the *Today* programme on,' adds Chappers, 'and they've asked if you could stand in for John Humphrys tomorrow. . .'

That's me – the new Paxman of cricket.

Away from that show and *TMS*, I welcome any other chances to talk cricket and in 2006 I accidentally make myself very unpopular with the entire Australian team with some comments I make in an interview. I'm at a pub doing a promotion for a lager company, when someone approaches me with a camera and a mic and asks me to give a message to the Australian cricket team. I assume it's got something to do with the promo, which is a light-hearted affair, so I poke fun at the Aussies for losing to us in the previous year's Ashes series: 'Oi, Ponting, why did you bat first at Edgbaston you muppet? . . . Glenn – unlucky for stepping on the ball. . .' – that sort of nonsense.

A few weeks later, I get some texts from friends in Australia saying either: 'What have you done?' or 'Good on yer.'

At first I've no idea what they're on about, but then I discover that my little video was played at the Allan Border Medal awards dinner. Named after the great former Australian captain, it's the Oscars of Australian cricket where the cricketer of the past season, as voted for by his peers, the media and umpires, receives the Allan Border Medal. When my message was played, some of the Australian Test boys promptly got up and walked out and now my name is plastered across the press Down Under for disrespecting them. Oops.

I further endear myself to the Aussie boys when they next come over to England for an Ashes series in 2009. As part of a promotion with Marmite, before the second Test, a fifteen-metre-high image of me naked is projected onto the side of the hotel where they are staying (see, I told you Dawn doesn't mind me baring all if it's for a laugh. . . just not when I'm presenting a cheque to a very worthy charity). My coy side-on-looking-over-the-shoulder pose mimics the famous stunt when a photo of TV presenter and model Gail Porter in the buff was projected onto the side of the Houses of Parliament back in 1999. Instead of Gail's curves, any Aussies coming back late to the hotel are treated to the sight of me at seven times my normal size with a 'Too tasty for the Aussies' label covering my bum and a big Marmite pot covering the crown jewels. So much for Vegemite. . .

In 2007, I'm recruited as a reporter for the BBC's new weeknight magazine show, *The One Show*. Again, I'm delighted because in my role

I'm given the chance to report on all sorts of subjects beyond cricket (more in Chapter 6), but occasionally I'm given some cricket-related assignments too.

One I'll never forget is meeting up with the brilliant sports illustrator Paul Trevillion. Born in 1934, Paul attended his first Test match at the age of four when his dad took him to the Oval and he saw some of Len Hutton's famous innings of 364 against Australia (he didn't see all the runs because Hutton's innings lasted more than thirteen hours). Fifteen years later, Paul witnessed England's legendary win over Australia in the 1953 Coronation Ashes, this time as an illustrator for the *Sporting Record* newspaper.

We meet in the Lord's library in 2013, the sixtieth anniversary year of that series. I've been warned that he is an eccentric character, but nothing can prepare me for the whirlwind that hits me. He has long silver hair in a Seventies footballer mullet style and cuts a dash in black trousers, shirt, white waistcoat and black cowboy hat. He has met and drawn everyone in his career – from Muhammad Ali to Michael Jordan, Jack Nicklaus to Andy Murray – not to mention inventing a revolutionary golf putting stroke, having a showbiz career as a stand-up comedian and setting a world speed-kissing record. At the age of seventy-nine, he's still full of energy and working full-time, illustrating books and producing his ever popular *You are the Ref* and *You are the Umpire* newspaper strips. All of which he's happy to tell me about at length, speaking a mile a minute and shouting the more excited he gets. I can barely get a word in edgeways as he talks me through the anecdotes behind his fantastic original artworks of the great players from that 1953 Test series, including my dad's favourites, Keith Miller and Denis Compton. Our poor old director has to remind Paul that the entire item will only last for six minutes on the show and to try and shorten his anecdotes.

As we're leafing through his old drawings, I discover he's got a lovely surprise for me among them – a pencil drawing he did specially of one P.C.R. Tufnell appealing for lbw in my heyday. Howzat.

There's a minor match going on in the ground, so we then go out together and sit in the stands where he shows me how he goes about drawing cricketers.

'So what are your plans now? Are you ever going to retire?' I ask to round off the item.

'No, I'm eighty next year,' he replies. 'All that you've seen before is just the blossom on tree, now you're going to get the fruit.'

It's a hilarious morning. I love him and when *The One Show* production team see the rushes, they decide they've got to get him in the studio for the live show with hosts Alex Jones and Matt Baker. Sure enough he causes merry chaos.

'Now we can say hello to the fully blossomed fruit, Paul's in the studio and it's a pleasure to have you with us,' says Alex by way of introduction.

'I'm so happy to be here, I tell you, I'M HAPPY! I'm ready to go!'

Alex asks him which sporting moment stands out from his long career and he nominates the 1966 World Cup and talks about getting to know all the players.

'And what did they think of all the sketches you did then?' says Matt.

'Loved them, didn't they? Loved 'em. I'M THE MAN!'

'You are the man!'

As well as his lifelike portraits, he also does animalistic ones where he morphs animals into famous sportsmen (check out his 'Pelephant' on YouTube, where he transforms a drawing of an elephant into a picture of Pelé's face).

He shows Matt and Alex a drawing where he visualises Wayne Rooney's face as a bulldog. 'What people don't realise is that he's a very good-looking footballer,' he concludes. 'Photographs badly.'

Next up, Gareth Bale's face as a chimp – 'I always think he looks like a cheeky chimp who steals the nut. He steals the ball, bang, it's in the goal. TOP MAN!'

They've got Shane Filan, formerly of Westlife, in the studio and, while the next six-minute VT is on, they challenge Paul to draw him.

'Well, Shane's going to be tough, because he's a good-looking boy – he's just eyes and teeth. . . listen, I saw you in that group Westlife and them three backing singers didn't do you any favours.'

'Now, there's no need for that,' replies Shane.

'It's going to be tough – it was easier drawing Tuffers. He's got a lot of lines – he's lived in his face.'

'Tell you what Paul,' says Matt, desperately trying to introduce the next item, 'while you get your pens out. . .'

'You haven't asked me what animal you look like,' interrupts Paul, pointing at Matt.

'Go on then, what do I look like?'

'You look like a bear, A POLAR BEAR!'

Everyone's pissing themselves. I've never looked at Matt and thought, 'Polar bear', but Paul sees the world differently.

'I tell you why, because polar bears look lovely and cuddly and then they crush you. When I came in you shook my hand – and look at my hand now, there's no life in it. . .'

What a character.

When I appear on the BBC's *Room 101* programme in 2012, the Aussies are again in my line of fire as I nominate 'the Australian cricket team 1990–2002' as my first choice to banish into Room 101.

'Does that coincide with your own career?' asks host Frank Skinner.

'It does as a matter of fact.' (Actually, come to think of it now, my last Test against Aussie was in 2001. . .)

'I thought it might.'

'They made my life a misery. I played in five Ashes series, never won one. Won the odd Test, but never won a series. I think that side that we came up against, statistically, was the best side that's ever played the game, and I copped it.'

'The only thing you ever won in Australia was *I'm a Celebrity*. . . *Get Me Out of Here!*' notes Frank. True.

Incidentally, the other two pet hates I nominate on the show are canapés and tipping.

I hate canapés. It's impossible to hold a polite conversation with a high commissioner or someone important, while holding a glass of wine in one hand and trying to eat a mini-burger pinned together by a cocktail stick in a serviette in the other or without spitting puff pastry from a mushroom vol-au-vent all over them.

As for tipping, it's got to the stage where it's ruining the end of meals.

Dawn always tips, but I never quite know what to tip: is the service included? If the service is on the bill, do you tip on top of that? If the service has been bad but the tip is included on the bill, do you get it taken off? It's a nightmare, especially in America.

One time, in Miami, I go into a sandwich shop and order a couple of ham sandwiches to take away. The guy makes the sandwiches, which are about two inches deep with ham. He says, 'That'll be ten dollars,' so I give him the exact money and walk out.

I've got about fifty yards down the street, when I hear two fellas from the shop calling after me: 'Hey, hey, where you going?'

'What's up?'

'You didn't leave a tip.'

'Er, well, you told me what I owed and I paid you. . .'

I'm frogmarched back to the deli with my arm behind my back. They make me feel like I've nicked the sandwiches and threaten to call the police. I have visions of being arrested, taken to Rikers Island and being buggered senseless by a load of gang members just for the sake of a couple of ham sarnies.

They point out a sign which says that you have to tip and make me hand over an extra couple of dollars.

'Why didn't you just say that when I gave you the money? I had no idea you had to tip in a takeaway, even in the States.'

Anyway, sorry, I've gone off on a massive tangent, but *Test Match Special* habits die hard. Back on the subject of *TMS*, I must tell you that I have something of an epiphany during my first commentary assignment of 2015 – England versus. New Zealand at Lord's. It proves to be one of the most exciting matches any of us have seen in years, with both sides having periods of dominance and playing great attacking cricket.

The game is still in the balance going into the last day. England are batting and have four wickets remaining and the pressure is now on England captain Alastair Cook to decide when to declare and set New Zealand a target that leaves England enough time to bowl them out and win, but also enough of a lead that they don't lose. The tendency is to play safe and not to leave a chaseable target due to the fear of an embarrassing defeat – if Cookie gets it wrong, he's liable to be slaughtered by the press, especially as there's just been a big controversy about leaving out star batsman Kevin Pietersen.

As a twenty-three-year-old lad in the dressing room, my attitude would be 'Give them **** all.' But on this Bank Holiday morning I wake up feeling very jolly after four days of exciting cricket and think to myself: 'Why does it matter so much if you win or lose? Don't settle for a draw – go for the win. This game deserves a result.'

When I get to Lord's, there's a huge line of people snaking all the way around the ground to get tickets. Everyone's buzzing about the match so far and the club are even letting kids in for free, so it's going to be a full house – which is very unusual for a fifth day in a Test.

I'm thinking, 'This is great.' In the modern day, when people supposedly have the attention spans of goldfish, Test matches that last five days still have the power to grip people when the game is played in the right spirit.

That's why I love the way the Kiwis play under their brilliant captain Brendon McCullum. He says we're going to go out there and attack when we bat, and then bowl with five slips to our fast bowlers and try to win. In this game, England have played with the same sort of daring approach, and it's been wonderful to watch the two sides go at it, with the momentum shifting this way and that.

When the final day's play gets underway, the declaration problem is taken out of Cook's hands as England are bowled out quite quickly. It's the best thing that could happen for the game, because it leaves New Zealand a very tough but gettable target of 345 runs. You can guarantee that McCullum's boys are initially planning to get it, but an inspired England bowling attack reduce them to twelve runs for three wickets by lunch and leave them batting for survival.

The Bank Holiday crowd, with all the excited youngsters, is slightly more boisterous than usual, and they are roaring the England boys towards victory.

We have our window open and, when England's new hero, all-rounder Ben Stokes, bowls McCullum for his second wicket in two deliveries during the afternoon, we literally feel the noise. It's like a shockwave. I feel my hair move and there's no breeze; it's quite uncanny. Aggers also comments on it. When Ed Smith comes back from his break, he tells us that he was sitting in the Mound Stand at the time and felt it too. Alastair Cook says in the press conference later that he's never heard a sound like it.

Whoosh.

I'd forgotten the power of Test cricket to bring that sort of energy and excitement when it's played aggressively, and it's so refreshing. It's an absolute joy to be here and I can't wait for my half-hour shifts. I want to get on and be part of it.

Someone sends me a tweet, saying, 'Your commentary when Ben Stokes was coming in to bowl to McCullum reminded me of my four-year-old in a toy shop. That's what makes you a great commentator.' Well, I do feel like a kid again.

At 6pm, after a thrilling day, with less than ten overs remaining, Moeen Ali takes a fantastic running catch on the boundary to complete victory for England, despite a spirited rearguard action by New Zealand.

I go down on the pitch to do a round-up with Aggers. We interview Alastair Cook, who tells us it's been one of the most enjoyable Test matches he's played in his life. Okay, maybe that's partly because England won, but Brendon McCullum says the same. Enjoyable? That's a word we hear too rarely from modern sportsmen. It's usually, 'pressure, pressure, pressure'.

Enjoyment is kind of the point of sport, and it's got lost a bit.

McCullum's team have lost the match, but he's not crestfallen: 'Great game. We'll learn from it and do better next time.' Brilliant attitude. A breath of fresh air and all sports teams could learn from it.

In the evening, on our cricket show, me and Vaughanie say that if England play with that spirit every day and we lose a series 5-0, we don't really mind. It's great to watch. You see there's a passion. The reality is that if you play like that, you won't lose all the time. The Aussies have proved down the years that playing ultra-aggressive cricket can actually make you a dominant force.

There's so much emphasis on winning in sport now that it's very hard for coaches and managers to have that devil-may-care attitude for fear of getting the sack after losing a few games. Too often the game itself seems to become the backstory. It's all about the 'W'; the win is the only thing that matters. In football, it's the José Mourinho philosophy with Chelsea. Nick a goal, then park the bus in front of your own goal. They win the league, but the fans are bored out of their minds.

A win, a trophy, a statistic becomes more important than the experience of the game, and when you think about it, it's rather a boring way to live life. Sport is so much more fun to play and watch when it's played with freedom.

The pressure the money men, us in the media and the fans put on the results, ultimately leads to us watching a less exciting game because we are increasing the fear of failure. Why are we all going mental when our cricket team loses? They're eleven blokes – if they all give their best, try everything to win, learn from their defeats and improve, why crucify them and call for them to be dropped and sacked when they don't?

After all, as Keith Miller, my granddad and dad would have told you (and Ed Smith will tell you now, too, if you're half-listening), playing cricket is not like having a Messerschmitt up your arse. Let's enjoy the game.

5

LET'S GET QUIZZICAL

I made my first appearance on *A Question of Sport* as a guest in the early Nineties, soon after I made my debut for England. Bill Beaumont and Ian Botham were the captains and we all went up to do the recording on a Sunday. A nice Sunday lunch, with quizmaster David Coleman sitting at the head of the table, made it feel like a family get-together. Beefy brought out the red wine and we all teetered off into the studio to do the show.

I absolutely loved it — it really was a dream come true. When I was a kid, Mum, Dad, Greg and me all sat round the telly watching the show and playing along, so to be asked to actually appear on it — well, I thought I'd made it.

After Bill and Ian, Ally McCoist and John Parrott took over as skippers in 1996, with Frankie Dettori replacing John in 2002 and Matt Dawson — when he had hair — then replacing Frankie in 2004. I probably appeared half a dozen times on the show during those years. In 2007, Ally goes off to become assistant manager at Rangers FC and for a while the Beeb invite various guest captains to sit in Ally's chair – including Jamie Redknapp, Darren Gough, Ricky Hatton, my old spinning nemesis Shane Warne. . . and me.

I'm very chuffed to be asked to have a go. Strangely enough, I was never asked to captain a side during my eighteen years as a professional cricketer. For some reason, I was not marked down as a potential leader of men except, perhaps, to the bar at the end of the game.

I've always thought I know quite a lot about sport – I follow cricket, football and rugby in particular – but the prospect of captaining a side on *A Question of Sport* makes me start to doubt that in the week before filming the show. I don't exactly revise for the show like an exam – not that I ever revised for an exam in my school days – but I watch the sports news on telly a bit more closely than normal. Then on the day of the recording, on the way to the studio on Wood Lane, Shepherd's Bush, I get the driver to stop off at a garage and, rather than buy the *Daily Star*, I pick up copies of the *Daily Telegraph* and *The Times*. Scouring the latest stories in the broadsheet sports pages for a few minutes, I'm sure I will soak up knowledge of the entire history of sport.

At the studio, as I'm waiting to go on set, I get chatting to one of the guys working behind the scenes who I've met before:

'Go on, tell us – who's the mystery guest this week?' I say.

He looks horrified: 'You what?'

'Go on, give us a clue, I won't tell anyone. . .'

'What?'

'Well, you know, I'm just a bit nervous on my first show as captain, I don't know too much about other sports.'

'Oh no, sorry, mate. All of that is top-secret. I wouldn't ask anyone that again, if I were you.'

'Ooh, crikey, er, only joking. . .'

It's like I'm asking him to help me steal the Crown Jewels.

It is dawning on me that looking over the papers for half an hour on the way to the studio might not be sufficient. Unlike *They Think It's All Over*, which was a comedy panel show with a quiz element, *A Question of Sport* is not scripted at all and no clues are given about what to expect before you get out there. It's a sports quiz first and foremost, with a bit of banter thrown in, and I think that's one of the reasons it's maintained its popularity for so many years.

Aside from the last-minute swotting up and unseemly attempt to cheat, I'm not panicking too much though. I've been made to feel so at home as a team member in the past, I plan to just go on and enjoy it.

Once I'm in the studio, however, I soon realise that the dynamic completely changes when you are captain. Previously, I've been expected to know my cricket and if I get a couple of general sporting questions right too, happy days. As skipper, you're supposed to have a bit of a wider knowledge of sport so you can help your team-mates out. You're also expected to lead the conversation. Sometimes even the most confident, successful sportspeople aren't so comfortable appearing on a show like this, so you have to help them along.

Presenter Sue Barker will ask one of my team-mates if they wanted to 'go home or away' on their question and I'll just be sitting there quietly until I remember I'm captain and supposed to be giving them advice, getting them talking and helping to drive the show.

That takes some getting used to, but Sue and the production team are very helpful in guiding me (well, helpful within the rules).

In the absence of any great depth of sporting knowledge, I revert back to my days in a cricket dressing room, making fun out of whatever's available. I'm terrible at remembering the dates of when things happened, though, and I give an answer that's a good decade out.

'Is it 1982, Sue?'

'No, 1995.'

'Well, the Nineties were a bit of a blur for me. . .'

My team loses to Daws's by a country mile, but we have a laugh doing it, have a drink in the green room afterwards with everyone, get in the car and go home.

I thoroughly enjoy the experience, but don't really think about it again until I get a phone call a few months later from Mike saying that the producers want me to do a full series as captain. I'm amazed and absolutely thrilled. It's a real wow moment for me: 'Hold on – me, a captain on *A Question of Sport*?' All those legends who've done the job: Cliff Morgan, Henry Cooper, Freddie Trueman, Brendan Foster, Gareth Edwards, Willie Carson, Bill Beaumont, Beefy Botham. . . and now me? I do feel immensely proud and honoured to be asked.

I'd watched the show with Goughie, Warney and Ricky Hatton as captains, but didn't realise I was a part of some sort of audition process. It was never put to me like that – as far as I was concerned, I was a guest captain and I was excited just to get asked as a one-off. Looking back, I'm glad I wasn't aware I was in the running to be a permanent captain, because I might have panicked and tried too hard.

Even when I do my first series, in 2007, I don't feel too daunted because the production team make it all so natural and relaxed. After seeing how badly my team did when I was guest captain, they clearly didn't pick me for the breadth of my sporting knowledge and I don't feel like a new era of the show is resting on my shoulders. They always just encourage me to go on there and have a laugh and I've continued to do that ever since.

I like to think I have raised my game a bit when it comes to my sporting knowledge, too, though, so I can at least give my mate Daws a run for his money. I knew I had to when he first invited me round to his house – you can barely move for stacks of sports trivia books in his downstairs loo.

In recent years, since the BBC has created a new northern base in Salford, Greater Manchester, the show has been recorded up there. We usually do a two-day stint, so I get up there early on the first day, record three or four shows each day and then drive back home. They come so thick and fast that sometimes you can get blasé about the succession of brilliant sportsmen and women we have on the show – Sir Chris Hoy, Michael Johnson, Dame Tanni Grey-Thompson, Rory McIlroy, Dame Kelly Holmes, Shane Warne, Martina Navratilova – the list goes on and on. What's great is that whenever we have someone on for the first time, they are just as excited as I was when I made my debut all those years ago. It is such an institution; most sport-loving Brits grew up watching it, it's like a badge of honour to be on the show.

The spotlight is focused on Daws and I when it comes to the 'Captains'

Challenge' round and it can be, well, challenging. Like the time we have to play sports-related tunes on a piano, earning a point for every one our team-mates guess correctly.

Daws is first up and has a slight advantage as he can play a little bit. . . but I mean only a little bit. He plays slow, but vaguely recognisable versions of the *Match of the Day* theme and the French national anthem, which his team-mates Andrew Castle and *Football Focus* presenter Dan Walker identify. Then Dan somehow guesses the *Question of Sport* theme tune within two notes.

When my turn comes, I take my sheet music from Sue and approach the piano like Les Dawson doing his concert pianist act, hamming it up, bowing to the audience, flexing my fingers, swishing the tail of my imaginary dinner jacket out of the way to sit down. That's where the problems start, though, because whereas Les played the piano badly brilliantly, I have never played the piano in my life. My old cricket captain, Mike Gatting, used to say that I had delicate 'hands like a pianist', but that was because I didn't particularly enjoy catching balls smashed at me at 100mph.

To help us out, the producers have put stickers on the keys identifying which note they are, but hitting the right keys in the right order is a challenge, let alone at the right tempo. I end up singing the notes as I poke them with my left forefinger: 'G-E, G-E, A-E-A. F-A, F-A, G-E-G. . .'

My team-mates, the former World Superbike champion James Toseland and ex-rugby league star Martin 'Chariots' Offiah, are looking at me in a state of total bemusement. It brings to mind Les Dawson's gag: 'Oh yes, ladies and gentlemen, where would we be without good music? Here.'

'Just listen to the beginning. . . I've nailed the beginning, big time,' I urge them. 'Ready? Ready? Feel it, feel it. . . G-E, G-E, A-E-Aaaaaa!'

'Sounds like *Snoopy Loopy*,' says James, which is near enough. *Snooker Loopy*, it is.

Buoyed by this success, I then launch into a confident one-fingered rendition of Baddiel and Skinner's *Three Lions*, which James recognises instantly.

'Here's the next one. . . What sport do you think of when you hear this tune?' asks Sue.

'Right listen carefully, because it's quite difficult, this. . .' I say.

'It's been difficult from the start,' says James. Then, within four notes, he blurts out, 'Formula 1!'

'What?' says Sue.

'Formula 1. . .'

'. . .is the right answer.'

Three out of three, which is definitely worth my deep bows to take the applause from all sides of the audience. But Daws' and my efforts are put to shame when Sue invites James to the piano. He's brilliant and has the whole audience clapping along. It turns out he's not only a motorcycling superstar and a very handsome chap, he's a talented singer-songwriter who has performed around the world. Some guys have it all.

Playing the piano is not my forte, but at least it doesn't hurt, unlike the occasion when we have to answer questions for 45 seconds while 2012 Paralympic silver medallist Sam Ingram chucks us about on a judo mat. Sam has a genetic eye condition called conal dystrophy, meaning he can't see colour and has no central vision, but, as the amazing performances of the athletes at the London Paralympics showed, it's all about ability rather than disability, and he certainly has a lot more ability at this than me.

We have five minutes with him before the show just so he can explain to us how to hold and how to fall. I half-listen to him.

'You will go easy on us, though, won't you, Sam?'

When it comes to the show itself, we get dressed up in the judo gear. Sam walks out all smiles and I'm hiding behind Daws, who is up first. Sue gives him the choice of whether to name Olympics or Commonwealth Games host cities and he opts for the Olympics. Being an ex-rugby player, Daws is strong and used to a bit of rough and tumble, and he manages to blurt out fifteen correct answers while he's being thrown about: 'London. . . Bei-jiiiing. . . Athen, Ath-ens. . . Sydney!. . . Atlanta. . . Barcelon-aaaaagh. . .' and so on.

I think the fact that Daws gives Sam a good little tussle riles him up a bit. When I take to the mat, I can see from his demeanour that he's a bit more up for this one. On the other hand, I'm feeling rather reluctant.

'Okay, let's have it. . . Is there a doctor in the house? Paramedics? Lovely, thank you. . .'

My first move is to run away from him and get a couple of quick answers in — 'Melbourne. . . Kuala Lumpur. . .' — but he soon catches up with me and has me down.

'Kuala Lumpur. . . oh my God. . .'

He lets me get up, but the next thing I know, he's got me upside down above his head with my feet almost clipping the studio lights then slamming me down on the mat – 'Edinburgh, Montreal, er, Japaaaaan. . .!'

Of course, doing it for the first time ever, I don't have time to remember how to land properly so I land more on my back and the back of my head, than my feet. Thud! The studio shakes with the impact and there's a big 'Oooooooooh' from the audience. When I see the playback of the show, they cut to Sue's face. Her mouth is wide open in shock: 'Oh God, I think he's killed Tuffers. . .'

I can feel my back twinge-ing but pull myself up to take more punishment.

'Maaan-chester. . .'

Sam's dragging me around like a rag doll and I realise my judo trousers are falling down. The audience on one side of the studio are on the verge of seeing a half-moon. I manage to pull them up just in time to receive my second overhead slam for luck (two more than Daws got). 'Syd-neyyyyyy.'

When Sue mercifully calls an end to the ritual slaughter, it takes me about twenty seconds to get up. Daws, Sue and the studio audience are in fits of laughter.

As is traditional in judo, I eventually bow to my opponent, but drop my trousers at the same time to give my team and the audience behind me an eyeful.

In the circumstances, my score of six isn't too bad.

When it comes to the pure physical challenges, I'm always struggling against Daws, but sometimes I can overcome him with my superior technique. That's the case when we have a kayak race in Salford Quays which I win. Daws magnanimously paddles over to congratulate me, shakes my hand and deliberately capsizes me. I have to rush back to London after filming and when I take off the kayaking gear, my underpants are sopping wet, so I have to quickly take them off, wring them out and stuff them in my bag. Sod's law; when I go through security at Manchester airport, my bag gets pulled for a baggage search. I do feel sorry for the security guy who physically recoils as he pulls out my damp grundies.

'Urrrrgh.'

'Just been kayaking in Salford Quays. . .'

When it comes to sheer terror, nothing will ever match the time Daws and I have to answer questions while wingwalking. 'Ah, Tuffers doesn't like heights or flying – let's not just put him in a plane, let's strap him to the top of one while it does a loop-the-loop over the Gloucestershire countryside.' It's just horrific – freezing-cold wind battering your face, and pulling a few G as the plane flips around all over the place. Sadistic Sue Barker chose watching Daws and me doing that challenge as one of her top five moments in the entire history of the show – I'm so glad she enjoyed watching it.

Much more enjoyable for me is the penalty challenge we do at Wembley. It's not the first time I've played there, because I was lucky enough to play as goalkeeper in a test game played there, before the stadium officially opened for professional football in 2007. That even earned me a cameo appearance on that evening's *Match of the Day*, as former Crystal Palace striker Mark Bright slipped the ball past me for the first ever goal at the stadium.

This time Daws and I run out on the hallowed turf like kids, me wearing Arsenal's classic yellow and blue 1979 FA Cup final kit, Matt in the 1985 Cup final kit of his beloved Everton.

We've got three shots each against each other. Daws wins the toss and opts to strike first. I give him the old Bruce Grobbelaar wobbly legs routine, but make the mistake of diving to my left as he drills it straight down the middle where I had been standing.

Then, as the commentator Steve Bower puts it, 'It's the first chance we get to look at that sweet left foot of Phil Tufnell.' I hit it pretty well, squeak it under Daws' body as he dives to the left and celebrate in front of imaginary fans like I've actually scored in a cup final.

Taking his second penalty, Matt forgets where he is, leaning back and striking it way over the bar more like a penalty-taker at Twickenham.

'Hit it well again,' I shout up to him as he treks up the steps and searches for the ball under rows of empty seats.

I score with a delightful shot, this time to Matt's right just under the crossbar to take the lead, while Matt scores his next to even it up, leaving me with a chance to take victory. I go for power, but I slice it over the bar like Chris Waddle at Italia '90.

It's a couple of days before the FA Cup final and the groundsmen have been poised by the edge of the pitch watching this saga unfold, grimacing at each wild hack at their lovingly prepared turf. When our director asks if they mind if we have a sudden-death shootout to decide the winner, the answer is a swift no. So we shake hands on a draw and both head up to the royal box and together lift the FA Cup which has been brought out for us specially, a great thrill. Meanwhile, down below, the groundstaff are already prodding anxiously at the turf around the penalty spot and goal line.

Over the years, we do the occasional celebrity special and in one of them my unparalleled ability to forget dates comes to the fore again.

Sue asks Daws' team: 'Which of these happened in 1990? Theo Walcott was born; Phil Tufnell makes his England Test debut; Nick Faldo wins a Major for the first time; and Tony McCoy wins for the first time in his career.'

'The first six years, Tuffers didn't even realise he was playing for England,' says Patrick Kielty.

'If we hadn't had Ceefax, I wouldn't have even turned up,' I say. 'That's how I used to find out. "I'm playing for England tomorrow – look, it's on Ceefax."'

'We are going to go with the legend. . .' begins Matt.

'Phil Tufnell,' says Patrick.

'No, AP McCoy.'

'AP won for the first time in his career in 1992. The legend that is Tuffers made his Test debut in 1990.'

My team is celebrating when Patrick pipes up: 'What I love about it is that there are very few shows you can do, where a professional sportsman is the answer, he's in the room, he's the answer and he goes: "Was it me?"'

'Do you remember who you played on your Test debut, Tuffers?' asks Sue.

'He was just camping in the next field and just went across for a game of bat and ball,' replies team-mate Bradley Walsh.

Later, in the final Picture Round, we only need seven points to win, but I make a right mess of it and don't give Bradley or my other team-mate DJ Spoony a cat in hell's chance. First photo: starting grid.

'Oh, oh, motor racing at the start. . .'

'Er. . .'

Before they have time to think: 'Pass!'

The next one is the San Siro stadium and I can't even begin to think of how to explain that without saying the words.

'Oh pass, pass. . .'

Then I lie down flat on my back to try and imitate someone doing the luge.

'What's this? What's this?'

'Toboggan,' shouts Bradley.

'No, no, pass!' I reply as I leap to my feet to give the next clue.

And so it goes on. All I keep saying is 'Pass' before they can get more than a word in.

As I walk back to my seat at the end of my minute, the audience, Sue, Daws and his team-mates Patrick Kielty and Ronan Keating are pissing themselves at my frantic and almost totally ineffective efforts. Bradley and Spoony are looking at me in disbelief at my, um, passing ability.

'Pass! Pass! Pass! We didn't have a chance to speak!' says Bradley in mock fury at me. 'Give us a chance. We only needed seven to win – you've thrown it all away! I'm not coming on this show again – it's a joke. Call yourself a skipper?'

A couple of years later, in 2011, Bradley reminds me of my meltdown when I'm a guest on a celebrity special of ITV show *The Chase*, which he presents.

Another offshoot of going into the jungle is that I get invited to go on a lot of these general knowledge-type quizzes. Dawn and I have got a good stock of board games in the cupboard at home and enjoy them with family and friends, so I'm always up for having a go. I usually turn up thinking, 'Oh, this will be fun and it's a chance to raise some money for charity.' But as the time approaches to actually walk out on set there is always a horrible realisation: 'I could make a right tit of myself here – I don't really know too much.'

Films, entertainment or who wrote this and that – I'm not great at any of that. Or, as I've shown many times on *A Question of Sport*, the dates when things happened. Most of my knowledge comes from little snippets I've heard here and there on radio, TV or just in random conversations. Things just pop into my head. No one is more surprised than me if I do well – and, oddly enough, over the years I've had a few good results and won a lot of money for various good causes.

When I'm waiting in the green room before *The Chase*, having a chat with my team-mates – interior designer Laurence Llewelyn-Bowen, presenter Ulrika Jonsson and Jennie Bond, the journalist and former BBC royal correspondent – someone pipes up: 'So what's your general knowledge like, Phil?'

'I know nothing!'

'But you always seem to do well on these quizzes.'

'I don't know how!'

Then Bradley pops his head in to wish us good luck and, remembering his appearance on *A Question of Sport*, says: 'Phil – whatever you do, don't say "Pass". It's multiple choice – just say one of them, you might get it bloody right.'

When we get out there, we all have to do the 'Head-to-Head' where each member of our team competes against one of the show's resident 'Chasers', trying to correctly answer general knowledge questions to reach the end of the 'Money Board' before they do. The Chaser gives you either a two-, three- or four-step start, depending on how much you are willing to gamble. Take the harder option, you get less of a head-start but more money if you reach the end. If the Chaser catches you, you get nothing and you're eliminated.

Laurence, Ulrika and Jennie all opt for the safer option and they all manage to stay ahead of the Chaser to stick £13,000 in our prize pot.

I'm the last on our team to have a go. Before starting the Head-to-Head, though, I have to do a 'Cash Builder' round where I'm given a minute to answer as many questions as I can, with a grand awarded for each correct answer. I get four right, which means I have the option to start my Head-to-Head three steps ahead of the Chaser and play for £4,000.

The Chaser I shall be facing is introduced; he strolls on wearing a rather snazzy white suit and black shirt combo. He takes his seat at the top of the big sloping game board, some ten feet up. His name is Paul Sinha, but on *The Chase* he goes by various nicknames: 'The Sinnerman', 'The Smiling Assassin' or 'Sarcasm in a Suit'. Paul is a qualified doctor, stand-up comedian and broadcaster. More importantly, he's also an expert quiz player who has competed in everything from *Mastermind*, through

University Challenge to *Brain of Britain*. To put his intellectual CV in context against mine, an Australian cricket fan once shouted at me, 'Tufnell! Can I borrow your brain? I'm building an idiot.'

On paper, it's a mismatch, but at least I have a head-start and The Sinnerman offers me the chance to start the chase another step away from him. From there, I'd only have to answer four questions correctly to reach 'home' (the end of the board), but the reward would reduce to £1,000. Then he has to reveal the amount I can play for if I take the harder option of moving back a step closer to him. That will mean him only having to get two more right than me to catch me up.

'Come on now, give us something big now, let's see how tough you are,' I say to The Sinnerman.

'Do I look like a man who's done any competitive sport in his life?'

'I dunno, I think I have played cricket with you. . . Think you were the stump.'

Doesn't really make sense as he's not a slim man, but people laugh anyway.

Then The Sinnerman reveals the big-money option: 'Come on, be brave – £67,000!'

Blimey. That would be a massive wedge for our charities, but this fella I'm up against is obviously a fountain of knowledge and I'm, well. . . I'm me.

'Have a chat with your team-mates,' says Bradley.

I turn round and ask them what to do: 'You've gotta go for it,' yells Ulrika and my other team-mates are urging me on, too. So I take up the challenge.

'Right, Tuffers, for £67,000, the chase is on. . .'

They're all multiple-choice questions with three possible answers and I get a handy one to start:

The 'Mexican Wave' is so-called after it became a regular feature at which of these sporting events held in Mexico?

Answer: B 1986 FIFA World Cup.

We both get that one right, so I'm on my way, but the next one has me stumped:

Nevus is the Latin name for which of these bodily features?

A: Bald patch; B: Belly button; C: Birthmark

No clue, but you only have a few seconds to make a choice, so I press the button for C.

'Could be a belly button, but birthmark sounds like a *Nevus*. . .' I say, in an unconvincing attempt to apply some logic to my wild guess.

'Correct answer is. . .' says Bradley.

Ding – answer C lights up on the screen. Get in.

Time to see if the Chaser got it right, too. He's looking pretty smug so I know the answer to that before it's confirmed. Oh well, I'm not shaking him off, but at least I'm moving in the right direction and I've got lucky once already.

Which of these is a flaming dessert?

A: Baked Alaska; B: Crêpe suzette; C: Rum baba

'They're all flaming desserts. . .'

For a second I lose track of what I'm supposed to be doing.

'What's happening?'

The Chaser is laughing.

'It's up to you,' says Bradley.

'When?'

'Now! You can put him under pressure if you wish.'

'How?'

'By pressing the button!'

We used to make crêpe suzette pans at my dad's silversmiths. He also used to hang one in the garden as a target to help me improve the accuracy of my bowling – the satisfying sound of leather on pan meant I was on the right line and length.

I hit B, but immediately have second thoughts: 'Oh no, I might have got that wrong.'

But my instinct proves correct. Even better, the Chaser plumped for rum baba, much to my team-mates' astonishment and delight.

'Rum baba? What happened there?' asks Bradley.

'My GP has banned me from eating desserts for two years, so I can fit into this suit. I don't know what any of them are because I just don't eat them.'

He's comfortable in his suit and I've got a bit more breathing space on the game board.

Next question asks in which Eighties sitcom Vincent Pinner and Penny Warrender were the central characters.

The Chaser hits his button immediately while I'm wracking my brain.

'Press the button, Phil!' urges Bradley.

I go for *Just Good Friends* on a vague memory of the series and then realise Vincent is 'Vince' as I remember him.

'Ooh, I got that right,' I announce before the reveal.

So does the Chaser but I'm now just two questions from glory.

The next question pops up on the screen and I start reading it out loud to myself before Bradley interrupts:

'What is the only country outside Africa in which. . .'

'I ask the questions! What is the only country outside Africa in which lions are still found in the wild?'

I discount option C, Saudi Arabia, but am torn between India and Iran. With time running out I hit B: Iran.

'Might be India, but that's the tiger. . .' I say, pulling my hands up to look like cat paws, but ending up frozen in a Tommy Cooper-like pose.

'Yeah, but what's a lion like?' asks Bradley.

'He's a bit more like this,' I say, moving my paws wider. 'Not like that, like this.' (Apologies, Tommy, RIP.) Whatever, I'm wrong – India is correct and the Chaser catches up a step: 'Yes, you're right,' he says. 'It's associated with the Royal Bengal tiger, but there is a small population of lions in India.'

I still need two correct answers and the next question lands so nicely for me that I'm punching the air before Bradley has even read the question out. Boxer David Haye blamed his loss to Wladimir Klitschko on a broken toe. Definitely right.

One away from £67,000 and still a couple of steps ahead of the Chaser.

Which magazine holds the Man of the Year awards?

A: Esquire; B: GQ; C: FHM

Not sure but hit B.

'I've got a gut feeling, even though I'm on a diet. . .' I explain.

'Alright, you've gone for *GQ*,' says Bradley, pointing at the big screen.

'To go through with sixty-seven thousand pounds, the correct answer is. . . C'mon, Tuffers . . .'

Ding. B.

Yessss! I'm celebrating like I've taken a five-fer, punching the air in the direction of my team-mates and then giving Bradley a big bearhug.

A total of £80,000 in the prize pot, and Head-to-Head victories for all four members of our team, means we'll be playing for a massive twenty grand each for our charities in 'The Final Chase'. This involves a two-minute round where we have to answer as many questions correctly as possible. First person to press the buzzer has to answer and we move forward one space for each correct answer.

As four of us have made it through, we get a four-step head-start on the Chaser.

This is where Laurence Llewelyn-Bowen's massive brain comes into play – he knows just about everything. He's first on the buzzer for almost every question and gets them right, too. Awesome.

The rest of us don't have much to do, except for when a sports question comes up – which Laurence knows nothing about – and he looks at me. I manage to chip in with a handful of correct answers, but our score of 30-odd is almost totally down to him.

The Chaser has two minutes to try and catch us, but can't manage it. If he gets one wrong, it's thrown over to our team and, again, Laurence keeps getting them right to knock him back a space. Even the Chaser says: 'Whoah, you should be sitting up here.' So we all walk away with £20k each for our charities.

Getting lucky with the questions and having a clever bloke on your team like LLB can take you a long way, but sometimes you just need the questions to fall right for you. That happens when my old mucker Martin 'Chariots' Offiah and I pair up for a charity edition of *Pointless Celebrities* in November 2012. Martin's on my team whenever he comes on *A Question of Sport* and we have a laugh because we always struggle – we always say 'We're hanging on, we're hanging on. . .' That's on a sports quiz; neither of us would claim to be oracles of general knowledge, so we think we've got no chance on a quiz like this.

The three pairs we're up against are: Mark Bright, who slotted one past me at Wembley, and 1966 World Cup hero Martin Peters; two-time Olympic gold-medal-winning rower Pete Reed and modern pentathlete Samantha Murray, who won silver at the London Olympics; and ex-snooker star (and *A Question of Sport* captain) John Parrott with sports presenter Hazel Irvine.

The first-round question is simply to come up with a UK city's name that begins with 'C', 'I', 'T', 'E' or 'S'.

Brighty goes first and plumps for Stoke, which isn't that obscure, but scores him a creditably low score of 14.

Then presenter Alexander Armstrong turns to me to nominate on behalf of our team, but the duvet of stupidity instantly descends upon me. My mind just goes blank and of all the cities in the UK, literally the only one I can think of which starts with any of those letters is Coventry.

'I've got one I'm going to go with, I think. . . stay in the game, stay in the game. . . I'm going to go with Coventry.'

'Coventry, says Phil. Coventry. . .' repeats Alexander with the practised politeness of someone who has heard some crap answers over the years.

'Let's see if he's right. Let's see how many of our one hundred said Coventry. . .'

As the totaliser starts going down, I go 'Ooh', as if it's some achievement to know that Coventry is in England, but it soon stops at 53.

Martin's got his arms folded and shaking his head. Alexander says: 'Fifty-three!'

'That's a lot,' I agree.

Alexander turns to his sidekick Richard Osman: 'Richard?'

'It's not my fault.'

'No, I'm just saying it's a big score.'

'Yeah, it's a lot, and Martin doesn't look happy. He's thinking, Chris Kamara got me knocked out in round one, now Tuffers is going to do it. Come back a third time – bring one of the Chuckle Brothers.'

'They did very well. . .' notes Alexander.

Martin does much better than me when it's his turn, but Hazel, who's very bright, goes for a very obscure Scottish place that turns out not to be a city, so we sneak through into round two, despite a big aggregate score.

'Yes! In your face with the Coventry!'

We continue in the same vein and somehow luck our way into the final, and then just when we need one out of three pointless answers, we get two.

We have to name groups that have won Best International Group at the Brit Awards. Martin knows his music and pulls out Bon Jovi (who won in 1996) and I dig out INXS (1989 winners). The only reason I know about INXS is because, a week or so before filming, I'd been listening to a radio programme about lead singer Michael Hutchence on the fifteenth anniversary of his death, and they were talking about what an underrated band INXS were – and that people forget they won a Brit Award. Total fluke.

As the winning pointless answer pings in, Martin and me are running around the studio celebrating like we've scored in a cup final. Big Richard has got his head down on his desk in disbelief, Alexander and the audience are laughing, clearly all wondering how these two herberts have managed to see off reasonably intelligent people and win.

Ever since, whenever Martin and I see each other we go: '*Pointless* winners! Anyone else here won *Pointless*? We have. . .'

I generally prefer the quiz shows where you don't need such a wide range of general knowledge, as there's less chance of showing myself up. Mind you, the pressure is on a bit in 2008 when Dawn and I agree to appear together on *All Star Mr & Mrs*, a revamped version of the old family favourite show, hosted by Phillip Schofield and Fern Britton. You have to answer multiple-choice questions about your partner's habits, likes and dislikes, while they sit in a booth with big earmuffs on (and vice versa); then they come out and see if they can guess what you have said. It would be a bit embarrassing to go on national TV and get loads of questions about each other wrong. Happily, we do really well and beat the other two couples on the show to win £30,000 for our charity, The Children's Trust, of which I'm honorary vice president. The only one I get wrong is when I'm asked: 'What is the worst thing your partner has ever cooked?'

The answer is beef stroganoff, the first thing Dawn ever cooked for me round at her house soon after we met. How I forgot that, I don't know. Let's just say Dawn is a better cook than she showed that night, as our meal concluded with me involuntarily pebble-dashing her back garden. And they say romance is dead. . .

Another quiz show story that will go down in Tufnell family legend is our hapless effort on *All Star Family Fortunes* in 2006. Our team consists of me, my brother Greg, my dad, his second wife Val and her daughter; we're up against Dame Kelly Holmes and her family. Again, this is a show that's more about using a bit of common sense than requiring encyclopedic general knowledge, so we fancy our chances beforehand. Well, we win a couple of hundred quid, which may just be the lowest total in the history of the show. That's partly because my old dad's common sense is quite different to the average Joe. This is best highlighted when the host Vernon Kay asks: 'If you saw someone you fancied across a crowded bar, what would you do?'

'Smile,' I say.

Greg says, 'Wink.'

Then it's dad's turn: 'Buy her a fur coat.'

What? Everyone falls about laughing. 'Well, it always worked for me,' he says, deadpan.

Genius.

Despite the pre-show stressing out and occasions in the studio when the duvet of stupidity has smothered me, I think that's why I'm pleased to be invited on so many quizzes – they're usually great fun and something memorable always happens. The new Channel 4 daytime quiz for spring 2015, *Benchmark*, is no exception.

The concept of the show is quite simple – one contestant has the chance to win thousands of pounds with the help of a team of ten people, aka 'Benchmarkers', and I take part in two celebrity episodes, both as a contestant and Benchmarker.

In the quiz, the Benchmarkers have to give their answers to a series of numerical general knowledge questions and the average of all the ten answers sets the benchmark. The contestant then has to decide whether the correct answer is higher or lower.

Paddy McGuinness is the host, and we have a good bunch of people playing, including the presenter and actor Joe Swash, Olympic silver-medal-winning gymnast Louis Smith, England international rugby star James Haskell, Geordie comedian Chris Ramsey and darts' king of bling Bobby George. It's quite hard to make a fool of yourself playing *Benchmark*, because the show's definition of 'general knowledge' is so broad, the answer often could be anything. In fact, it's so broad, I do get a bit annoyed when I'm the contestant and one of the questions is: 'How many lies does the average person tell per day?'

The benchmark is four, and I go higher, but the answer is three – I mean, how does anyone know the exact answer to that? The people they asked could be lying. I wouldn't mind, but I'm playing for the Brain Tumour Charity and want to win as much as I can for them. I win a grand in total, but the jackpot is £50,000, so I would have liked to do better.

I say it is hard to make a fool of yourself, but when it's my turn to be a Benchmarker, I have a right good go.

'What percentage of journeys in Holland are taken on a bicycle?'

I'm going: 'Well, Holland, nice and flat, everyone's on a bike – sixty-five per cent.'

The answer is twelve.

'They do have cars as well, Phil. How many tonnes of sausages are consumed per week in Britain?'

'Well, a ton is like a transit van, and Brits do like their sausages, so, erm – sixty tonnes.'

The answer is 3,500 tonnes.

The funniest one, though, is when we're asked on average how many pints does a man drink in his lifetime. I say, 'Well, your drinking career's about forty years, couple of pints a day, the odd day off – what's that, say 25,000?'

James Haskell goes for 24,000.

The answer is 7,000.

We're miles out, but nothing compared to Bobby George, who'd guessed 54,000.

'If anything, I knocked a few off. . .' he says with a shrug.

It's a really enjoyable show and I think people will get hooked on it.

But whatever quizzes I do in future, the daddy of them all for me is and will always be *A Question of Sport*. As I write, I'm coming up to nine years as captain on the show, a fact that I can hardly believe. I've been there to celebrate its forty-fifth birthday in January 2015. Before that, for the thousandth episode in March 2013, I teamed up with former skippers Bill Beaumont and Ally McCoist, while Willie Carson and John Parrott played for Daws' team. We had a great laugh – and my team won! – but more than that, that day underlined again for me what a privilege it is to be part of Britain's longest-running quiz show. In New Zealand, they say that when rugby players play for the All Blacks, they are just taking care of the shirt to pass on to the next generation. That's how I feel about *A Question of Sport*, a TV institution.

One of the joys of my working life over the past few years has been the sheer variety of things I've been asked to do. Between my regular sports-related work on *Test Match Special* and *A Question of Sport*, all sorts of surprising proposals come in that give me access to places I might never otherwise visit, meeting interesting people and allowing me to experience all sorts of random activities.

When it comes to random, I couldn't ask for a better job than being a reporter for *The One Show*. Three or four times a month I catch a plane, train or automobile to a different part of Britain to cover a story. Quite often, other than the location, I don't know too much about what I'll be doing or who I'm meeting before I get there.

I'm always happy when my final destination turns out to be a pub, like the time I went to Wendover in the Chiltern Hills to meet the world's oldest barmaid, an extraordinary lady called Dolly Saville. Dolly was born in 1914, just months before the outbreak of the First World War, and when she did her first shift at the Red Lion Hotel in 1940, a pint cost 8d (3½p). When I visit, she's ninety-nine years old and a great-great-grandmother, but she looks at least twenty-five years younger, and is still doing three lunchtime shifts per week in the hotel bar. She's a great advertisement for the benefits of staying in the pub all your life.

Over the years, Dolly has met everyone from Dame Vera Lynn to former prime minister Edward Heath, and shows me photos of her with Sir Stanley Matthews and Pierce Brosnan.

Dolly tells me the secret of her success is meeting people, keeping active – and her favourite tipple of whisky and tonic water. As a treat for her, the show commissions artist Carne Griffiths to paint Dolly's portrait. Carne is renowned for working with unusual liquids, including teas and alcohol, so he adds a dash of whisky to his painting. He really captures her cheerful spirit (excuse the pun) in the picture and, when we reveal the finished portrait to Dolly, she's really thrilled with the result.

Dolly worked at the Red Lion all the way up to the end of 2014. I understand that she passed away in February 2015, but not before reaching the big 100, when Wendover threw a big party in her honour. A brilliant century, Dolly; RIP.

A lot of the reports I do for *The One Show* have an artistic element. Art was the one subject at school (apart from PE) that I really liked and I've always maintained that interest. I like to paint and enjoy the sense of freedom and creativity it gives me when I work from a blank canvas.

It's a pleasure to meet different artists and see how they go about their work. I've had the opportunity to talk to very famous artists like Antony Gormley and Quentin Blake, and others who've created their own niche working with different media. I once met a fella who made incredibly realistic images out of food and another guy who made fantastic 3D pavement art.

Sometimes I get to have a go myself. For instance, I had a very enjoyable day in Cambridge with paper artist Justin Rowe, who makes paper sculptures out of books. Justin works in a bookshop and only started carving them up in 2010, when he was asked to make a Christmas window display for the shop. His wife suggested trying paper sculpture and then he thought, well, why not make them as if they are actually emerging from books. He made three at first for the shop window and the response to them was so positive, that ever since he's been doing more paper carving than serving in the shop. The only negative comments he's had are from people saying that it's wrong to cut up books, but he buys all of the old books he uses from junk shops, as they would otherwise end up in landfill.

To me, he brings new life to these unwanted old books. He makes all the sculptures by hand with a scalpel; they are incredibly intricate. They are often inspired by scenes described in books, especially children's books like The Lion, the Witch and the Wardrobe, and they really have a magical quality – talk about making a story jump off the page.

I go round to his house and cut out a tree to help him finish off a forest landscape he's making. Almost immediately I manage to chop off a branch.

'That was meant to be – the tree was always meant to be that shape,' Justin tells me kindly, although I think he might chop my tree down from his forest once I leave.

Before I do, he brings out an amazing sculpture he's made of *The One Show* studio, complete with presenters Matt Baker and Alex Jones sitting on the couch, and a grizzly bear as a cameraman.

'Just got one finishing touch to add,' he says, reaching for another cut-out he made earlier. 'I've got this chap here. . .'

And there I am, immortalised in paper, ready to sit on the sofa opposite.

As well as making art, I enjoy going to art exhibitions and museums, but as you will have gathered from my fortieth birthday trip to Venice, I'm too impatient to queue for the most popular shows and tourist attractions. Actually, the worst example of that was when Dawn and I went to Rome on holiday with the intention of enjoying a week of culture. The problem is, we're staying at a beautiful hotel on the outskirts of the city, which, unusually for Rome, has a pool. It's red-hot and we end up spending most of the week having a lovely time roasting by the pool, only moving as far as local restaurants for dinner. But as the end of our holiday approaches, we start to feel guilty that we haven't experienced any of the art and culture of Rome and must see it properly.

'Today's the day.'

So we go to one of the drivers at the hotel and say, 'What's the way to do it? It's so hot – do you know all the places to go?'

He says, 'Yes, I can take you.'

'Is there going to be a lot of queuing to get into these places?'

'Well, yes,' he replies to my stupid question. 'There are a lot of tourists in Rome. . .'

So he ends up ferrying us around Rome in his lovely air-conditioned car, pulling up at a bus stop near a famous building – we jump out and take a picture.

At the Trevi Fountain, our driver points out the balcony of a building from which Mussolini used to give speeches. We're so comfy in his car, rather than even get out, we get him to drive around the roundabout four times to take a photo out of the car window ('Can you go round again? . . . one more time').

The nearest we get to art is when we spot a human statue dressed up as a Roman centurion in a lay-by by a busy road – 'Stop, there's a Roman!' We give this fella a tenner and he lets Dawn wear his crown and sash for a photo with him.

We do all the 'culture' and we're back to the pool in about three hours. Terrible, but we do have such a laugh.

Another day we do make the effort and go to the Vatican, but they've run out of headsets and, while it is very beautiful, looking at a succession of one-armed statues with little nobs can get rather tedious without any background information. When we get to the Sistine Chapel it's like being a sheep in a pen – we're funnelled through so quickly there's barely time to look up at the ceiling.

Luckily, waiting around to get into museums and galleries or being shepherded past great artworks is never an issue when you're doing a bit of telly. You get VIP access and the chance to look at things properly, in the company of an expert who can explain the story behind the exhibits.

My favourite of all the art historians I've met working on *The One Show* is Sister Wendy Beckett. She's an amazing person who, as a consecrated virgin and hermit, has devoted her life to solitude and prayer. She has only ever allowed herself two hours of work per day to earn a living, so whenever we were filming with her we had to be quick!

I guess we made for an odd couple, wandering around art galleries together, but she's incredibly knowledgeable about the history of religious art and has this very soothing way about her. We've had a laugh working together and I've always enjoyed her company.

One time we visit a church and she shows me a little outbuilding where the entrance is bricked up apart from a small hatch. She tells me that a nun would go in there, that it would be bricked up and she'd stay in there for years on end.

My first reaction is: 'What? That's barbaric! Poor woman!'

'Oh no, Phil, she chose to do it. I would have loved to do it, too. Having the quiet space to contemplate would be wonderful. . .'

It's all about completely abstaining from worldly pleasures to pursue spiritual enlightenment, something I personally might struggle with to that extreme.

Now in her mid-eighties, Sister Wendy still lives a simple life in a mobile caravan in the grounds of a monastery in Norfolk. I'm told that she still prays for me, bless her.

When it comes to privileged access, it has never been more so than when I went to Buckingham Palace to do a report marking the sixtieth anniversary of the Queen's coronation. On the day of the coronation, legendary fashion and society photographer Cecil Beaton took a famous picture of the Queen in the palace, flanked by her six maids of honour. I'm visiting to get a close-up view of the original photo and meet the six maids of honour sixty years on – sadly, the Queen can't make it.

In his diary, Beaton said how nervous he was, because he had to get the portraits taken very quickly. The interior of the palace is magnificent and, as I enter wearing a suit and tie – a first for me as a *One Show* reporter – and walk up the wide, sweeping staircases edged with gold banisters, I can imagine how he felt.

I sit down and have a chat with the former maids of honour who recall their memories of the day. They are all Ladies with a capital 'L', and I'm on my very best behaviour. During a break in filming, I ask the producer to remind me of the name of one of the women.

'Not sure, but I think she owns most of Scotland,' he replies drily.

They tell me a nice story about Prince Philip. He had wanted his mate, another famous society photographer who went by the single name of Baron, to take the photo, rather than Cecil Beaton. The Queen Mum adored Beaton though, and had insisted that he got the job. On the day, as the photo shoot started, Prince Philip was hanging around and telling the women where to stand for the photo, to the growing irritation of Beaton. In the end, Beaton, as politely as he could manage, turned to Prince Philip, and said: 'Would you like to take the photo, sir?' After that, the Duke of Edinburgh backed off and let him get on with it.

Another *One Show* assignment that takes me to the Sandham Memorial Chapel in the village of Burghclere, Hampshire, gets me thinking about my granddad. I'm there to see the paintings by Stanley Spencer. Spencer started as a hospital orderly in Bristol before serving on the front line in

Macedonia in the First World War, and he spent six years living in Burghclere afterwards to create a series of nineteen paintings in the chapel to record his experiences. They are wonderful paintings and really different to how you'd imagine war paintings would be. They're not about gruesome details of combat, but more day-to-day life. People doing the laundry, carrying tea canisters, washing their hair – all the routines that helped Spencer get through an awful time. There's one of patients sitting round a table eating bread and jam, but you can see the more seriously injured soldiers lying on their beds in the background, giving a clue to the battles raging elsewhere.

Covering the entire wall, probably 30-feet high, at the far end of the chapel behind the altar, is Spencer's interpretation of the resurrection; but rather than the resurrection of Christ, it's the resurrection of the soldiers. His idea was that they were rising from the burial ground to a happy place and it's a very moving piece when you think of the thousands that died, and underlines how fortunate my granddad was to survive.

Previously, in 2008, I had the chance to learn more about my grand-dad's own experiences of that conflict when I took part in a BBC One documentary series called My Family At War. Bill Tufnell – or Mechanic 1st Class William Tufnell, to use his official army title – was a coppersmith in the No. 46 Royal Flying Corps. His job was to help manufacture and repair biplane engines and, as my dad had mentioned before, part of his job involved risking his life venturing into no man's land to retrieve parts of planes that had been shot down.

I have the privilege of going up in the only operational replica of an Avro biplane, which only forty-odd other people, including Bill Clinton, have done before. I'm nervous about flying at the best of times, but when I sit in the cockpit on a wicker chair on top of a tank of fuel and get a sense of how flimsy and flammable the original planes were, it brings home just how brave the pilots that flew them into enemy territory were. The generals in charge cared so little for their lives that they initially just supplied the pilots with pistols instead of parachutes so they could shoot themselves rather than burn to death in the event of being blown up. It was only later in the war that the pilots were given parachutes and that was just because they realised the pilots were more important than planes – remember, this was only a few years after the Wright brothers first ever flight, so skilled pilots were hardly two-a-penny. No wonder my granddad did everything in his power to stop my dad suffering the same fate in the Second World War, and got him in the army band.

In a very odd way, back in the days when I was Foster's ambassador post-jungle, I did an event which triggered my dad's own memories of that. On this particular day, my arduous duty is to play cricket with a load of bikini-clad girls on a beach Foster's have created in the middle of Trafalgar Square, and tempt passers-by to join in and have a drink at the beach bar (I told you this was the best sponsorship deal I've ever had. . .).

Dad's told me he's in town and might pop down and say hello, but I don't see him.

When I get home in the afternoon, he calls me up.

'Hello, son, I must have missed you. . .'

'Oh, sorry, are you there now?'

'Don't worry, I've just been having a beer on the beach with the girls.'

'Haha – oh, good, I hope they're looking after you.'

'Do you know what, son? This is where I played the trumpet on VE Day. Just three flagstones along from here . . . I tell you, we had a great party that day, but we were also sad about the ones who hadn't made it. How lovely to be here again now, where no one's got a care in the world.'

In a way, he's saying, 'How easy you've got it now,' but not in a bitter way. He's happy for me that I've not had to go through what him and Granddad did.

Away from television and endorsements, I've fronted a few public health campaigns in my time, too, including a memorable fortnight in summer 2009 when I launched the eleventh annual Gut Week and then, um, spearheaded a campaign on erectile dysfunction.

I turn up for the first job knowing it's something to do with promoting better digestive health, but I've no idea what they want me to do to support the cause. The location for the photo shoot is a lovely little park in a London square and when I arrive the art director comes over to fill me in on the details.

'Alright, Phil. Thanks for coming. Nice and simple shoot today. Just need you to go and sit on that toilet over there.'

'Okay. . . er, say, what now?'

I look across the way and a couple of assistants are placing a toilet on the grass.

'Yes, just sit over there, take your trousers down and we'll give you a few props to hold.'

So far, so weird, but there is a reason for all this. I'm handed a bit of paper with the results of a recent survey which shows that many Brits multi-task while they are sitting on the loo and 65 per cent of those polled were unaware that sitting on the throne for too long can cause haemorrhoids. Apparently, men and women do everything on the toilet from emailing on their laptop, making phone calls or playing sudoku to eating a sandwich (which can lead to gastroenteritis). I have to admit, when I was a cricketer touring the sub-continent, through no fault of my own, I spent quite a lot of time on the toilet, so having a read while there was understandable, but clearly this has got out of control in Britain.

I must do my duty, so I duly unbuckle and sit down with my trousers round my ankles and pose for photos with a computer on my lap, a tea cup in one hand and a sandwich in the other, while builders heckle me from a nearby building site. All good fun.

A week later, I'm filming at a cricket club with a doctor talking about impotence. Forty per cent of men over forty – over five million people – suffer from erectile dysfunction, but people wait ages to go and see their doctor through embarrassment. My job is to encourage men of around my age to take action immediately so they can 'bowl their maidens over this summer'. I must admit that the immature side of me nearly takes over and I'm quite tempted to begin by saying, 'Now some people can have problems getting an erection – so a friend tells me. . .'

That Ashes summer of 2009, I also do my bit for the British pig-farming industry by supporting the 'Love Pork' campaign. My role is to encourage people to be more adventurous with what they cook on the barbecue and to try and cook whole joints like pork shoulder and belly.

The Love Pork people know I am the man for the job, because two years previously I'd demonstrated my fine palate for meat-based products as a judge in the Legendary British Bangers competition. I spent British Sausage Week traversing the country in search of the best sausages in each region. The organisers were so pleased with my efforts – despite an unfortunate chunder at the Midlands regional final, caused by excessive sausage consumption – that I was presented with a magnificent golden sausage on a plinth 'for outstanding service to the Great British sausage'.

More recently, in April 2015, my pork expertise was called upon again when I hit the mean streets of Primrose Hill with *Celebrity Big Brother* star Casey Batchelor to promote Peperami's spoof 'Pork Juice' diet drink. We park up in a big green van, put on 'Pork Juice' aprons and tempt the well-heeled locals with the drink – which is not actually raw pork juice, but rather a healthy blend of alfalfa sprouts, acorns, truffles and beetroot. The idea of the campaign is to poke fun at the trend for detox diets and as a meaty kind of guy myself, I'm happy to ham it up (sorry) for the cameras.

Another unusual promotional day – and definitely the longest one I've ever done – was for Powwownow, a conference-call service provider. Their idea is to stage the world's longest ever three-way conference call; to this end, they place me, glamour model Jodie Marsh and comedian Pat Monahan at different train stations around London on a Friday in September 2010, to chat to each other for 24 hours. The company sets up a stand with a bed, screens and the conference-call technology at each station – for Jodie at Waterloo, Pat at London Bridge and me at Victoria. Considering I got my 'Cat' nickname because people said I could fall asleep on a clothes line, putting me in pyjamas and on a bed – and expecting me to stay awake for a whole day – is a big ask.

We start off by doing a group photo together early in the morning – the first time I've met either Jodie or Pat in my life – and then we're all dispatched to our stations ready to begin.

At 8am, the curtains are opened around our beds, the digital stopwatch above the beds starts and the conference call begins. At first, as we're total strangers, Jodie, Pat and me have got quite a bit to talk about. We've also been given a sheet of paper with a list of topics to stimulate conversation, but we exhaust those in about half an hour.

Luckily, all three are really busy stations, so there's always people coming past during the day. We're all grabbing people to come and sit on the bed and join in the discussion. People with dogs are always good and parents with babies are usually happy to sit down and take the weight off. At one point, we have a conference-call dance-off – while Pat and Jodie start some sort of ramshackle group dance, I get lucky as a dance teacher happens to be standing nearby, so we inject a bit of class into the occasion by doing a waltz.

Pat is a very funny guy and he can talk about anything, so we can always rely on him to rattle on when Jodie and me start flagging a bit as he keeps us going. He also makes the most imaginative use of his bed when he gets about twenty people to cram onto it and crowd-surfs across them.

Around 5pm, the commuters start passing through again. As the night wears on, we get all the Friday-night revellers and drunks coming through, so it gets a bit lively – I have some beer sprayed over me, but at least it's keeping me awake. Once the last train has departed, though, I'm left sitting on this bed in an almost deserted station, which is very eerie.

Even Pat is running out of things to say and the three-way conversation degenerates into incoherent mumbling and, if anyone goes suspiciously quiet, there are shouts of 'Are you still awake?'

'Huh? What? Yeah, I'm here.'

We've got no security, so when an aggressive drunk man tries to get in my bed at 4am, I have to wrestle him off with the help of a bloke from Powwownow who's hanging around to make doubly sure we all stay awake.

Somehow I get through the night and, as the trains start disgorging their passengers again, I can see the finishing line. With a few minutes to go, the company CEO calls upon me to make a speech. Delirious from a combination of lack of sleep and massive intake of espressos and Red Bulls, I ramble on about what a wonderful world we live in, before concluding: 'It's been emotional, Victoria'. A little crowd has gathered around the beds at each station and we're all handed certificates and pop champagne to mark the end of an epic conversation. Then I stagger out to a car to take me home; I lie down in the bedroom with the curtains closed for the whole day.

Looking back on the hundreds of corporate dos and after-dinner speeches I've done I'm pleased to say that, almost without exception, they've gone pretty well. Not wishing to tempt fate, but there have only been a handful that have fallen a bit flat, which is a pretty good strike rate.

If I'm booked for a cricket club awards dinner or similar, I turn up safe in the knowledge that the members of the club have specifically chosen me as their guest. Going in, I'm confident that they'll be up for a laugh and give me a good reception. In contrast, I was a bit more nervous before doing a Q&A for the Metropolitan Police in 2011. After my run-ins with the Old Bill in my younger, wilder days, it was nice to get paid to be interviewed by them this time and it proved to be a lot more fun.

When I'm booked for a company event, there can be a few more butterflies. Some of the audience may not have a clue who I am, and I'll have a bit more to prove. There have been occasions when I feel like there's a few people looking at me, thinking: 'Come on, then, show us what you've got.' There's no worse feeling than standing up, chatting away, while people just sit there, stony-faced, in silence. I've had a few that start off like that, but normally I've managed to win them over. In fact the only real disaster I can think of came at one of my early book-ings after the jungle.

I'm a guest speaker at a company away day and I get dropped off at this very plush country manor. I walk in, thinking it's just another gig. There's someone there to greet me, a German chap who explains in impeccable English that it's a company do for a German bank.

'Oh, right, okay. Lead on. . .'

As I walk into the conference room, I'm introduced to the other speaker, Steven Norris, the official Conservative candidate to become Mayor of London. Hmm, this seems a bit highbrow. Germans are not known for their love of cricket, are they?

'Am I in the right room?'

'Oh yes, Phil. We're delighted to have you here.'

I wander around mingling before the dinner, it's a relatively small affair with about eighty of their top executives and I discover that a large proportion of them don't speak English very well.

I'm in a mild state of panic all through dinner, which isn't eased when Mr Norris gets up and gives a talk about politics and business which I can barely understand, while the audience nod their heads and applaud. Then it's my turn and I die on my arse.

'Oh, do you remember the time when I bowled Sachin Tendulkar?'

A sea of blank faces. I get the impression that no one here knows who the greatest Indian cricketer of all time is, let alone recalls me bowling to him.

Where am I? What am I doing here? It's half an hour of absolute torture.

Whoever booked me for that gig, I have no idea why. I can laugh about it now, but no one was laughing at the time I can tell you.

Another slightly random fish-out-of-water experience occurred in 2010, when I'm hired by the Chartered Institute for IT to present a short film about Sir Clive Sinclair, talking about his pioneering contribution to the development of home computers. Anyone who knows what a techno-phobe I am might be surprised that I was chosen – I have just about got to grips with an iPad, but I tend to leave the computer to Dawn. It's only fairly recently I've got myself a smartphone to do a bit of tweeting – for many years I had a prehistoric brick of a Nokia phone given to me by the ECB when I was playing for England. I quite enjoyed the fact (as did my dad) that years after I retired, they were still paying my phone bill. Despite my lack of IT skills, I enjoy my day filming the tribute to Sir Clive and learn a few things along the way – for instance, did you know in 1953, there were less than a hundred computers in the whole world?

A few years before, when I first started doing telly outside of sport, I think I would have really struggled to do a job like this, but because of doing things like *The One Show* I'm now pretty confident I can adapt to unfamiliar subjects and do a good job.

These sort of experiences have helped when I get asked to do bigger things as, for example, I am in 2012 when I co-present a prime-time series for the BBC called the *Flowerpot Gang*. The idea of the show is that the 'gang' travel around the country and transform neglected plots of land to benefit local communities.

I love a nice garden, but I'm no expert on flowers and shrubs. At home, Dawn and I have a gardener called John who comes in. John used to be a jockey and he's really short, under five feet tall – very good at weeding, not so good at pruning. His nickname is 'Little John' and his partner is a tiny Thai lady who works in Boots. They are a very cute, pocket-sized couple.

One summer Dawn's dad Neil came to stay with us for her birthday. A friend of ours, Chris, who was my driver at the time, picks him up from the airport. Chris previously had had a motorbike accident and lost the use of one arm, so his car is specially converted for him to drive.

He drops Neil off and a bit later we're sitting in the garden having a drink, when Little John pops in and says hello before disappearing behind some low bushes down the garden to work.

The next morning, there's a knock at the door. Dawn's dad is first down to answer it and he gets to meet our transgender postman, Hazel (formerly Harry).

At breakfast, Neil says to me: 'So I've met your one-armed chauffeur, the world's smallest gardener and your transgender postie – very eclectic bunch you have round here. . .'

Indeed, although sadly Hazel has since moved on to pastures new and is no longer delivering our post.

Anyway, my point is, I'm not much of a gardener, but the *Flowerpot Gang* is a really fulfilling show to be involved in because it brings communities together and creates places that improve people's lives.

We create four gardens in all: at a young carer's centre in Sunderland; on an unused plot of derelict land in Poplar, East London; for a nursing home on the edge of Sheffield for people suffering from dementia; and for a student support centre in Bristol, helping kids who've been excluded from mainstream schools.

My co-presenters are Anneka Rice and gardener Joe Swift, who are both lovely. Like many teenagers of the early Eighties, I have fond memories of Anneka running round in a jumpsuit on Channel 4's *Treasure Hunt* and, of course, her famous 'Rear of the Year'-winning bum – she's still got it, by the way, and she's great fun to work with. Joe's a fellow Gooner, so we have a bit of chat about Arsenal and it's interesting to learn a few gardening techniques from him.

The gardens require week- or fortnight-long builds and although Anneka and I get stuck in on the days we're down there to do our presenting bit, most of the hard work is done by a brilliant full-time team of professional landscape gardeners working under Joe's direction. Local volunteers also pitch in, giving loads of their time and skills and make a huge contribution. At the two children's projects in Sunderland and Bristol, the kids get involved – for some of them, especially in Bristol, it's the first time they've ever seen a project through from start to finish and there is a great sense of achievement for them. The projects bring the whole community together.

The amount of work that goes into preparing the gardens is incredible. I've never seen people work so hard. I'll introduce an item, saying: 'Right, we've got to build this wall,' help to lay a few bricks – cut – and when I come back a few days later there's a beautiful walled area completed. Meet people, get my hands dirty, but not actually have to finish anything myself – it's the perfect job for me!

The other part of the show is for Anneka and me to meet the people involved in the projects. We speak to the families of people with dementia and find out how it has affected their lives, or get to know the kids who've had problems at school (which I can certainly relate to). When we hear the backstories, a lot of which are very moving, it gives everyone involved in the programme a real understanding of how important the new garden will be and pushes everyone on to finish it.

The day of the big reveal is just a joy. At the dementia home in Sheffield, previously there was just a bit of scrub outside the building, so the residents were looking out on nothing. The team create lovely little places where they can sit outside with friends and family, and installed all sorts of sensory features, such as a recording of waves lapping on the seashore to trigger memories of seaside holidays. Everyone has a tear in their eye as we see the delighted reactions of the sixty-odd residents as they explore their new garden.

The funniest reveal day is in Bristol. It's an absolute miracle there's any sort of garden there, because from day one it has rained almost constantly. When I say rain, I mean torrential – the whole site is waterlogged. I understand that it's the highest rainfall in a month the city has ever had. The pro gardeners who are working there full-time say it's the hardest bit of graft they've ever done, because every time they dug a hole, it filled up with water. The days I'm down there we are knee-deep in mud.

When I turn up on the final day, I can't believe how good it looks, but the boys tell us that everything has been cosmetically enhanced so it looks good on camera. When I look more closely, the slabs of turf are wobbling around on the swamp below. The garden is moving in front of our eyes as if it's floating on top of a calm sea, but our filming schedule is immovable, so we have to get the reveal done today.

As we lead all the staff and kids out to see the finished garden for the first time, everyone is told to stay on the path in the middle because it's the only bit that's solid. If anyone deviates they will sink waist-deep. It's like quicksand – we could lose a small child in there: 'Come on everyone, let's see your new garden and have a party... STAY ON THE PATH!... Let's have fun... DON'T TOUCH THAT!'

Luckily for us, the sun breaks through for the first time in a week. Everything is being shot on cameras high on booms and the garden looks amazing. It looks bright, new and colourful.

We end up all crushed into this little paved area. The only way we're going to be able to dance at this party is by doing a Riverdance with our hands locked down by our sides, but we managed to get our arms above our heads to wave goodbye to the overhead cameras.

It is hilarious. I hasten to add that when the weather gets better and the garden dries out, the team go back and put it all right.

The show doesn't get recommissioned, unfortunately. The feedback is that from a viewer's perspective it's two programmes in one – people were tuning in more for the gardening or the documentary side, but there wasn't time to do it all. It didn't quite work as a TV show, but it was really satisfying to be part of the experience. It's one of those times when the power of television really does work to create something with a lasting impact.

My efforts when I appear as a contestant on *Celebrity Antiques Road Trip* in summer 2012 are less effective, although I'm really delighted to be invited to do it. It's the first series of the celebrity version of the show and I've watched the non-celebrity version before and laughed at some of the tat people buy in the hope of auctioning it off for a profit. I reckon I know a bargain when I see one, so I quite fancy my chances of doing alright at it and finding some gems among the junk.

In my episode I'm matched up against TV presenter Chris Hollins, who won *Strictly Come Dancing* (see Chapter 7) the year I did it. He's an absolutely charming chap, Chris, and he was a very good cricketer in his youth, too. He played first-class cricket for Oxford University, gaining a blue before deciding he wasn't quite good enough to play professionally and going into the media instead. Sporting ability runs in his family. I remember watching his dad, John, who was a professional footballer at the top level for twenty years, playing for Arsenal in the late Seventies and Eighties.

Chris and I are each paired with experts to give us advice and sent off on a two-day jaunt, plundering various second-hand shops dotted along the Kent and Sussex coast for items to sell at auction.

My expert/travelling companion is auctioneer Philip Serrell. I find out that we have a love of cricket in common. He played both cricket and rugby for the Royal Grammar School in Worcester, where one of his schoolmates was a future legend of the game, Pakistani all-rounder Imran Khan. After uni, he became a PE teacher, before changing course to become an auctioneer.

The BBC have laid on a classic Ford Zephyr car for us and, even though it's not the easiest motor to drive, scooting along the coast with the top down and stopping off at interesting little places along the coastline is a joy. We also make time for a couple of nice seafood lunches and after-noon tea with a slice of cake.

It's great fun, rummaging around in bric-a-brac stores and learning from Philip about the provenance of different objects. His speciality is Worcester porcelain, but he also has a love of wooden objects like big old butchers' blocks and tables. Wood proves to be a theme of our shop-ping trip.

Indeed, as a little diversion, we stop off at the cricket bat manufac-turers, Newbery, one of the few companies that still finish bats by hand. We meet their master bat maker, who has personally made over a quarter of a million bats in his lifetime.

He shows us how to pick a good bat. You're looking for a nice tight grain; the deeper and more mellow the sound when you hit the middle of it with a hammer, the more reactive it will be when it hits a cricket ball. When I was batting in Test matches — and in county matches for that matter – I never really heard that lovely sound. The wood in all my bats must have been rubbish.

Anyway, back to the business at hand. We pick up a pair of old wooden crutches, which apparently date back to the First World War. They are a bit broken and don't look like much, but when I'm told the story that they may have been used by a soldier on the battlefield, injured fighting for his country, I'm sold. Someone at the auction who collects war memorabilia might be too and they only cost us a tenner.

Another wooden item catches my eye in one place – a large trolley on metal rollers.

'What is it?' I ask the shop owner.

'It's a Victorian nut trolley – which people used to move big sacks of nuts in a factory,' he says with an air of authority, as if it could hardly be anything else.

A nut trolley? I've never heard of one of those and, despite his confident answer, I'm looking at this bloke wondering if he really knows any more than me, but for some reason it captures my imagination. First, my mind is transported back to a nineteenth-century factory, with men loading big sacks of nuts onto it. Then I envision it taking pride of place in a modern-day loft conversion. . . in Shoreditch. . . owned by some hipster with a pencil moustache, wearing an ironic T-shirt, rolled-up skinny jeans with brogues and no socks. Place a piece of glass on top of the trolley to upcycle it into a coffee table, stick copies of *Fantastic Man* and *Monocle* on top of it, and away you go.

Philip has never seen a nut trolley before either, but carried along by my enthusiasm and, perhaps, his weakness for wooden antiques, he seems to think it's a good buy. Even after a bit of bargaining, it costs us about £350, which is a good chunk of our budget, but I walk out of the shop feeling buoyed that I've thought outside the box and that someone's going to pay a grand for it.

We pick up a few more items – including a water-stained vintage photo of a cricketer – so that by the end of the trip I'm really fancying myself as the new David Dickinson. I reckon I've picked up some right bargains and that nut trolley is a winner. Philip seems to think I've done alright too. We high-five as we say goodbye to each other and I go home and gush to Dawn about the items we've bought.

'Oh, well done Phil. Sounds brilliant.'

There's a couple of weeks between buying our bits and pieces and the auction sale. I have other jobs to do in between, but a couple of days before, I'm having a shower at home, thinking about the forthcoming auction and debating the merits of the nut trolley with myself:

'Hmm, actually, it's just a couple of planks of wood with pram wheels on it?. . . No, no, it's a beautiful piece of British industrial history. . . where factory workers once dumped big sacks of nuts, now metropolitan hipsters will put their canapés before a dinner party on it. . . Or is it planks of wood on wheels?'

By the time I arrive at the auction house on the day, the 'plank' argument is definitely winning inside my head. Have I lumped three-and-a-half hundred quid on a bit of old scrap?

'That nut trolley – what have we done?' I say, when Philip greets me outside.

'No, Tuffers, it's great, it's great. Let's go into the showroom and have a look at it. Yeah, it's great. . .'

So we walk inside and there it is. And, yes, sure enough, it's a couple of old planks of wood with pram wheels.

We look at each other. 'Oh dear. . .' he says, as we dissolve into nervous fits of laughter.

'What have we done? What *have* we done?'

When the lot comes up, even the auctioneer sounds dubious about it:

'And here we have lot number so and so. . . er, a Victorian nut trolley. . . a Victorian nut trolley?'

It's obviously not something that has come up for sale before and I'm starting to doubt such a thing ever existed.

'Right, who's going to give me one hundred pounds. . . two hundred pounds. . .?'

Someone from the back of the room shouts: 'Tenner!'

It ends up going for thirty quid.

I can feel myself blushing with embarrassment. Meanwhile, Chris Hollins and his mentor are absolutely pissing themselves.

'They've got no vision – it's an antique of the future,' declares Philip defiantly, trying to make me feel better.

We make a couple of quid profit (literally) on the crutches. The water-stained vintage picture of a cricketer only sells when, in desperation, I offer to write my signature on the back and someone in the showroom takes pity on us.

The idea of the show is that whatever money is left at the end of the show is donated to Children in Need, but I've actually managed to lose a substantial amount of our seed money, which I feel quite bad about.

At least someone went home the proud owner of a rare – possibly unique – nut trolley. . . or more likely, took it home and smashed it up for firewood.

A show I do for the Dave TV channel in May 2014 seems much more geared to my skillset – the ability to lose money.

The series is called *24 Hours to Go Broke*. Each episode sees a pair of comedians/sportspeople/TV personalities sent off to different places, where they are given a load of 'Dave's hard-earned money' and tasked to spend it all in a day. Comedians David Baddiel and Richard Herring go to Armenia's capital city, Yerevan, and attempt to spend £8,000 worth of Armenian currency on things like chess with human-sized pieces and sabre-dancing in drag. Boxer David Haye and comedian Seann Walsh go to Cork in Ireland where, among other activities, a local man agrees to be punched by the former world heavyweight champion for money. London 2012 gold-medal-winning long jumper Greg Rutherford and comedian Josh Widdicombe go to Bavaria, where they challenge locals to a Pub Olympics and Greg pays skiers on Wank mountain to tell him jokes. Meanwhile, in Thessaloniki, Rachel Riley and Joe Wilkinson from *8 Out of 10 Cats Does Countdown* splash their cash on ancient fertility rites and a fancy-dress football game.

Billed as 'the world's weirdest day trip', it's basically *Brewster's Millions* on a budget and with a slightly tighter money-losing schedule, with a bonus of giving the local economy of places visited a little boost.

I'm appearing in the fifth and final episode with the Scottish comedian

Susan Calman, and we have a right laugh filming it. Our day begins in a location outside Reykjavik. The two of us clamber across black volcanic rocks and between natural hot springs. Ahead of us, through the swirling mist of water vapour and eggy-smelling sulphur, we see a suitcase. When we open it, it's filled with wodges of cash – £10,000 worth of Icelandic Krona (ISK) to be precise. There's roughly 200 ISK to the pound, so it looks like an impressive amount of wonga.

Inside the case, we also find a list of five rules we have to abide by:

1. You may hire anyone or anything you need, but you must not pay more than the reasonable going rate.

2. The money should be spent on experiences and cannot be given away. 'We can't just give it to puffins or seals, then,' I note.

3. You must not spend more than ten per cent of the total on any one experience. 'So you can't just go, here's ten grand, give me a massage,' says Susan. 'That would be a good massage. . .'

4. Any spend that goes against the spirit of the challenge may be vetoed.

5. Takist þér ekki ad eyda peningunum hiytur refsingu en ef þér tekst það færdu verdlaun. 'Look, penguins,' says Susan. 'It's something to do with penguins. . .'

So, it's not going to be quite so simple, but Iceland is notoriously expensive so we're quietly confident of spending all the cash. Thankfully, there's a list of three people who may be able to help us, with their phone numbers.

First job is to get a taxi to take us back into Reykjavik and the time starts once we're onboard. The driver rebuffs Sarah's offer of paying him a tip to translate the Danish phrase on our rule sheet.

'No, no way,' he replies, looking rather offended at the idea. 'There's no tipping in Iceland.'

It's the one time I've been abroad and wanted a cabbie to rip me off, but, unfortunately, this fella's only willing to take us for a ride into town, not take us for a ride. The trip costs £16 so we've got a long way to go.

When we're dropped off, we look around for someone else to help us translate rule five, just in case it's something that gets us into trouble. Reykjavik has a population of 120,000 people and most of them speak English I've been told, so shouldn't take a minute.

We see a fella across the road pushing a baby in a pram and rush over to him:

'Hello, sir,' I say, 'we need a little help translating this. Are you from Iceland?'

'No.'

'Where are you from?'

'Luton.'

Good start.

Then we ask a girl with blonde hair and blue eyes, who couldn't look more Scandinavian if she tried, but she appears to be the exception to the English-speaking rule and just giggles in reply.

Third time lucky, we ask a sensible-looking bespectacled fellow in a uniform who informs us that it means: 'If you don't manage to spend your money, then you should be punished. If you succeed, then you will have a prize.'

Reward or forfeit: *peningunum* doesn't mean penguins.

I go off to talk to locals in search of recommendations to splurge our cash, while Susan phones the first of three contacts.

Some people look alarmed and hurry past when I run up to them, but one couple suggest going for a bath at the famous Blue Lagoon Geothermal Spa, which sounds appealing, but probably not that expensive. Another fella I stop thinks carefully for a few seconds and says: 'There's a liquor store over there. . .'

I'll bear that in mind.

I go back to Susan to see how's she's getting on: 'Phil, I phoned the last number. Hjörtur. Hijuuurrrter – lovely name – and he says we should meet him at his museum.'

'Ooh, very cultural.'

'Do you like museums?'

'I love 'em.'

So we wander down to the address given and on arrival we discover it's a very specialist museum: the Icelandic Phallological Museum – or, in plainer language, the Icelandic Penis Museum.

The curator, Hjörtur Gísli Sigurðsson, is waiting to give us a guided tour. Hjörtur is a very well-travelled man, a skilled hunter-fisherman, a self-taught master chef and most importantly, as a second-generation phallologist, a huge penis expert (as opposed to an expert in huge penises).

The museum's founder, Sigurður Hjartarson's, um, interest in collecting mammals' penises began as a kid in the Seventies when he went on summer holidays to the countryside and was given a bull's penis as a whip for the animals. By the time he opened the museum in Reykjavik in 1997, he had collected 63 specimens. It was moved to a fishing village

LEFT: 7 July 2005 - marrying my perfect woman on a beach in Mauritius.

RIGHT: Completing a 584-mile walk, and helping to raise £620,000 for the Macmillan Cancer Relief Fund in 2004, was one of my most worthwhile challenges.

ABOVE: Surfing in Newquay in 2006. As you can see, the instructor was impressed with my technique.

LEFT: Playing in goal at the new Wembley in 2007, when I made history by letting in the first ever goal at the stadium.

RIGHT: Chatting with Meat Loaf at Ant and Dec's Ryder Cup–style celebrity golf match, the All*Star Cup in 2006.

LEFT: Chris Evans invited me to take part, but after Europe's captain Colin Montgomerie saw us play, we spent more time drinking in the clubhouse than on the course.

ABOVE: Over the years I have become one of Britain's premier pork ambassadors! In 2007, I was a judge in the Legendary British Bangers competition.

ABOVE: Leaving my Aussie rival Jason 'Dizzy' Gillespie trailing in my grass clippings during the 2009 Betfair Lawnmower Grand Prix.

LEFT: Getting ready for a 7km race through the streets of London, dressed as a gorilla, in 2007. As you do.

RIGHT: Where am I? Sitting on a loo in a London park to launch the eleventh annual Gut Week, naturally.

BELOW: That's a very big pot of Marmite... A 15-metre high photo of me projected on the side of the Australian team's hotel in 2009.

TOO TASTY FOR THE AUSSIES

RIGHT: I love painting and was thrilled to be asked to put on an exhibition of my work at the JAG Gallery, Brighton, in 2014.

RIGHT: Talking cricket (and pigeons, probably) with 'Blowers' for *Test Match Special*.

LEFT: On air with 'Aggers'.

BELOW: It's a joy and a privilege to be part of *A Question of Sport*, Britain's longest-running quiz show, with Daws and Sue.

LEFT: I preferred ballroom over Latin dances on *Strictly Come Dancing*, but a Tufnell bum-shake always seemed to be a crowd-pleaser.

RIGHT: One of my more understated outfits…

All the gear, no idea... I felt like a super hero wearing my custom-made ski suit for *The Jump*, right up to the point when I had to actually ski...or skeleton...or ski jump.

With my Dawnie, my angel. If we hadn't met by chance in 2001, I might not be here now.

Me and my dad. The time we had to talk in the fortnight before he passed away has given me a sense of peace I've not felt since I was very young.

in 2004, but Hjörtur took over in 2011 and relaunched it in Iceland's capital.

Hjörtur tells us with pride that the museum now houses nearly 300 specimens from 90-odd different species and is probably the only one in the world to contain a collection of phallic specimens belonging to every kind of land and sea mammal found in a single country. It's very popular and they have over 200 honorary members (stop sniggering at the back. . .). What you have to do to become an honorary member I don't know, but I'm sure the competition to be nominated is very stiff.

All the penises are lovingly preserved in formaldehyde and displayed in clear Perspex containers, and as I'm wandering round looking at them with a mixture of wonder and horror, I spot a massive, rather pointy nob.

'Whoah, whose is that bad boy over there?'

'Yeah, that's the biggest one we've got – from the sperm whale,' explains Hjörtur.

'Wow.'

'That's the same height as me,' says Susan.

'I think that's just a touch bigger,' I say. It's about eight-feet long – that's almost two Susans.

It's a very odd experience, as Hjörtur guides us round pointing out the most notable cocks. 'This one is from a walrus,' he says, gesturing toward a gnarly four-feet-long branch of a penis.

'Walrus. . .' I reply, not really knowing what else to say. 'Big one,' he adds, unnecessarily. 'Hmm.'

It's not all mammal penises. We are shown a wooden cabinet full of what look like silver-plated dildos of various sizes. Hjörtur explains, very matter of factly, that to mark the Icelandic handball team winning the silver medal at the 2008 Beijing Olympics, the whole squad had casts of their penises made.

Susan covers her eyes, while I find myself transfixed by the silver nobs standing proudly in the cabinet, trying to process this information. Why on earth would Iceland honour their Olympic heroes by getting their cocks cast in silver? And, as they are handball players, wouldn't casts of their testicles have been more appropriate?

Where am I?

I'm still reeling from this bombshell, when I get a tap on the shoulder.

'Hello, Phil.'

'Hello.'

'I'm Nick Hancock's sister. . .'

'Ooh, hello, what brings you to Reykjavik?'

'We're here on holiday. . .'

Fancy bumping into a Hancock in the Penis Museum.

Hjörtur points up at the lights hanging from the ceiling. 'What do you think the shades are made of?' I don't want to say what I'm thinking, but I have no choice. 'Ballsacks?' I venture.

'Yes.'

I'm becoming an expert in this field. 'Yes, nutsacks. . . from what?'

'From bulls.'

'Ohhh, that's just what we want at home, me and the wife,' says Susan. 'Over the dinner table – lovely.'

Thinking we have completed our penis odyssey, we thank Hjörtur, but he's not finished.

'You can't miss this one. This is the only human penis we've got.'

I tentatively step forward for a closer look. There's a rather grim-looking bit of furry skin inside the capsule and a newspaper cutting on the wall with an obituary and a photo of a jolly-looking pensioner called Páll Arason.

'He was 96 years old when he died, so it's a bit shrunk, but he was a famous womaniser in his youth,' explains Hjörtur.

'Oh so he's done well then. . .'

By this point, I think Susan is all cocked-out as she is hiding behind me, unable to look at this wrinkly member.

Amid all the mind-blowing phallological insights, we've almost forgotten why we're here. Enough nob-watching, we need to spunk as much money as we can in the gift shop. They've got quite a comprehensive range: keyrings with little penis key fobs, nob-shaped ashtrays, back scratchers and what Hjörtur describes as 'ball scratchers' with nob-shaped handles. Even a delightful set of cheese knives with hand-carved nob handles.

'Do you sell many of the cheese knives?' I ask.

'Yes, they are quite popular.'

In the end we plump for a pair of the bull scrotum lights costing £175. Hjörtur hands them over to me by the wires and I'm standing there with these two testicle lightshades dangling in front of my chest.

'Shall we take a bag for it?' says Sarah.

'Yes, I think a bag would be good. . .'

Before we leave, it's Hjörtur's duty to reveal the forfeit we will face if we don't spend the entire £10k in a day. 'You will have to promote my museum,' he informs us solemnly.

'Your museum?'

'How would we do that?'

Just as the words come out of my mouth, a man comes into the room dressed in an inflatable cock and balls outfit.

With 23 hours left and £9,800 still to spend, the possibility of walking round Reykjavik literally looking like a nob certainly concentrates the mind. And somehow we've got to offload the testicle lamps to a local, because we're not allowed to have anything left to show for the money.

Next, we head down the Reykjavik harbour and pay a commercial fisherman £854 to take us out fishing with his crew. He looks incredibly happy, so I'm not sure we've strictly kept within the rule about only paying the going rate, but hey-ho.

Half an hour later, we're line-fishing in the choppy waters of the Atlantic. It's good fun and we both catch a couple – in fact I somehow manage to catch two on my hook in one go.

What we haven't really thought through is the time element of doing this. While we're floating about in the Atlantic, the clock is ticking. Luckily, we've paid the fisherman so much money, he's happy to cut short the day's work and bring us back to shore.

On the way, I call the second contact on our list, Rikka Hjördís, one of the country's top chefs and a presenter on the Icelandic version of *Masterchef*.

'Rikka! Yes, we've got loads of fish. Can you help us?'

We offer to pay her a daily rate to cook us a bit of whiting and cod on our return to port.

'Are you very expensive? Yes. . . good. Right, we'll send a very nice car for you and we'll see you at the harbour.'

We book a chauffeur-driven vintage 1957 Buick Century car, but it turns out she only lives down the road, so that only comes in at a measly £87. Rikka's daily rate is 100,000 ISK, but we manage to barter her up. 'No, you're better than that,' I say.

'Okay, 125?'

'Listen,' says Susan, 'I'm offended on your behalf.'

'Look, I don't want to rob you guys. . .'

'150 or we're walking away. . .'

The deal is done — another £919 spent — and then it's a matter of finding a place to cook the fish. We look around the harbour for the biggest boat and ask the captain — we know he's the captain because he's wearing a cap with 'Captain' on it — how much to hire it out? He wants a 100,000 ISK, but after a little negotiation settles for 125,000 ISK (£730).

Rikka knocks us up a delicious, if pricey lunch, with the fish we've caught, served on a bed of mashed potatoes, and gives us a couple of suggestions of how we could spend some more money.

'You could go horse-riding on a lava field — that is like riding on the moon — and you could go and meet some Y-kings. . . Have you ever met Y-kings before?'

'Oh, Y-kings,' I say, accidentally mimicking her pronunciation of Vikings.

'And we have elves.'

'I love an elf,' says Susan.

'Actually, I have a friend who knows about elves, but she's quite expensive. . .'

'Good, don't worry about that. . .'

Four-and-a-half hours in and we've still got three-quarters of the money left, so we need to start spending. I'm lugging this suitcase around Reykjavik and it's not getting much lighter. It's time to split up and double our cash-frittering potential.

I head off on a lava pony trek (£175) combined with a 'Viking Surprise' experience (£900). It's an amazing place and a lot greener than Rikka was making out, because the lava fields are covered in moss. It's like something out of the Hobbit films. I dismount to take some photos, when suddenly half a dozen blokes in full armour come charging out at me from behind a hillock – oh no, it's the Y-kings. Within seconds, I'm on my knees in surrender with the tips of spears and axes inches from my neck. The fact that I booked the surprise myself does take away the surprise element from the attack, but the boys give it plenty of humpty.

Then the Vikings carry me away on their shoulders to their village, where I'm given a lesson in swordsmanship, join in with a Viking sing-song and drink beer out of an animal horn.

While I'm doing this, Susan goes for a half-hour consultation with Rikka's mate, the elf expert, which sets her back a pleasingly outrageous 70,000 ISK (£409). Iceland takes elves very seriously – apparently this woman is often consulted by councils to ensure that new roads aren't routed through the site of elf dwellings. The Vikings say to me that you don't mess with the elves because they will stab you and kill you, so it's no wonder the road-builders are a bit wary.

With over six hours gone, we've done over four grand and we're on a roll now.

It's half past three in the afternoon when we ring our last contact, a guy called Henrik who turns out to be a tour guide. At £400 for an afternoon, he's not cheap – everyone's day rate seems to be going up which is good news for us – so we immediately hire him to take us on a whistle-stop tour of the wilderness around Reykjavik.

He takes his time coming to pick us up and Susan and I do some body-popping and moonwalking for some reason while we wait. Henrik then takes us for a drive, stopping off at a typical elf habitat (allegedly). The elf expert told Susan that the elves like you to leave presents, so she's bought a ridiculously expensive bunch of flowers (£35) from a garage for them. We ceremoniously place the flowers down close to some bushes, while Susan quietly sings a Björk song: *'It's oh so quiet. It's oh so still. . .'* As we drop the flowers on the grass, Susan turns to me and says: 'Ooh, I can feel them. . . can you feel them?'

'I can a little bit. . . I can feel something. . . I dunno if it's because I haven't been to the loo for a while.'

Then bang on cue, the sun bursts out from behind the thick clouds above.

'That's the elves, Phil!' says Susan.

Next Henrik takes us to the edge of Langjökull, the second-biggest glacier in Iceland. It's an absolutely stunning, otherworldly black-and-white landscape of snow and volcanic ash. Henrik sorts us out a 20-ton truck (£730) to drive us up the glacier.

We stop off for a lie-down in the snow 'to harness elf energy' as instructed by Susan's elf advisor. Then we have to stand up and lift our 'antennae' (arms) to the sky and make a wish. It is actually rather a spiritual experience. I'm getting right into this elfishness.

Back to business, though, and in order to maximise our spending while we're in the middle of nowhere, Henrik has a team of climbing experts (£885) and hire equipment (£233) on standby to take us abseiling down a crevasse.

It's freezing cold — must be a good ten degrees below zero with the wind-chill factor — and I start getting a bit worried about what's in store. Then a blizzard rolls in and, even though I've now got a scarf covering most of my face, sharp hailstones are coming in sideways and really stinging.

'Oh my God. . . my eyes!'

Susan has a bit of a sense of humour failure: 'Can we do this fairly quickly? Because it is ****ing freezing.'

They give us climbing helmets and crampons and attach us all together with a climbing line; we're told to stay on the path behind the man leading us, because if you're not careful you can accidentally stand on a hole in the ice and plunge to your death.

The new rule that the director has just made up is that if we don't reach the bottom of the crevasse, the climbing company will have to give us a full refund, so the pressure's on.

We're edging towards this crevasse on climbing ropes in a line — one of the experts at the front, then Susan, then me. I peer over into the abyss. . . and it's a ditch, about twelve-feet deep. Nonetheless, they film me abseiling down and climbing out like I'm Scott of the Antarctic.

After offloading wedges of Krona from our suitcase to pay for a spectacular and spectacularly expensive excursion, we've got just around £2,600 to spend as darkness descends and we head back into Reykjavik.

We're both ready for a drink and by 9pm we're in a bar recommended by Henrik, buying a round of drinks for everyone there. We still need to find a couple more really expensive activities to burn through the remaining cash, though.

We ask a local man for some hints. Susan is all for hiring a tank from the Icelandic army, which I think might be tricky at this time of night, and more so, as the man explains, that Iceland doesn't have an army or any tanks. Instead, he suggests trying the 24-hour golf course.

The bar tab comes to 68,000 ISK (£400), but the girl behind the bar gives us the heart-breaking news that it's happy hour, so we get fifty per cent off.

It's past midnight, we've still got just under two-and-a-half grand in our case and we're looking down the barrel of walking round Reykjavik dressed as a cock and balls tomorrow morning.

We head to the golf course. It's members only, so we ask to join (I'm not sure that would normally be possible, but the power of television makes it happen), hire some clubs and we're on the first tee for 1am. Considering it's an open-all-hours course, it is not very well lit. I remember the young Seve Ballesteros's style of play was said to be, 'hit it, find it, hit it again' – well, this is another level.

After hacking around blindly for a couple of hours – at a cost of over

£900 – both Susan and I are exhausted and need at least a couple of hours' kip before trying to spend the rest of the cash first thing in the morning.

We find a hotel and ask for the most expensive room – it's the honeymoon suite at 44,000 ISK.

'Forty-four thousand for a night in the honeymoon suite with Phil Tufnell,' cheers Susan. 'Cheap at the price.'

It's 4am and time to sleep, but not before Susan has ordered a bottle of champagne and the entire room service menu to eat up a bit more cash.

Two-and-a-half hours later, we're up and out again to try and spend the remaining £663 in ninety minutes.

There's not much open at this time of the morning, but I see a convenience store and I have the bright idea to buy some lottery scratchcards. The first problem with this plan is that you have to get them from a coin-operated machine and the woman behind the counter says we can only have enough change to buy three tickets. Secondly, as I realise once we've bought the tickets, which costs about a fiver, there's a possibility we might win. Luckily we don't.

Susan spots that they rent out DVDs, so we rent their entire stock for 30,000 ISK (£175). The shop assistant bags them up for us, we walk out the front door of the shop, walk back in and return them.

'Thanks very much, they were great.' Back outside, we try to work out our next move. 'That seemed such a waste of money,' I say to Susan.

'Look, do you want to dress up as a. . .'

'No.'

'Well, spend some money!'

Four hundred and eighty-three pounds and twelve pence left to spend in fifty minutes.

Next stop is a hot-dog-stand and we buy hot dogs for our breakfast plus thirty more for the next thirty customers, which earns us a round of applause from the people behind us in the queue.

At this point, the director reminds us that we still have two scrotum lamps and we need to offload them or we'll lose the challenge. To achieve this, we run in a shop and ask a woman for directions to the nearest bike rental store. As a thank-you gift, we give her the lamps, which she seems rather non-plussed about, but we run out before she can ask us what they're made of.

We rush down to the Bike & Segway Tours shop in the harbour and arrive with eighteen minutes to go and 70,000 ISK (£330) to spend. They've got Segways and bikes of all shapes and sizes, and we ask the owner how much to hire each of them. By doing the shortest Segway tour in history, and making 12 other quick return journeys up and down the street on different hire bikes, we can do it. Halfway through I notice he's got a tandem, which is twice the price, so that saves a bit of time. With just over a minute remaining, we return the final bikes and hand over the 70k ISK. The owner of the shop is delighted. 'You are the strangest customers I've ever had, but I like you,' he says as he closes early for the day.

After 24 hours of nobs, scrotum lamps, elf offerings, glaciers, crevasses, night-time golf and extreme bike hiring, we've done it – the money is all gone.

Back at the hotel, we receive our reward, which is an Icelandic delicacy: *Hákarl* (rotten shark meat) washed down with a shot of an 80 per cent proof local spirit called Brennivlín. We both knock back the shot. The plastic container contains little chunks of the shark meat which smells worse than anything I encountered in the jungle. Susan is not having any of it, but I prod a piece with a cocktail stick and give it a go. Sadly, it doesn't stay down.

As I'm glugging water to try and get rid of the rancid taste, my phone beeps. When I've stopped retching, I reach into my pocket to retrieve it. There's a message from Nick Hancock which begins: 'Hello Tuffers, I've just received the most unlikely text from my sister...'

7

CHALLENGE TUFFERS

Spending ten grand in a day is one thing, but since coming out of the jungle and discovering I'd become a 'celebrity' I've been set some much tougher challenges. Without meaning to sound like Paul Whitehouse's spoof DJ, Mike 'lotta great work for charidee' Smash, the most fulfilling ones are those that benefit causes close to my heart. That's the best part about having a bit of fame. By winning I'm a Celebrity I became so much more widely known, which meant that when I put my name down for something, I can help raise much more money than I would have been able to before.

The one I'm still most proud of is the npower 500 Walk to raise funds for the Macmillan Cancer Relief fund, which I set off on at the end of March 2004.

It's only a year after the jungle and my profile is still as high as it's ever been, so the aim is to raise £250,000. The route will take me from

Sussex's cricket ground in Hove, visiting twenty village cricket clubs and a total of six Test grounds, finishing at Trent Bridge in time for the start of an England versus New Zealand Test match. Groups of charity walkers and famous names, such as England rugby captain Martin Johnson, author Jeffrey Archer and royal equestrian eventer Zara Phillips, will join me on each leg to help push me along.

I have to average twenty miles, which is seven or eight hours' walking per day. This fact doesn't really hit me until sometime after myself, Dawn and the other first-day walkers stride off from Hove, waving to the crowd while The Proclaimers' *I'm Gonna Be (500 Miles)* blasts out of the speakers. I've always had trouble with my Achilles tendons during my cricket career, something I neglected to tell the physio who gave me a check-up before clearing me to do the walk. As we're walking along an A-road, just our group and support cars, after what seems like hours, my left Achilles is starting to aggravate me.

'Have we nearly finished yet?' I ask Dawn.

'Er, no, Phil, we've only been going for two-and-a-half hours.'

'I don't think I can do this.'

'Well, you're going to have to bloody do it.'

We've just moved into a new house in Kingswood, a couple of days before, and Dawn was only planning to do the first day or two on the walk before going home to oversee the installation of a new kitchen. She ends up staying with me for twenty-three out of the twenty-five days, while her mum looks after Alana and keeps an eye on the renovations.

Having Dawn around to kick my arse, thinking about my mum and talking to other walkers, some of whom are in recovery from cancer, keeps me going thereafter. After a few days, despite the aches and pains, I just get used to walking the distance every day. Ian Botham, who's famously done many charity walks the length of Britain, told me that you become a 'prisoner of the walk' and I learn what that means. You just have to keep going; there is no other choice.

It helps that we've got two really good physios who give us massages and treatment for blisters along the way. We park up at a Travelodge hotel every night and they even put bricks under the mattress at the foot of the bed for us, because it's best for the circulation in your legs to sleep with your feet up.

Staying in different Travelodge rooms gets a bit disorienting though, because while they all have the same fittings, the layout of the rooms varies. A few times Dawn gets up in the night to go to the bathroom and walks straight into a wall.

We're very lucky with the weather. It's the best spring weather in years and only rains on about three days; walking through the heartland of Britain, we really do come to appreciate what a beautiful country this is. Most days we finish up in a lovely little village, where the local cricket club has arranged a fete with a barbecue, raffle and a Twenty20 match, with all proceeds going to Macmillan. To start with, the idea is that I might play in the cricket match and when we're a bit behind schedule, they'll wait for us to arrive before starting. As the days go past, and I get more and more knackered, it becomes clear that playing might be over-ambitious.

'Can I just play the first five overs?' . . . 'Can I just bowl the first over?'. . . 'Oh, can I just bowl the first ball?'

On a few evenings we retire to the pub for drinks with locals. When we overdo it a bit, Ian Botham's recommended morning-after hangover cure – orange-flavour Tango with a shot of tequila – gets us walking in a straight line again.

The welcome we receive en route and the atmosphere among the walkers makes a huge difference and, after my early mental wobble, there are surprisingly few down moments. The only major physical worry comes at the end of one day when I'm striding down a hill into a village in the Peak District. As I put my left foot down, it feels like I've been shot in the Achilles and I collapse in a heap. At first I fear it's a rupture, which would be game over, but luckily it's not and the physios patch me up to walk another few days.

The other low moment is when, around the halfway point, the organisers say that it looks unlikely we'll hit our target of £250k. Npower pledge to make it up to that figure no matter what, but Dawn and I are a bit down, thinking that we're doing this crazy walk and it's not even going to generate the money hoped for. So it is a huge surprise and relief when we are presented with a cheque at the end for £620,000. As news of the walk spread, there has been a massive spike in donations. All the pain has been worthwhile and there's a tremendous sense of achievement.

Afterwards, I go on Des O'Connor and Melanie Sykes' show and they ask me if I came out with any injuries.

Rather than talk about my Achilles heel, I say: 'Well, I lost my big toenail. . .' Afterwards, Dawn is not amused: 'My toenail fell off, not yours – you nicked my injury!'

In some ways, the walk got me as fit as I've ever been – including my cricket career – but long term Dawn and I both end up needing hip operations because of it. You don't realise it, but walking many miles – and due to some police diversions we actually walked 584 miles in the end – on the slight camber of the road, means that your hips get out of line. No regrets though, it was one of the most worthwhile things I've ever done.

Post-jungle, the most popular show I've participated in – and a major personal challenge for me – is *Strictly Come Dancing* in 2009. I actually have to choose between *Strictly* and ITV's *Dancing on Ice*. I'd previously been invited for a trial in front of the legendary Torvill and Dean, which proved to be both painfully embarrassing and painful – I was terrible, and being bad at ice-skating means a lot of falling over on ice, which hurts. Despite my bruising mishaps, they still wanted me to be on the show – but then *Strictly* come in with a late invitation to replace another former cricketer, Matthew Hoggard, who's pulled out.

We're on holiday in Spain when Mike calls me up with the *Strictly* offer and I have to decide between the two shows. Even though *Dancing on Ice* is more lucrative, I don't really fancy it. Dawn loves *Strictly* and if I do it she'll get tickets to see the show, so it's an easy choice in the end.

Before the celebrity line-up is officially announced, everything is kept top-secret; so much so that all the contestants are given code names. Mine is 'Squirrel', and when I turn up at the gates of the BBC for meetings, the driver winds down his window and announces: 'Mr Squirrel'. The security guard checks his list and lifts the barrier to let us in. All very covert.

My professional partner is Katya Virshilas. She's beginning her first year on the show and is very keen to do well so that she will be invited back next year. As we get into training (which is really intense, six or seven hours per day at a dance studio in Wimbledon), I do feel a responsibility towards her to put the effort in. The fact that two of my former cricket team-mates – Darren Gough (2005) and Mark Ramprakash (2006) – have won the show, gives me an added incentive to do well, but I am under no illusions that I'll win the famous glitterball trophy. My aim is just to learn to dance and not make a total tit of myself on live TV in front of ten million viewers.

The show lasts thirteen weeks and Dawn keeps driving me on because I only receive complimentary seats for as long as I stay in the competition. I get four tickets for the green room and two complimentary seats for the studio itself, and our family and friends are lining up to come to the show.

Every week Dawn says to me: 'You've got to get through, because I've promised so-and-so I'll get them tickets for next week.'

'But Dawn – it's the salsa – it's not my dance.' (I soon discover I'm a ballroom boy; the Latin dances – not so much.)

'Well, you better get training – I've got your cousin and uncle George coming along the week after. . .'

So not only am I doing a full day's training, I'm under pressure when I get home. I end up in the kitchen helping to cook the dinner, salsa-ing over to the cooker to put the shepherd's pie in. Then *cha-cha-cha*, holding the saucepan with one hand while stretching out my other arm to perfect my armography.

I actually suffer a major setback in the fourth week, when I injure my knee in training for the salsa; I have to have an emergency cartilage operation. I dance on the next show wearing a knee brace. I can tell you, when you've just had a knee op, the last thing you want to be doing is twisting around on a dancefloor – something that some of the judges seem oblivious to with their low marks – but the viewers' vote helps me through to the next week anyway.

It's good fun being in the sparkly *Strictly* bubble of rhinestones and sequins – and I like the spray tans because people keep telling me how healthy I look – but I never quite get into the dancing, like some of the other contestants do. We're doing so many hours of training as if we are professionals, so some of them feel like they are dancers by the end, but I never lose that five per cent of self-consciousness, especially doing the sexy dances.

That five per cent comes to the fore at the Blackpool Tower Ballroom in week eight. Everyone's been desperate to get to Blackpool, because it's such a beautiful venue and the iconic home of ballroom dancing. I've qualified after doing quite a decent tango to Amy Winehouse's *Back to Black* in week seven and I'm really hoping to be given a nice ballroom dance to do in Blackpool – a waltz or a quickstep, which I'm quite good at. Instead, I'm lumbered with the rumba. It's the 'dance of love', and I hate it from day one of training. I just don't want to do it.

Even worse, we get six complimentary tickets for the actual ballroom for the show, so Dawn and five friends are out there watching me get all soppy in a frilly shirt. There's a bit where I have to do a solo and sort of caress my own body. It's horrific – I can hear people giggling. Just as well I've got the spray tan, because I can feel my face going redder and redder. Dawn tells me afterwards that she loved it. . . which must mean she really loves me, because it was really not good.

The viewers take pity on me and I squeak through to dance the following week back in the BBC studio. That's where it ends for me though, when I'm controversially defeated in a dance-off with *EastEnders* star Ricky Groves, despite doing what many observers thought was a rather elegant American smooth to *Come Fly With Me*.

My *Strictly* journey is not over yet though. Three years later, in winter 2012, I get a call from Michael Vaughan, who's just been on *Strictly* himself: 'Tuffers, I'm going on the live tour in the new year and they're going to ask you too. Come on, we'll have a laugh. . .'

Like me, Vaughanie was useless when he started – no, actually, he was worse than me – but surprised everyone by becoming half-decent and, also like me, reaching week nine. If he wasn't doing the live tour, I'd probably have said no, but I think it could be fun. Also, January can be a quiet month for me work-wise because I don't go abroad to commentate on the winter cricket tours and it'll be a nice extra few quid in the pocket to start the year. Win-win.

It turns out to be an absolute blast. The tour takes us up and down Britain for three weeks – Glasgow, Newcastle, Birmingham, Brighton, Liverpool, etcetera – playing to packed houses all over the place. After each show, we all bundle onto the coach and head up to the next city. Every time, there's bottles of Bollinger on ice waiting for us (which

Vaughanie has wangled from his contacts), so we just sit at the back of the coach drinking bubbly all the way.

Vaughanie and I arrange to meet up with a load of old cricketer mates during the tour too; we see the ex-England fast bowler Stevie Harmison up in Newcastle and a few of the others come along to the shows.

It's a lovely group of people – seven professionals (Pasha Kovalev, James and Ola Jordan, Artem Chigvintsev, Robin Windsor, Natalie Lowe and Karen Hauer) and seven of us amateurs (Dani Harmer, Denise Van Outen, Fern Britton, Lisa Riley, Louis Smith, Vaughanie and me) – and we become a sort of dysfunctional family. Vaughanie and Fern are Mum and Dad, Denise is Aunty Den, little Dani Harmer and Louis Smith are the kids. I'm the slightly strange Uncle Phil.

'Come on, children. . . let's all go out on the stage and play. . .'

It's a bit simpler than doing the TV show because we all do the same two individual dances every night; I do the American smooth and swivel my hips for the salsa. My pro partner for the tour is Karen Hauer, who becomes known as 'Phil's labrador' (i.e. leading the blind). Karen just talks me through the dances: 'And shimmy, and turn and turn, and shimmy, shimmy, turn. . .'

There are also a couple of group dances for which Vaughanie and I are strategically hidden at the back. The first couple of times, we're a bit nervous and just want to get them done, but after a while we get to do them quite well. Then towards the end of the tour, some of the pro dancers try to confuse us, just for a laugh. They know we keep an eye on them to help us remember where to go next, so they deliberately go to the wrong place and suddenly we're wandering around the stage bumping into each other in front of a few thousand people. Once you lose the beat, it's so hard to get back on it, but when in doubt, I just put my hands above my head, clap and smile.

The funniest one is when we do a team salsa at the O2. There's a move in the dance where the girls go down on their bums, you hold them, spin them and pull them up, and then carry on. Before the start of the penultimate show, one of the pros says: 'Let's spin them round and leave them' and we all agree to do it.

The pro female dancers and Denise – who's like a pro – spring up like nothing's happened and run after their partners, but while the rest of us get into formation, poor old Lisa Riley and Fern Britton are left spinning on the floor, on their back like beetles, in the spotlight in front 10,000 people. It's hysterical.

Kate Thornton presents the show and the three judges are Craig Revel Horwood, Bruno Tonioli and Len Goodman (opinion is split among the rest of the cast as to whether Len or *Strictly*'s TV presenter Bruce Forsyth – they say I bear an uncanny resemblance to both – is my long-lost dad). Because we're doing the same dances, the comments from the judges are similar every night, so after a couple of shows, Vaughanie and me say different things in response, just to throw them off. I'm actually quite good by the end, but I still seem to be getting scores of two.

I do get rather self-conscious that people are paying very good money to watch me dance the salsa very badly. Then again, for brilliant dancing, the spectators can watch all the pros and Louis Smith, who is just amazing and wins almost every night with his partner, Ola Jordan. Denise is also excellent and a couple of the other celebrities know their way around a dancefloor. I come to realise that I'm here more for the comedy value. My ridiculous bum shake during the salsa, where I stand on my own, put my hands on my bum and rotate my hips lasciviously, is always a winner with the crowds, so I just go for it.

The reviews are positive wherever we go: 'Pure Strictly magic – as good as it gets' (*Mail on Sunday*); a 'sizzlingly entertaining show' (*Birmingham Post*); 'Strictly is the perfect way to banish the January blues' (*Liverpool Echo*). All in all, it's a real feel-good show – we have a laugh doing it and the audience enjoys it too.

Participating on BBC One Saturday-night show *The Magicians*, in January 2012, offers another fun challenge, but it causes me to have mixed feelings. In the show, three celebrities are each paired with a professional magician to perform tricks. On the one hand, it's great to learn magic – after forty-six years on the planet not knowing how they do it, it's a box ticked – but on the other, a part of me dies when I discover some of the, er, tricks of the trade.

I'm teamed with Jason Latimer – or simply 'Latimer' to use his stage name – and for one of our tricks, we go to a studio in the Candid Arts gallery in Islington, just round the corner from my dad's old workshop. There's a huge 40-feet-wide canvas on the wall and loads of paints, spraycans, brushes, sponges and rollers (with long handles to reach the top of the canvas) ready for use.

Jason introduces the item for the viewers at home. 'Phil and I have made a prediction,' he says, pointing to a parcel wrapped in brown paper and string, locked up in a Perspex container and suspended from the high ceiling above. 'It's locked, it's bolted, it will not come down until this work of art is finished. All we need now is you and your imagination. . .'

The studio is then opened to members of the public – men, women and children – who spend the next hour or so enjoying themselves painting whatever they like, from squiggles and splatters to birthday cakes and figures. When the Pollockian masterpiece is finished, I ask for a volunteer and a little girl steps forward. I give her a foam ball and ask her to throw it over her head for one of her fellow painters standing in the group behind to catch. A man catches it and then we ask him to throw it again, and the next person. It ends up being caught by a young woman in a faux-fur coat who steps up as our volunteer.

We give her a sticky-backed, rectangular cardboard frame and ask her to place it wherever she likes, at any angle, on this giant abstract. When she's placed it on the painting, Jason goes across and cuts out around the frame with a Stanley knife.

We ask the lady to hold her painting and then invite all the people who helped to make the artwork cut off their own bits to take home as souvenirs, which takes a few minutes. 'Now remember,' I tell the watching audience at home, 'our prediction has been locked up for three days and no one has touched it.' Hanging from the high ceiling above us is the framed canvas, sealed in its container. A couple of studio assistants get up on a stepladder to detach it and place it carefully on a table. In full view of the painters, Jason and me then unlock the padlocks, unscrew the top layer of Perspex and put it aside. Jason cuts the string and unwraps our framed canvas and shows the audience the back of the canvas which has our signatures and the date three days ago written on it.

I turn to our volunteer who is standing next to us holding up her chosen piece of the giant artwork, asking her again to confirm she chose to place the frame by herself, 'completely ad hoc?', which she does. Time for the reveal.

'Ladies and gentlemen,' says Jason. 'Let's see how we did. . .'

Hey presto, when he turns around our effort, it's almost an exact replica of the shapes and colours in the section chosen by the volunteer.

'*Wooooooh*.' Applause and looks of astonishment fill the room.

'Do you know what?' adds Jason. 'I liked it so much, I got the phone cover!'

He pulls out his phone, which has the painting on the back.

As the crowd go wild, I slam a cardboard box down on the table: 'I liked it so much, I got the cell phone covers and mugs printed up with it!'

Without missing a beat, Jason unbuttons his shirt to reveal a T-shirt underneath with the painting printed on: 'And I got the T-shirt!'

Afterwards they interview the people who are all amazed at what they've seen.

How did we do it? Well, read the above again carefully and you might be able to work it out. (Note: the volunteer wasn't in on it.)

More nerve-wracking, though, was performing a trick live on the Saturday-night show in front of about six million viewers. I had to get a volunteer from the audience to pick a card and then get Jason – standing twenty feet away, on top of a box – to guess which card had been chosen.

'What was your card, young man?' I asked the volunteer, after he'd chosen one from the deck.

'Seven of diamonds.' He shuffles through the cards but can't find it.

'It's not there. . .'

'That's because it's here,' smiles Jason, holding up the card.

To make the trick work requires some sleight of hand on my part and it can go horribly wrong, so I'm pretty chuffed to get it right under pressure on live TV. I'm also quite pleased to win the viewers' phone vote, beating former *Strictly* judge Arlene Phillips and the pairing of John Torode and Gregg Wallace (who once eliminated me from *Celebrity Masterchef* after I accidentally made a *beurre blanc* sauce without the *beurre* – it was rather thin).

Being selected as a contestant on a new ITV talent show, *Get Your Act Together,* in late 2014, gives me a chance to learn another skill. At first, the producers suggest that I do mime.

'Alright, think I might be able to do that. . .'

People do say I have very expressive hands. But after sleeping on it, I wonder whether it's a bit old hat. Who wants to watch mime anymore? I can imagine myself out there alone on stage, flapping about with my hands, creating my own imaginary self-made box of pain. Help me!

I go back and ask if they've got anything a bit more athletic I can do. Something I can really get my teeth into.

So they came back with another option: aerobatic basketball.

Apparently, it involves springing off trampolines and shooting hoops as part of a team. I think I'll enjoy that. When I was a little boy I remember our first holiday in Spain, where they had trampolines sunk into the beach. In the early evening, while Mum and Dad were relaxing and getting ready for dinner, my brother and I would go down and bounce on the trampolines. I had a lemon T-shirt and a matching long pair of lemon-coloured socks on, white Bermuda shorts, sun-bleached blond hair, brown skin. I looked really smart. My mum used to say to me, 'Ooh, my little blond bombshell.' After a couple of hours flipping about on the trampoline, my previously immaculate T-shirt and shorts would be dirty, but I had a big smile on my face when we came back.

'What've you been doing, Phil?'

'Bouncing on a trampoline.'

Then Greg and me would wolf down sausage and chips and go down there again and carry on bouncing while Mum and Dad ate their paella.

On holiday, we'd spend full days in the pool. As an adult, you stay in the bath for a few minutes and your skin wrinkles like a prune. Back then, I'd be in the pool from about 7am to 5pm, stop to have a burger for lunch and get straight back in. (Why doesn't your skin get pruney when you're younger?) Nowadays, after oysters and a couple of beers for lunch, I'm scared to get back in the pool in case I get the bends; instead, I'll just stay on the sun-lounger and read a book.

Great childhood memories, and I'm hoping that those evening trampolining sessions will stand me in good stead, forty years on.

Every contestant on the show is given a mentor to teach them their new skill; in my case, I get a whole troupe, called Face Team, from Hungary. They reached the semi-finals of *Britain's Got Talent* in 2012 and do exhibitions all round the world. I look them up on YouTube and they do some great tricks, but I think it's doable – at least there's a mini-trampoline to help get me up near the basket.

I fly over to Budapest with a film crew to meet the team. Their training camp is a flat-roofed, monolithic slab of a building that looks like a remnant of the Soviet occupation of Hungary after the Second World War. An old bloke takes us through some rusty gates round to the gymnasium at the back. It's a dimly lit room with a basketball court. Some of the slats on the floor are missing, there's the odd broken window. It's a facility in some need of modernisation.

A guy called Danny from Face Team, who speaks really good English, comes to say hello.

Some kids – from pre-teens to teenagers – are training, launching off a mini-trampoline towards the basket and landing on an old mattress that has been stitched together. All these kids are amazing. Little girls sprinting the length of the gym, leaping into the air, twisting and somersaulting.

We sit and watch that for a while and then Danny introduces me to the Face Team guys; they show me what it's all about. Watching them perform in the flesh is incredible; they're like little monkeys. The trampoline is set back about four metres from the hoop, but they jump so far and high, they can leap onto the top of the backboard, back-somersault off there and then slam dunk the ball through the hoop.

'Oh crikey, well, that was very impressive – what do I have to do?' I say, hoping the reply will be that I can just pass the ball to them and let them do the running and jumping.

'You have a go, Phil – first thing, just get used to running up and hitting the trampoline,' says Danny. He tells me that I need to run as fast as I can, hit the trampoline and I'll naturally go forward.

'Righto – but aren't you going to put the trampoline a bit nearer for me?'

'No, no, that's where we do it from. . .'

I stand, ready to run up, with the entire Face Team and all these acrobatic little kids watching me, wondering who this English ex-sportsman is and if he's going to be any good. The Face Team lads are all lean, athletic professionals – a mixture of gymnast and acrobat. They've all got their hi-tops on, NBA singlets and shorts. I've turned up with my old plimsolls, a Ted Baker T-shirt which I usually wear for going out and my old England cricket team tracksuit with a Tetley Bitter logo on it from 1990 when I first toured Australia. I feel like such a nob.

Where am I?

On the other hand, I'm half-expecting that this little trampoline ahead of me will transform me into Michael Jordan. So I sprint towards it – well, what I think is sprinting, although my sprinting days are over if I ever had them – hit the trampoline and. . . I barely make the mat. I just go *doink*, splat – flat on my face.

Everyone laughs.

You have to really pop up off the trampoline with your knees, which I haven't, so I go back to my mark and have another go. This time, I think, let's really have a go. So I sprint down, spring through the air. The hoop is in my sights and I reach towards it. But about a metre away from it, I start losing altitude. As I flail and plummet, I feel a twinge in my left hamstring. I drag myself up, clasping my leg and have to get it looked at by a physio. It's not a tear, or I'd really be in trouble, but I have to keep it strapped up. I can feel it every time I do a practice leap. It's a novel experience for me because, in eighteen years of playing cricket, I've never pulled a hammy.

It's quite physically demanding. You're sprinting and using your legs and knees and arching your back to launch yourself off the trampoline. Even with the mat, the landing is jarring for the knees, back, shoulders. You do that for an hour and it knackers you.

Later the same day, one of the pros severely sprains his ankle when he lands slightly awkwardly on the side of his foot, coming down from a height of around twelve feet. He lands, screams, has the injury iced and puts his foot up, but it swells up like a balloon. It's terrible for him because he's one of the five who is supposed to be coming over for the show. His trip to England is now gone, because that injury takes four to six weeks to heal. I've only just started and we're already a man down.

After two days in Budapest, I go home and Danny comes over for two days a week over the next three weeks to train me. When he first walks into the gym in Carshalton, his eyes light up: 'Wow! Oh my God.' It's just a normal leisure centre, but he's blown away by the facilities compared to what they have back home.

Danny's a lovely bloke and he shows me how to get maximum height off the trampoline – it's all about getting the technique and building muscle memory. Within a couple of weeks, I'm pretty good at it and Danny's very pleased. 'You've got this down,' he says. 'Now, it's just a case of keep doing it, keep doing it.'

The hamstring problem continues to hamper me throughout the training but icing it, strapping it up and getting some physio keeps it manageable. After doing four or five hours a day at the start, as I get the hang of the technique, we cut the sessions to just two hours or so. Any more and my hammy starts to get a bit tight and I don't want to ping it and have to pull out of the show.

A couple of days before the show, the whole team come over. I meet all the guys again, minus the guy with the ballooned ankle. They bring the music to accompany our routine and we have a chance to practise the part involving the whole team. . . and a cricket bat.

I point out that although I was a cricketer, I wasn't much cop with a bat in my hand, but Danny seems unconcerned: 'No problem. This is easy. . .'

First I have to run up and nail a slam-dunk (yes, by this time I can do that), then after landing quickly grab the bat. As three members of the team run up one after the other, they bounce the ball and I have to flip it up with the bat to just the right height as they somersault through the air to grab it and then slam-dunk it.

In Hungary they obviously don't get much cricket on the telly, because it's actually quite difficult to get the speed and trajectory of the ball off the bat just right three times in a row. A big basketball and cricket bat are not made for each other. Sometimes it comes right off the middle and springs off out of the jumper's reach, sometimes I *phat* it and they're left grasping below their knees for the ball.

But with practice I manage to get two or three out of three most of the time. The boys time their runs like clockwork, so for me it's about getting the rhythm – bounce, hit, catch, *bom-bom-ch, bom-bom-ch.*

While Danny was impressed by the facilities over here, one thing they don't have is big landing mats. Instead we have a few pushed together and that proves disastrous on the last day of training, when one of the lads comes down and one of his feet goes between the mats and he snaps his ankle. Another one bites the dust. There's no time to bring in a replacement so we're down to four Face Teamers, plus me, for the show.

The following evening, half an hour before showtime, we're all warming up together as a team. We're pacing around, getting psyched up and the nerves are jangling. It's like my old Test match days – the only difference is that this time my team-mates are called Laszlo and György rather than Gatt and Goochy.

When we get the call that it's time to get out there, we're high-fiving and geeing each other up. I still love that buzz, that feeling of 'Come on, let's do this boys'. Equal to the excitement is the fear that we're about to perform a choreographed, synchronised show which depends on me to some extent. It could go horribly wrong.

We're first on and all walk out wearing ridiculous sequined tops, give the audience big smiles, the music comes on, the light show begins. . . and I slightly balls it up.

In practice, I've been getting my alley-oops right every time. I have to spring off the trampoline, put the ball under one leg, then the other, then bounce it off the back board for the next man following me to do his skills, pass it on to the next man and so on. . .

I run up, boing off the trampoline and have plenty of time to do my under-the-leg thing, throw it towards the backboard, but clip the rim of the basket and it rebounds high into the audience as man after man of the Face Team come piling in after me. A ball boy chucks another ball in so they aren't leaping through the air for nothing, but my heart sinks because I *never* get that wrong.

When it comes to my slam-dunk/cricket bat sequence, I'm so pumped up that I get some massive air, a big arc and absolutely nail the slam-dunk. I really do feel like Michael Jordan. That adrenaline doesn't help so much when I grab the cricket bat for the next stage though. The first one, I hit right out of the sweetspot and it rattles one of the studio lights as my man slam-dunks thin air through the basket. The next one, perfect. And the third one I *phat*.

Despite the odd mishap, we still finish our routine to a massive round of applause – everyone in the studio seems to have enjoyed it. As an ex-sportsman, I do miss that buzz and it's a really joyous thing to hear the cheers again.

Equally, though, when we get back to the dressing room, the old sports pro inside me beats me up for a few minutes. When I played cricket, this self-analysis – or 'The Churn' as I call it – could last two, three days or even a week if, say, I'd not bowled well in the last innings of a match and missed out on a win.

But the Face Team boys soon snap me out of it.

'Phil, you did very, very well,' says Danny. 'For someone to do that in the time you've had to learn it is amazing. We make mistakes all the time, we just know how to cover it.'

Then I remember I'm not actually an acrobat. When I think about it, I've thrown myself into it and done pretty well for someone who's had eight days' training, and made only a couple of errors in a two-and-a-half minute routine. Everyone backstage says it looked spectacular.

I sit and watch the rest of the acts on the screen in the green room. I'm up against model Amy Willerton, who is roller-skating on podiums with a partner from the Moscow State Circus; actor Chelsee Healey (aerial silks), *Emmerdale* actors Matthew Wolfenden and Natalie Anderson (quick-change act) and the great actor James Bolam, who is singing with Michael Ball.

As they are waiting to go out, I do find myself gently 'sledging' the other contestants. Amy Willerton is on her roller skates, nervous about doing her act, and I'm saying stuff like: 'Oh careful, Amy – there's something on your wheel!'

'What? What?'

'No, only joking. . .'

Watching the others, I think I actually have a good chance of winning right the way up to the last act. The crooning Bolam-Ball dream team are charming, though, and it's no surprise when the audience vote decides that they will go through to the live final.

Even though the show got my competitive juices flowing for a while, as soon as the result is announced, I'm delighted for James. He's a hero of mine, having grown up watching him in the classic Seventies' sitcom *Whatever Happened to the Likely Lads?* and I was chuffed before the show when he told me how much he enjoys listening to me on *TMS*. Afterwards, I sign the cricket bat that earlier sent basketballs flying everywhere in the studio and give it to him, which he's very happy about.

It's been a great experience. I've enjoyed springing about for the first time since that Spanish summer holiday as a kid and the Face Team guys, aside from being really talented, are such a nice bunch. Very humble, very smiley. A couple of them didn't speak much English, but we've communicated through the language of, um, acrobatic basketball and had a right laugh.

The episode, filmed in December, isn't screened until Saturday 1 February. The same evening people need only to flick TV channels to watch the culmination of another challenge – a much more dangerous one – I've been working on for the past two months. . .

MEDIC!

In November 2014, I get a call from Mike. He's been approached by the producers of a Channel 4 show called *The Jump*. I've never seen it, but I know it's something to do with winter sports and that my old England team-mate Darren Gough appeared in the previous series. The last (and only) time I went skiing was on a school trip to Bulgaria thirty-plus years ago, but, I reasoned, after I'd already followed his twinkling toes onto the *Strictly* dancefloor, if Goughie could do it, how hard can it be?

A meeting is scheduled one afternoon at a hotel in Hoxton, East London, to discuss it further. On the day, I have a few drinks at lunchtime because it's coming up to Christmas – okay, it's still November, but I like to start my Christmas celebrations early – so I'm full of the joys of the season when I rock up there.

Three members of the production team greet Mike and me, and I have a couple more glasses of wine with them. They tell me a bit about the show, which is broadcast from the famous Innsbruck ski resort in Austria, and it sounds like great fun. I haven't really learnt how to ski before and as a cricketer, I always followed the sun – there isn't much snow in Barbados or on Manly beach in January. I have never been in that sort of environment before, so I think it might be an enjoyable challenge. They've got Olympians lined up to teach us, so I'll learn something new from some of the best in their sports.

With hindsight though, perhaps, in my 'festive' state, I wasn't paying close enough attention to the detail of what they were saying. The name of the show – *The Jump* – doesn't even raise alarm bells, despite my fear of heights. Instead, when I'm told that there are three different jumps to choose from, I'm bullish: 'You think I'm not going off the top ski jump? I'm not ****ing around going off some little jump. I'm going all out. . .'

I'm giving it all the bravado and they're lapping it up. They must think I'm a right daredevil, but I've got no idea what I'm talking about.

In my mind, I'll be getting paid to have a nice holiday, meet some nice people, have a laugh, do a bit of skiing with some après-ski thrown in. Lovely job, I'm in.

A few days later, I phone up my mate Darren Gough to get the lowdown.

'I've just signed up for *The Jump*, Goughie. What's it like?'

'Well, y'know, it's reet dangerous, Tuffers. . . a couple nearly didn't make it back.'

Probably should have called him before, really. Oh well, what can possibly go wrong?

I'll be heading for pine-fresh air in the Austrian Alps at the beginning of the new year, but first the less glamorous prospect of an indoor ski centre in Hemel Hempstead beckons for a couple of weeks of basic training. This means 4am alarm calls for 6am starts, so we can have the slope to ourselves for four hours before it opens to the public.

The full line-up for the show is: ex-England rugby captain Mike Tindall; *Strictly* dancer Ola Jordan; Sally Bercow, wife of the Speaker of the House of Commons; Steve-O of *Jackass* fame, JB Gill, former singer with boyband JLS; former member of the Pussycat Dolls Ashley Roberts; ex-RAF serviceman and Paralympian cyclist Jon-Allan Butterworth; athlete Louise Hazel; dancer Louie Spence; *Made in Chelsea* star Louise Thompson; philanthropist (and the former Mrs McCartney) Heather Mills; Dom Parker of people-watching-TV TV show *Gogglebox*; pop singer/TV personality Stacey Solomon; socialite Lady Victoria Hervey; and TV personality/Essex legend, er, Joey Essex.

When I rock up bleary-eyed for the first morning's training, a few people are missing due to previous work commitments, so I don't get to meet everyone. I do get to meet Lady V's dog who she's brought with her, a handbag-sized little fella called D'Artagnan.

The purpose of the Hemel Hempstead sessions is just to get us up and skiing – learning how to parallel ski, go over a few rollers, little jumps. I soon learn that I'm one of the worst skiers in the group.

Experienced skiers like Lady V and Louise Thompson, who I think have spent a few winter vacations on the slopes, just zip down. Heather Mills, who, I discover, used to be in the UK disabled skiing team and won a World Cup silver medal a couple of years before, is also really, really good. At the other end of the scale are the absolute beginners and novices among us – namely Louie, Joey, Ola and myself. We are all struggling to start with and stack it into the safety nets on a few occasions.

The first thing you need to learn as a beginner is the snow-plough technique, where you put your skis in a V-shape to control your speed, turn and stop. On the second day, Ola is practising this when she topples over gently. It's nothing dramatic, so the rest of us don't think anything of it at first. The next thing we know the medics have appeared and she's being stretchered off the slope and taken to hospital.

Never see her again.

Turns out she's torn the ACL (anterior cruciate ligament) in her knee which could put her out of dancing action for nine months, poor thing.

I should have twigged then that this was going to be rather harder than I had imagined. Chloe Madeley, freelance journalist, TV presenter and daughter of Richard and Judy, is drafted in to replace Ola.

I throw myself into the training, though, which results in a few falls, but I'm reasonably happy with my progress as the days go on. I'm not doing too badly, but this is a relatively gentle indoor slope in Hemel Hempstead, not the Alps.

We are given a nice break for Christmas before flying out to Austria early on 2 January. Dawn and I throw a massive New Year's Eve party at our place – loads of friends round, hog roast in the garden, DJs, cocktail makers – a really good bash. That finishes around 7am so I only have one more proper sleep and then it's off to Austria on an early-morning flight.

With Dawn having a bit of a snooze on New Year's Day to recover from our party, I don't pack particularly well for the challenges ahead. Two pairs of ski socks, a couple of roll-necks and one thermal vest in my suitcase. I'm going to be out there for six weeks.

When I get to the airport, wheeling a suspiciously light suitcase, I'm still feeling a bit ropey, but excited. Everyone's there ready to go. Someone mentions that we should all look out the window as we fly into Innsbruck because it's a spectacular view. Apparently, though, it gets very windy between the mountains, and only the best pilots are allowed to fly in there. Being a nervous flier, this is not really what I want to hear.

The early omens are not good when one of the air hostesses puts a ski helmet in the overhead lockers. A few seconds later, she comes back, opens it again and the helmet falls out and smacks Chloe Madeley on the head. It leaves poor Chloe with a massive egg on her forehead.

I'm sitting behind Dom Parker on the flight over. Dawn and I enjoy watching *Gogglebox* and find him and his wife Steph absolutely hilarious, so I was really pleased when I found out he was in the line-up for the show. During the training sessions at Hemel Hempstead, we had the odd ciggy break together, but at that time of the morning, neither of us were exactly wide awake, so I'm looking forward to getting to know him better in Austria.

When the air hosts and hostesses come round to take breakfast orders, everyone's ordering cereals and juice. I suggest to Dom we order Bloody Marys – hair of the dog after the New Year's Eve festivities and a flight nerve-settler for me.

'Good man, here we go.'

It's the beginning of a beautiful bromance.

By the time our plane begins its descent into Innsbruck, Dom and I have had three or four glasses each. I'm glad I have because it does start to get a little bit bouncy as we get closer.

When I look out the window, I get my first glimpse of the Alps; proper massive mountains, whose snow-capped peaks are almost up by the side of the aeroplane. These are not Mount Snowdons, these all looked like Everest.

The plane flutters about a bit and then lands. The steel steps off the aeroplane are covered with ice and snow and, as we disembark, I slip and nearly fall off them in my desert boots (yes, I know, I know. . .).

There are lots of 'wows' at the scenery and people get their phones out to take photos and selfies. Everyone else seems to cooing in awe of the splendour of the mountains surrounding the airport, but when I look up at them, all I can see is their teeth, as if they're saying: 'I'm going to get you.'

I've never been a man of the mountains and it's starting to dawn on me that this whole thing really might not be the best idea. I turn round to Dom and say: 'I don't know if this is for me.'

'Come on, Phil, we've only just got off the bloody plane.'

We collect our luggage in the terminal and troop off to the waiting fleet of Mercedes-Benz Viano people carriers. On arrival at the hotel, walking the few yards to the entrance, I fall over and land on my arse. I pick myself up in as dignified a fashion as I can and walk through the revolving doors. They are the type that stop if you get too close to the front, which I do, so I headbutt the reinforced glass.

One slip, a fall and a headbutt and I haven't even reached the hotel foyer yet, let alone put my skis on. This is going really well.

After checking in and dropping off our gear, Dom and I take a stroll. This takes us as far as the local pub, which is also a micro-brewery. We decide to sit down and sample their entire range one by one, marking each of them out of ten. The beers are excellent and having conducted this vital preliminary research on behalf of the group, we shall return there on several occasions to unwind after long days on the slopes.

I awake the next day, Saturday, with a mild hangover and a strong sense of foreboding about what lies ahead. The weekend schedule allows us a bit of time to settle in, though. There's a couple of meetings, we're issued with our equipment and we head over to a place called Natters, just outside Innsbruck, for our first look at the three ski jumps which are the focus of the show.

To be honest, it would have been enough for me to look up at them from the bottom – which is scary enough – but instead we are herded onto a travelator. Perhaps the idea is to show us the worst thing first so the other events seem relatively easy in comparison? More likely the show's producers wanted to get some footage of us absolutely shitting ourselves in the bank for the show. If so, in my case and that of a few others – mission accomplished.

As we go past the little jump, I turn and take a peek down and think, 'Fuuuckin' hell. . .' We continue our journey on the human conveyor belt to the middle jump before hopping off. This in itself is a bit of a hairy operation, because it's still moving and you have to step onto a podium which is thinly crusted with ice. More ice and steel – there's a pattern forming here. I'm still wearing my desert boots, which probably doesn't help my balance either.

Then it's about thirty-odd steps up to reach the top of the highest jump, where *Ski Sunday* presenter and former Olympic skier Martin Bell is waiting for us, with a silly grin on his face. As we're all sitting there, looking down, I started whiting out. *Whoah, whoaaaahhh*. . .

Martin calls us up one by one to sit on the metal bar right at the top of the jump where you push off from to get an idea of what it's like.

Stacey's up first and she's like: 'Ooh God, it's a bit high.'

Then Dom: '*Brrrruuuhhhh*, bloody hell, dunno if I fancy that. . .'

When it's my turn, I gingerly inch my way along the bar to Martin's side. As I stare fixedly down this steep slope to oblivion, I can feel my bottom lip go and a tear wells up in my eye.

The last time I got tearful in a sporting situation was way back on New Year's Day 1991, during my first tour for England. During a one-day match against Australia at Sydney Cricket Ground, I botched a simple chance to run out their star batsman Steve Waugh. All 37,000 watching Australians laughed at me and I wanted the ground to swallow me up. If you want to revisit my pain, you can still find it on YouTube. Thanks.

I feel very queasy indeed. Suddenly, I retch and vomit, just missing my legs poking out in front of me.

'I'm alright, I'm alright, I'm okay. . .' I say to myself as much as to Martin, but a few seconds later I feel myself losing my balance – 'Ohhhh fuuuhhck. . .'

I slip off the bar and Martin catches my leg. Luckily, I fall upslope behind the bar, otherwise I might have become the first contestant on the show to do the jump without any skis on.

Soon after they get me to do a talking head to camera: 'If you asked me to do that right now, I'd bottle it,' I say.

I'm not the only one among the group who has a bit of a freak-out up there, but there's a few Billy Big Bollocks among us who show no fear. For instance, Steve-O of *Jackass* fame – unsurprisingly – is unfazed at the prospect. 'Oh, that's alright, yeah. I'll do that,' but you have to bear in mind this is a man who would happily staple his bollocks to his thigh as part of his day job.

On the Monday, training starts in earnest, and in keeping with what appears to be a policy of scaring the bejeezus out of us early doors, the day begins with a half-hour drive to Igls for our first skeleton lesson.

Igls is not the most welcoming of places. All I can see is steel – steel changing rooms, cold steel gratings, steel steps. And ice. There isn't a soft furnishing in sight. It's a really cold place – how I imagine a sacred burial ground. There is danger all around.

Despite my misgivings, being in a dressing room again ready to do a sporting challenge gets the old competitive juices going. Well, until I look across towards mighty Mike Tindall, that is. After putting on some armour over your thermals – padding for the hips, elbows and shoulders – we have to step into our Lycra onesies. It reminds me of getting ready to go out and bat, except wearing a giant condom. Mike has brought his own and it's got Iron Man decoration. There's me shivering in the corner and him looking like a cartoon superhero, muscles poking out everywhere. Makes me glad I played cricket, not rugby. Turns out Mike's got a mate who's made him a couple of different ones and he turns up another day dressed as Superman.

We put on the special spiked skeleton shoes, pick up our helmets and troop over to the top of the 'baby slope' where I see a familiar, friendly face – Amy Williams, the Olympic skeleton gold medallist, who I know through *A Question of Sport*.

'Oh, hello Amy. Nice to see you. What we doing here then?'

Amy gives us a short briefing before we have our first go. For those of you not familiar with the sport of skeleton racing, it involves a very small, low-lying sled with handles either side which, in theory, you use to push off before leaping on the sled and shooting head-first down a curving ice tunnel as fast as you can.

Amy's technical advice is alarmingly simple: 'The best thing to do is just hold on; do not let go of the sled.'

'Um, but how do I steer?'

'Just hold on.'

'Just hold on?! How do I go round corners?'

'Just hold on and go with it. . .'

Bloody hell.

Amy tells us that you can make slight head movements to adjust and 'feel' the corners. It's also possible to tap your feet down to straighten you up a bit, but novices like us will probably get into trouble if we try that because we might overdo it. No, the conclusion seems to be the best way is just to keep as still and straight as possible on the glorified tea tray – and hang on.

The only thing I can compare it too was the time when I did 'street luge' back in England once (don't ask me why. . .). The difference there was that you were on wheels and you went feet-first down a steep winding road. That was pretty terrifying, and although I came through unscathed, my enduring memory is of one of the experts teaching us getting his foot caught in a drain and wrecking his knee.

When it's his turn, Mike sprints off, leaps on the sled and zooms off.

For my first run, I take a more leisurely approach, opting for a lying-down start with Amy giving me a nudge to get me moving. As there's no real way to steer, I decide to keep my eyes closed and just hang on. It's fairly terrifying and feels pretty speedy for a supposed baby slope, but I arrive at the bottom in one piece.

Then we go up to the start of the middle track, where we are going to race from; it's a whole different animal.

Amy talks us through the course and a map of it, drawn on the back of a bit of cardboard, is passed around.

'Try to remember the corners so you know what's coming,' says Amy.

Dom and me are looking at each other, wincing at the prospect of hurtling head-first down a sheet-ice track at 70mph on a glorified dinner tray with no real understanding of how to steer or brake. We've been messing around coming up with ideas for TV shows we could do together and this in-at-the-deep-end experience has given him inspiration: 'How about: *Learn to Fly a Jet Fighter in Fifteen Minutes*, Tuffers? . . . What does this button do? Whoosh! Ooh, that hasn't gone well. . .'

The Jump's two resident paramedics, Dave and Wilko, are standing nearby. For the next few weeks they will be accompanying us everywhere, with backpacks containing defibrilators and oxygen and other first-aid equipment.

'Wilko, mate, I don't think you two should be at the start – I'm alright at the moment up here,' I say. 'Perhaps you should be somewhere at the bottom.'

'Oh, that's a good idea. . .'

I then overheard him ask Amy where fallers normally come off the sled. She says coming out of the notorious Kreisel bend, where the 'slider' (that's what you call the rider of the sled) is pulling something like 4G.

When it's my turn, I assume the racing position on the sled, Amy gives me a little shove to get me over the brow of the first hill, then, *whoosh*. This time I keep my eyes open so I can try and count the corners.

My face is a couple of inches from the ice and all you can hear is this relentless hard 'c' noise as the metal runners bite cut into the ice: *cccc-cccccccccc*. I reach the first corner and suddenly I'm up at about a ninety-degree angle skidding around a curving ice wall.

After that, any memories of the map of the course instantly slip out of my head. I don't have time to think 'Oh, this is corner two. . . and here comes corner three', I'm basically hanging on for dear life.

If you get it a bit wrong – which I do soon enough – you're bashing into the walls with your shoulders. Yes, we've got some protective padding in our suits, but it's a proper whack.

Amy has advised us to 'go with it, don't tense' when that happens, and let the ice wall flick you off. But that's easier said than done when you're scared stiff. Instead, I'm trying to shoulder-charge the ice wall – which is exactly what you shouldn't do, because there will only be one winner.

I career round the Kreisel corner where the G-force makes it feel like I've got a fat fella sitting on the top of my head, pushing it towards the ice. Then it's into the labyrinth section, a series of three gentle curves one way and then the other. You're supposed to go through it nice and smoothly, almost straight, like a fish meandering downstream, but I'm carrying too much speed. I feel like I'm going really quickly (and I am going over 100kph) and I veer above the blue safety line on the first curve. I haven't got a clue what to do to correct my line – no brakes, no steering, all I've got in my head are Amy's words – 'Just hold on!' I rebound off the second curve and then, on the third, I feel the sled turn and the next thing I know, it's above my head.

The frame of the sled is made of steel and its heavy – if it lands on you, it's going to hurt. In a split second, I'm wheeling around in mid-air, I think, 'So much for holding on to the sled – get rid of it.' That instinct comes from my days when I drove a few motorbikes and if you came off, you pushed the bike away from you because if it landed on you, you were in real trouble.

I push the sled off and thankfully it lands in front of me, otherwise that would have been chasing me down the track.

It was like being pushed out the back of the car doing the national speed limit on the M1. On an icy day.

The next few seconds are a confusing blur, but I'm told later that I slide backwards for a hundred metres on my backside, bashing the walls as I go. As I'm skidding along on my Lycra-clad backside across not-very-smooth ice, I'm wishing I had motorbike leathers on.

As I arse-skate to a halt, I become aware of Wilko's voice in the distance calling: 'Phil! Phil!'

Wilko tells me later he called my name five or six times before I responded, so I was probably knocked out for a couple of seconds. I look up and see two red blobs in a white haze.

Where am I?

The blobs gradually come into focus as two Austrian medics dressed in red suits and bobble hats, walk quickly towards me down the track. The medics haul me up and help me to their bus. As I sit down inside, I'm still shaking from pure adrenaline: 'Whoah, what the hell has happened there?'

I've never experienced a rush like that in my life. I'm physically shaking. This is why people like Amy do it – they love the adrenaline rush of racing. Me? Not so much.

I'm told to sit for five minutes while it goes out of my body. And it does take a few minutes before I feel alright again.

Playing a Test match in the Caribbean with Curtly Ambrose charging in and pinging down balls at my ribcage at 90mph used to get my blood up, but this is another level. I didn't mind people trying to hit me with cricket balls every now and then, but at least do it where the sun's shining and I can listen to some relaxing reggae at Millers Beach Bar at the end of a day's play. Not just cold, ice, that horrible *cccccccccccccccc* noise and constant feeling of dread from the fact that I've got no brakes, I'm completely out of control and I don't know what I'm doing.

I'm not the only one who struggles with the skeleton in training – Lady V also falls off and Dom cuts his chin up when the fat man sits on his head going round the Kreisel.

Aside from leaving me covered in bruises and ice burns, the fall knocks my confidence. 'Right, that's me done with the skeleton until the show.'

I can't see the point of risking getting hurt again before the race. If all you can do is hang on, how do you improve? Hang on better?

In the evening, I call Dawn up, still a bit shaken by my accident and fishing for some sympathy, but none is forthcoming.

'Come on Phil, man up. Grow a pair,' she says. 'Come on my lion. . .'

'Oh, alright, then,' I reply, feeling more like a pussycat.

Tuesday brings another terrifying prospect: our first crack at ski-jumping. Having puked and almost passed out going up there the other day, I've rapidly backtracked from my brave pledge to the producers back in November that I shall be soaring from the biggest of the three jumps. I've discovered that you reach a speed of about 70kph skiing down that one and 55kph on the middle jump. Even taking the smallest jump, you're skiing at 45kph down the ramp, which is more than quick enough for me.

Standing at the top, the scariest thing for me is that I can't see where I'm going to land — all I can see is the edge of a cliff. In the distance I can see people walking around in the town down below and they look tiny. Meanwhile, right next to me, there's a squirrel perched on a branch at the top of a huge fir tree, casually chewing nuts and looking over at me.

I gee myself up — 'Come on, do it, do it, do it. . .' — let go of the bar and the next thing I'm speeding down the hill — whoosh — and then leap off the end of the ramp. A second or two later, I'm like, 'I've landed, I've landed, great. . .'

The landing slope is as steep as a black run, though, so you're really moving before you reach the upslope. To stop yourself, you're supposed to do the snowplough, but in my relief at landing safely, I completely forget to do it until it's too late, despite desperate cries from Norbert, one of our coaches standing nearby: 'STOP! SNOWPLOUUGGGHHH!'

Before I know it, I'm speeding towards the barrier at the top. I'm still travelling at a fair speed when I hit it. My skis ping off in different directions and I only just stop myself going over the top. . . which is lucky because, as I notice on impact, it's about a ten-metre drop to the road below where I can see a lorry is rumbling along. If I'd gone over I'd have probably been killed.

Norbert, the rest of the Austrians and the film crew are all pissing themselves, but I'm not seeing the funny side. I gesture to one of the cameramen to point his camera over the barrier.

'Take a look down there. I could have killed myself. Why isn't there a net there? For ****'s sake. . . Health and safety!'

The film crew are all trying to calm me down, when Norbert comes over.

'Sixteen years I've worked here,' he says, shaking his head. 'I've never seen anyone not try to stop.' That does make me laugh.

Day three will take us to the tiny village of Kühtai – the highest resort in Austria, 2,000 metres above sea level – to practise parallel skiing in preparation for the skiing events. Just getting to the village offers the opportunity to enjoy another near-death experience.

It's about half an hour away from our hotel and a double-decker tour bus is laid on to take us there. Pop star Usher used it when he was touring Austria and it's very luxurious with a bar, lounge area, widescreens, state-of-the-art music system. The only thing missing is a hot tub.

Most people are taking the chance to get an extra bit of shut-eye before the day's exertions, but I'm sitting near the front of the top deck looking through the windscreen. The journey certainly keeps me awake.

We've got this big Austrian geezer driving and it's a job that requires a lot of skill and confidence. These mountain roads are narrow and icy, often with just flimsy barriers between you and a sheer cliff-face. Ten minutes outside Innsbruck, it's snowing so badly, the driver stops to put chains on the wheels ready for the really steep roads.

As we're rattling along into the mountains, the weather is getting progressively worse. Through the whiteness, I can just make out a car reversing out onto the road ahead.

'He ain't seen us! He's not going to stop, it's not going to stop. . .'

We swerve to miss it and screech to a grinding halt. Down below, I can see our driver getting out and so does the car driver, another big fella, and they start arguing and squaring up to each other. I go down and get out to try to help calm the situation, all the while, thinking: 'Where's Tindall? Wake Tindall up. . .'

Luckily, the medics have been following us up the mountain in their bus and Wilko steps in. He's ex-Forces, a powerful unit, and no one messes with him.

A truce appears to have been reached, but as I'm trudging back to the truck, a snowball fizzes past my head. I look round and a furious-looking bloke is striding alongside the truck towards me.

'You ****ing ****!' he yells.

'Excuse me?'

I soon discover that this Austrian fella was driving up the mountain behind us and is angry because he's had to stop his car and now, he says, he won't be able to get going again on the icy surface.

'Who are you calling a ****?'

'You ****ing English ****,' he elaborates.

I don't know what I'm supposed to have done, I'm just a passenger, but Anglo-Austrian relations are deteriorating rapidly.

(Dom, who was asleep in the coach, tells me later that he was awoken by the sound of me saying: 'D'ya want some? D'ya want some?' He wondered what the hell was going on.)

Like the other drivers, though, my tormentor soon calms down when Wilko makes his presence felt. Finally, peace breaks out and everyone returns to their vehicles.

Our driver now has the tricky task of getting our massive coach going again. Another Austrian chap comes out of his house nearby and kindly helps to guide us past cars parked on the road. By this time, most of our passengers are wide awake, sitting bolt upright, like meerkats, straining to look out of the front window. We see this guy walking in front, beckoning our driver forward. What he hasn't bargained for is that in such icy conditions, once you get a bit of momentum, you have to keep going. Suddenly he realises he's about to be mowed down, so he runs to the side of the road, kicks a post out the way and dives for it.

At first, we think we've hit him and he's gone under the coach, but when we look back there's two legs sticking up out of the snow by the side of the road.

Our man keeps driving, and further up we see a big van that's stopped by the side of the road. There's not much room to pass, and even less when the bloke inside opens the door – he just sees us in time to pull the door back in and we plough on up the mountain.

One of the cars taking the production crew has stopped further up and they're waving at us, but we just zoom past them.

We're speeding through huge tunnels carved out of the mountain like in a Bond movie, except instead of an Aston Martin, we're in a massive twenty-wheeler that has to go 50mph or it stops. This bloke is an amazing driver, but we're all saying 'He's going too fast', checking our seatbelts and screaming as he careers around another bend.

After a hair-raising ascent, we hit a downhill stretch into Kühtai. Ahead, there's a girl walking down the middle of the road in front of us. She's got her hood up and must have her headphones on because she seems completely oblivious to our monster truck coming straight for her at about 40mph. The driver's hooting his horn, rolling down the window and shouting at her and we're screaming and battering on the sides of the coach with our water bottles.

She turns just in time to run out of the way up against an ice wall to save her life.

When we finally reach our destination, I say: 'Well, that was an enter-taining journey, Dom. . . three near-death experiences just getting to the slopes. Fancy a cup of tea?'

'Might fancy something a bit stronger, Tuffers.'

We then take a gondola up to an altitude of 2,520 metres where forty-odd kilometres of ski slopes take you back down to the village. There's some swinging and swaying, and it's a bit of a white-out so when we get to the top of the run, I can hardly make out the lie of the land. It's minus eleven degrees. Can't feel my fingers, can't feel my toes. There's two instructors with us, and one says: 'We're going to have a nice ski down there.'

I set off gingerly, doing my best snowplough turns, the edges of my skis biting into the snow and ice. That ccccccccccccc noise again – like really bad interference on an old transistor radio with the sound turned up to the maximum. I'm trying to breathe – 'he-he-huh' – but it's not relaxing when you have very little clue what you're doing.

It's all going reasonably well, though, until we all reach a plateau and come to a stop. I take a peek over the edge and it looks like a cliff-face to me. I'm later told it's a red run, but almost a black.

'Right, we're going down there now.'

I'm like: 'What? I'm not going down there. No way.'

'Come on, Tuffers, you'll be alright.'

'No, I won't. I'll kill myself. I've only been skiing a couple of times in Hemel Hempstead.'

'Well, you can't go back because the gondolas are closed.'

'Perhaps you should have thought about that before bringing a load of beginners up here then! We're going to need a helicopter. . .'

No helicopter is forthcoming though, so there's no choice but to get down this slope somehow. The decent skiers among us zoom off, leaving the rest of us to our own devices. Louie Spence, who's not very happy about it either, goes down the hill – mostly on his arse. Chloe Madeley, who had never skied before doing the show, ends up taking her skis off and sort of clambering down.

I'm the last one sitting at the top and I have a moment – I feel short of breath and physically sick, like I'm going to pass out, and I'm looking over the edge of a cliff in minus eleven and a biting wind that makes it feel even colder.

'Medic! Mediiic!' I call out.

Dave plus a ski instructor and two of the camera crew come over to me.

Everything is white. I can't see anything. I don't know what's happening. I'm confused.

Where am I?

I'm frozen – in all senses of the word – to the spot, thinking I'm going to be stuck here for the rest of my life. Am I having a seizure, a stroke? No one else seems to be complaining, though – am I just moaning?

In the end, the ski instructor advises me to zig-zag down the hill – parallel ski across the slope, stop and then go back the other way. So in my woozy state I do that, listening to the awful sound of my skis cutting into the ice as I gradually make my descent: *cccccccccccc* – stop – turn around – *ccccccccccc* – stop – turn around. Repeat to exhaustion.

I keep getting disorientated, asking myself, 'Where is the piste?' There's a couple of poles here and there but no signs, and in a white-out, how do you know which direction to take? You could think: 'Oh this is alright, this is a little red run, there's the brow of a hill, it'll flatten out. . . oops, I've gone wrong, I'm falling 3,000 metres to my death.'

I just keep stopping every time I reach the brow of a hill and it takes me about forty-five minutes to sidewind down to the bottom of the run. The proper skiers who zipped down in about ten minutes and everyone else – even Louie – are all relaxing in the tent at the bottom having a drink by the time I arrive.

In the past couple of days – on the jump and on the mountain – I've discovered that I have a fear of skiing when I can't see the slope in front of me. Every time I see the brow of a hill ahead of me, I feel like I'm

going to ski off the edge of a cliff. And it could be the edge of a cliff –
during the time we are in Austria we hear of people *dying* when they go
skiing off-piste, accidentally or otherwise.

It couldn't be a more different environment, but it reminds me of
when I first went to Australia – 'Don't go in the sea – sharks. Don't go
in the Bush – snakes. Don't go in an outdoor toilet – might be a black
widow spider in there.'

I'm not seeing the beauty in the mountain landscape – all I can see
is danger, possible ways to get really badly hurt. Or worse. I'm genuinely
scared.

When I reach the bottom of the run, I'm exhausted, sweating and
soaking wet. I take my skis off and chuck them down, walk into the tent
and have a massive old strop.

'You are trying to ****ing kill me,' I say to the director.

'Alright, calm down, Phil. You'll get the hang of it.'

'I can't do it. . .'

In the hotel bar that evening, I tell Roman, the friendly manager of
the hotel, how I'd got all woozy and whited out on the slopes.

'That is altitude sickness. Did no one tell you about that?'

'Er, no. . .'

'Oh yes, the first couple of weeks you are here, you will feel funny.'

I thought I had something wrong with my brain up there.

The following days and weeks bring more opportunities to learn new
winter sports and to bash myself up. I get hurt every day. All I seem to
shout is 'Medic! Mediiic!' Wilko and Dave start to follow me round for
the first week or two, waiting for my next injury.

The whole thing is fraught with danger at every turn, not just the training, but getting to training. Joey Essex nearly has the worst accident of all when he slips, falls over backwards and is a hair's breadth from cracking his skull open on the sharp steel edge of a step. Dom is annoyed because he's been complaining that while the crew have crampons attached to their shoes, which give you a bit of grip on icy surfaces, we haven't. Eventually, they give us some crampons to shut him up. Sod's law, the first time Dom puts them on, he goes outside, gets stuck in a grate and takes a tumble: '****ing crampons!'

Dave – or 'Doctor Death' as he becomes known, is always on call to prescribe painkillers and anti-inflammatories. It becomes a routine for me to call him from my hotel room: 'Doctor Death. . . it's Phil – can you come round?' He's like our drug dealer. Of course, I hasten to add, Dave only gives us what is required and in safe dosages. He also tells us not to drink alcohol with the pills. . . which is advice Dom and me, for example, don't always stick to. I might, say, take mine with a pint of lager, while Dom prefers his with an evening snifter.

The evenings often end with me and Dom retiring to the smoking room of the bar in the hotel for a couple of drinks and plenty of gallows humour. After taking a hot bath and having dinner there's nothing much else to do, and a soothing drink helps: (a) you to calm down after the adrenaline rush of the past day; (b) anaesthetise the pain; and (c) take your mind off the sheer dread of what's to come the following day.

We have a similar sense of humour and we have some great chats – just two old men sitting around having a good laugh. As Dom says, in mock horror at the prospect: 'Without you here, I might have ended up going down to the gym or eating salad with the children' (the 'children', or 'kids', being the younger members of the group).

One day, we are given the afternoon off and head back to the micro-brewery to resample our favourite local brews. Afternoon turns to evening, by which time both Dom and I are three sheets to the wind. Most of the contestants are on WhatsApp, and Dom starts pinging out WhatsApps inviting the others to join us. Most people, sensibly, make their excuses. Mike Tindall replies saying he might pop down, to which JB says: 'Oh Mike, don't encourage them – they've been out since two o'clock and probably haven't eaten anything.'

As the night wears on, Dom's messages become increasingly misspelt: *'Thubk sonethng hsppned to Tiffers legs. Keep tring to get to door, but legs dont sem to work. Must be altitude sickness kickng in. Migt ned help geting bk to hotel. Weeeeeeeeee!'*

By then I think Mike has turned his phone off. No one comes to save us.

Dom has been skiing on and off for forty-five years, so he knows his way down a ski slope. He looked very good to me from day one, but according to the instructors, his old-school technique isn't seen as correct anymore. He does find that the new methods make skiing a lot easier once he gets the hang of them. But I'm the old dog who quite quickly starts to believe that I can't learn too many new tricks. Just putting on all the equipment is exhausting – the thermal underwear and mid-layer (which I have to go out and buy more of as I've packed so badly for the trip), salopettes, boots, jacket and then a jumper to fend off the cold, and gloves. . . and then you get it all on and realise you needed to go for a pee. There's too much gear knocking about. It's all a bit of a faff. Skiing holidays are not for me – sun, shorts, flip-flops and a copy of the *Racing Post* is more my scene.

I'm just in survival mode, trying to get through it, in contrast to the young ones like JB. He is a lovely fella, a real gentleman, and dead keen. JB loves the challenge and when he goes wrong, he bounces up and has another go: 'Let's look at the technique. . . let's do it again and get the technique right.'

Then you've got Mike, who's a bit older but still got about a dozen years on me. Another nice guy, and as well as being built like a brick outhouse, he's absolutely fearless. He has a fall in ski-jumping practice that would have broken my neck, but it hardly even registers with him; he just thinks it's funny.

The Paralympic cyclist Jon-Allan Butterworth has a similar attitude. He lost his left arm in an insurgent rocket attack serving with the RAF in Basra, so the dangers of winter sports are nothing to him.

Sally Bercow is really enjoying herself, too. Unfortunately for her, at the end of the first week, she has a nasty fall skiing and breaks two of her ribs. The same day, four other people have accidents that leave them needing medical treatment. She is forced to reluctantly withdraw from the show and the model and TV presenter Jodie Kidd flies in to replace her. (It's a mark of how much Sally loves skiing that, a month later, she brings her three children back out to Austria for a holiday, only to suffer an even worse accident and breaks her leg in nine places.)

By this point, I am on the verge of quitting myself. I feel beaten up and if I carry on I feel like I'll end up in the Betty Ford clinic because I'm on so many painkillers and anti-inflammatories. Dawn arrives in Innsbruck in the nick of time, to give me the bit of support and encouragement I need to keep going. She stays for ten days and ends up coming back for another ten days with Alana when the show's on. If she hadn't come, I think I would have been off. In our hotel room that night, I get undressed to get in the bath after another day's training.

'Oh my God,' she gasps. 'You're covered in bruises!'

I am black and blue – I must have thirty bruises. All down my arms, on my back, a couple round my ribs. I've even got two massive ones behind my knees which I haven't seen before until she points them out in the mirror. No idea how I got those. And this is after a week, we've got another month of this to go.

Dawn, who's tough, is shocked: 'Ooh, sorry Phil – perhaps I've been a little bit harsh. . .'

The threat of serious injury is constantly in my head, so I can never fully relax and enjoy the experience. I do improve gradually with practice, though. For instance, I eventually get alright at skiing, but I know my limits. I'll do a couple of runs, have a fall or two and our coaches will say: 'Go up and do it again.'

'No, I'm done, I'm tired, I'm going in.'

I become a bit of a ski psychic, developing a sixth sense for when something horrible is going to happen and I'm proved right almost every time if I go against my instincts – the days when I allow myself to be persuaded to go up and do an extra run are when I take a fall.

Snowboarding is one of the hardest disciplines to learn and the most painful. Unless you're a skateboarder or surfer or have a natural ability for it, you're going to fall over – a lot. Catch the wrong edge of the snowboard either way and you're down. Get your weight too far forward and you pitch forward and face-plant into the snow. Too much on the back edge, and you land right on your coccyx and get neck whiplash for good measure. There's a theory that you can only fall over backwards or forwards on a snowboard, not sideways, but Dom even manages to prove that wrong, pranging a bank of snow at very high speed. Every time you fall, the only way to get up from lying down is to flip your legs over your head. It's exhausting – a morning's snowboarding is like doing a full five-day Test match in the field.

Louie Spence and me get on very well. He's very similar to me in that he hadn't really thought about what was involved in the show before agreeing to take part. And, like me, now he's out here, he's realised that winter sports are not his thing.

After stacking it a few times, Louie turns to the instructor: 'Well, dahling, how many more times do you want me to fall over?'

A typical morning's snowboarding training for me consists of: face-plant, coccyx-crusher, face-plant, then shout over to Louie:

'Louie! Lou, love! Cup of tea?'

'Coming, Phil. . .'

Then we'd go in for a cuppa and a slice of Victoria sponge. Dom might join us and if it was particularly chilly, we might have a small glass of gluhwein at lunchtime to warm up.

'Very glad we brought the kids with us on this holiday. Nice to see them enjoying themselves. Another cuppa?'

There is one event that I really enjoy: bobsleigh. We do that on the same track we'd used for the skeleton run, but the big difference is that we have a professional driving the sled for us. You get the massive adrenaline rush, but without the terror of trying to steer the sled. You just have to push off, jump in and then it's like the best roller-coaster ride in the world.

The first time we do it, it's even easier because, to get us used to it, they stick two of us in a four-man bob with a driver and another bloke to push us off at the start.

I pair up with Dom and we record the fastest time of everyone. We have the largest combined weight and turns out that being heavier is an advantage in bobsleigh, which delights Dom: 'Oh great, a sport for chubbies – the fatter you are, the better you are!'

Before we try the two-man bob, our instructor, a short, stocky guy from the British bobsleigh team, demonstrates how to start.

'You have to hold here and here, one-two-three, push off and then jump in. . .'

So he does, but as he jumps into the sled, he cries out in anguish: '*Uuuaaarrggghh.*'

He's got cramp.

'Arghhhh, get me out, get me out!'

Me and Dom have to pull him out. It's hysterical.

Speeding down the track is a great buzz, but you still get really smashed about. The interior of a bobsleigh is not like a Bentley – it's all metal, no one's thought it might be a good idea to stick a bit of foam cushioning in there. This isn't so much of a problem in the four-man bob, because you're all squished in quite cosily, but doing the two-man in the same sled means there's more space to move around and bash into the sides. In the first season of *The Jump*, Melinda Messenger had given herself concussion doing bobsleigh.

You sit with your legs in front of you, knees bent, head down. When I come off the Kreisel corner, where you're pulling 4G, and the sled crashes down onto the straight, it's the nearest I've ever come to giving myself a blow job. As you've got a pro up front driving it, you feel a lot safer, though. Once you've pushed off and jumped in the bobsleigh, your only job – other than holding on tight and keeping your head down – is to pull the brake after the finishing line.

The brake is basically two attached metal pieces and when you pull the lever, the lower piece with teeth goes through the bottom of the bob and cuts into the ice to bring you to a halt. Well, that's the theory.

You have to really pull the brake hard to activate it and one day during a training run, the brake comes off in Jodie Kidd's hand. This great big Austrian driver is looking round at her screaming 'BRAKE. . . BRAAAAAAKE!'

'What, this?' she replies, holding the broken lever above her head.

The end of the track funnels into a sort of cone with foam either side and it's supposed to bring you to a gentle halt, but the poor Austrian fella and Jodie go smashing into it. It's comical to watch at the time, but the whiplash effect puts poor Jodie out for a couple of days.

Dom's initial enthusiasm for bobsleigh racing disintegrates when he does the two-man version. The Kreisel blow-job effect causes his back to go into spasm and he has to be lifted out of the bobsleigh in agony. At first, he thinks he's broken his back.

Despite the battering, I really love my first run in the two-man bob.

There's a people carrier to drive people back up to the top of the track again and on the way I'm all geared up to have another go. But then, as I get out of the car – 'Aaaarrrggghh' – my back goes into spasm too. It feels like someone has knifed me. I shuffle into the changing room, bent double like an old man, and collapse in a heap on the floor, yelping: 'Medic! Mediiic!'

Dave administers muscle relaxant and painkillers and then Dom and me are packed off back to the hotel to rest. I wedge myself into a corner of the people carrier, trying to find a position that doesn't hurt, which has me doubled up with my arse in Dom's face. By this time, he's had a bit of treatment and is not quite as bad as me but still in a fair amount of pain.

'Oh, Dom,' I say, 'I can't move me legs. . .'

'****ing hell, Tuffers – can't you get your own injury!' As Dawn could tell him, this isn't the first time I've been accused of this. . .

The journey is filled with both hysterical laughter and agonised yelps of pain. On arrival at the hotel, we both drag ourselves out of the Viano and walk into the reception like a couple of bow-legged cowboys who'd been out riding on the range for a year with no saddle. Roman sees us come in: 'Pheeel, Dom, what is the matter? What is the matter? What has happened to you?'

We tell him our tale of woe.

'Oh, don't worry. Go to bed lie down. I bring you some wiener schnitzel and strudel – make you feel so much better.'

Sure enough, after the show's masseur pays a visit to try and ease my back, I'm lying in bed and Roman arrives with a tray of traditional Austrian cuisine. For the next half hour, Dawnie patiently feeds me forkfuls of schnitzel followed by strudel by the spoonful.

After a day of rest and being nursed back to some semblance of health by Dawn, Roman's room service and the masseur, my back's eased a bit and the instructors tell me I need one more bobsleigh run before the show. Although I actually fancy another go, I say that I'd rather just do the show run because I don't think my back's going to handle it. The old 'ski psychic' again.

The following weeks' training in the build-up to the show continue in the same vein, mixing moments of pain and comedy. An incident one day, at the start of a slalom practice session, sums that up. It's a red run with ice walls on either side. One of our instructors Stuart says he'll show us what we need to do, and sets off down the course. After one neat turn, he clips the second gate, hits a rut and goes flying. His legs hit the ice wall, skis fly off in different directions and he topples over the wall. Warren and Phil – our other instructors – look on with us. 'Oh, I wonder what happened there?' says Warren, deadpan.

It's so funny. On the other hand, this is our expert instructor who's just gone flying so it doesn't say much for our prospects.

We do an event called snow-cross, which consists of a red run with curves and moguls. The experienced skiers struggle with it; for beginners, it's impossible. They don't make the run-off big enough, so everyone keeps smashing into the netting at the side of the course – we're all flapping around in there like fish caught in a trawler's net. Worse, in week three, poor Dom skids into the net feet first, flips over the top, headbutts an icewall and smashes his shoulder. He's knocked out and, as he's lying there motionless, two girls in the crew burst into tears. The next day, Dom himself feels quite close to tears and asks to see the medic.

The day after that, though, he walks in for breakfast, absolutely beaming: 'Can't wait to get out on the slopes today, Tuffers. I. Feel. Fantastic!'

We're all pleasantly surprised that he's feeling so chipper after his accident and he's in great form when we get out on the mountain, smiling and laughing. Throwing himself into everything, despite his bad shoulder.

Back at the hotel in the afternoon, though, I'm talking to him and all of a sudden for no obvious reason, he starts getting very teary and emotional.

'You alright, mate?' I say, putting a consoling arm around his dodgy shoulder.

When he's stopped crying, he tells me that the medic had told him to look out for mood swings.

'Ah, that'll be the concussion, then. . .'

Around the same time, one of the camera crew falls over and breaks his shoulder. It's all happening.

Every contestant on the show had four or five days when after training they'd be going, 'Argh, arggghh – me knee/back/leg/shoulder' (delete as appropriate).

Snowboarding continues to be my personal nemesis. A few days after my back spasm, we have another session and I'm not optimistic. I begin the day's training by turning to one of the cameras following us and saying: 'Hello and welcome to *Phil Tufnell Does Winter Sports Badly* – today, I will be doing snowboarding badly. Come with me. . .'

There's an Austrian fella in charge of the T-bar and as I approach, he says: 'Ah, here he comes – Churchill.'

I don't quite know what he means by that and as I step on the travelator I'm muttering under my breath, 'Alright, Adolf, don't take the piss.'

A few seconds later, twenty metres up the slope, I lose balance, fall off and have another back spasm.

'Medic! Mediiic!'

The nice part is getting to know the other contestants and we have some good nights out together. One evening Heather Mills lays on a party for the whole cast and crew at a local hotel, which is really nice of her.

They are an interesting and diverse bunch of people. No one more diverse than Steve-O. He's got some very strange tattoos dating back to his *Jackass* heyday, when people would dare him to do really stupid things. He's got a picture of a big penis with 'USA' written on it, a bloke behind prison bars saying 'Prison Love' and best of all, a tattoo of his own face – only bigger – on his back (someone had bet him that he wouldn't have a tattoo that big). I hear that him and Stacey Solomon started going out together after the show's over – didn't see that coming. Stacey's a great girl – funny, and very brave; braver than I was.

Lady V has brought D'Artagnan with her. The first weekend over there, I bumped into a bloke walking out of the hotel with him and my first instinct is that he's nicking him: 'Hold on, hold on, that's not your dog!' Turns out he's actually dogsitting for Lady V while we're out there. After that, we often see him taking tiny D'Artagnan out for walks alongside a massive St. Bernard, which always makes us laugh.

We don't see much of Louise for the first week, but she joins us in the bar a few times after that. She is good fun and very small — she's got tiny little feet.

'Maybe she's been here all the time and we just didn't notice?' says Dom.

Joey Essex is a nice lad and I piss myself when I discover that 'Essex' is his real surname. We call him 'Joey Innsbruck' for the duration of the trip. One afternoon out on the slopes, I ask him for the time.

'I dunno, I can't tell the time,' he replies. So I look at his watch for myself. It's about half four but it's set to half eleven. He's got a twenty-five-grand Rolex set to the wrong time, so even if he could tell the time, it would be wrong.

I think Joey's a little bit cleverer than he makes out, though. He's quite fearless, too, and throws himself into everything we do. He's done skating before and he picks up all the winter sports we do pretty quickly. He's also got a gleaming-white set of teeth and I notice that a lot of the group have impeccable gnashers. One day, there's a big group conversation about where they got their implants and veneers done – '2007 this' 'LA three years ago that'.

I turn to Dom: 'Are we the only people here with our own teeth?'

After a month of training, it's time for the actual shows. The format of the show is a bit strange. Having trained for all these different disciplines, you'd think all of the contestants would do them all over a few episodes and then the top three or four on the leaderboard would go through to a semi-final. Instead, the first episode, which just features the eight men, divides us into two groups of four, matching us up, one against one in skeleton races. The two winners of their races in each group qualify for the next round, the losers have to do the dreaded jump and the one with the shortest distance in that is eliminated from the show.

We actually did these skeleton races weeks before, not long after my training accident, but our times aren't revealed until the live show when we watch them together with the presenter Davina McCall. We've all been wondering how we got on.

In my group, I was matched up with Joey, who got similar times to me in practice, while Mike Tindall was up against Louie. On the morning of the race, Marcus, one of our instructors, who holds the record time ever at Igls, asks me how I want to get on the sled.

'Right, I'm going to run onto it.'

'Okay, but if you do it that way, you have to change your hand grip once you're on the sled.'

He shows me how and I have three practice gos at it as Marcus watches. Each time, I don't quite get my hands into the right position once I'm on the sled. After the third time, he says: 'Stop, stop, stop. . .'

'What?'

'You cannot do that. If you can't get that right on your three practice starts before your race, I cannot send you down there, because if you get that wrong, you'll break both your arms.'

Fair enough. So how am I going to do this?

Then Joey pipes up and says: 'I'm going to frog off.'

'Frog off? What's that, Joe?'

He tells me he's going to get a little plank of wood behind him, lay on the sled, get his hands in the right position and then push off with his legs. Right, I'll do that.

Despite my previous insistence that I won't have another practice run before the race, I decide I better do one just to get back on the horse. Thankfully, I manage to stay on this time.

We've all been given customised racing gear to wear on the show. Mine is decorated with a sort of cricket ball design. Lycra shows everything and me and the boys have to have a bit of padding put in to the groin area to, um, soften the outline, otherwise viewers would be able to work out our religion. It's top-of-the-range gear and I do feel a bit like a superhero wearing it. I walk out for the race, shoulders back, chest out, humming the *Superman* theme tune and feeling like a million dollars. Despite all the bumps and bruises of that first week, the old competitive spirit is kicking in.

There's quite a big crowd gathered to watch, cheering and ringing their cowbells.

I've got my Superman outfit on. I'm ready for this. Amy Williams is there, and all the camera crew, and I'm screaming to myself: 'Come on, Tufnell. Let's ****ing have it! Come on you ****!' I'm slapping myself round the face, pumping myself up.

Amy Williams is looking at me in disbelief, like, 'What is going on? Phil's gone mad.'

Watching me rant and rave, the crowd are probably now expecting me to sprint off and launch myself down the run. Instead, I assume a bow-legged stance and lower myself gently onto the sled – like a ballet dancer doing a plié. (Someone later sends me a photo on Twitter of me doing the frog start, but with the addition of a great big cock and balls, drawn on, hanging down between my legs.) I push off and only just make the brow of the hill to get moving down the track. I feel like such a twat.

I nearly come off again in the labyrinth section, but this time I have a bit more experience to know what to do. I smash into the third bend but, as I feel one side of the sled lift off the track, I slam it back down with my shoulder. By the time I cross the finishing line, I'm really travelling and just hanging on with my eyes shut. A few seconds later, I feel myself coming to a stop. I open my eyes, take off my goggles but can't see a thing.

The next thing I know an Austrian track official's face appears before me. He's pulling off the foam material I've got snagged up in at the end of the track. 'Oh, thank God for that. It's a miracle. I can see!'

As much as it terrified me to do it, it was an exhilarating experience and I thought I had a good chance of beating Joey. On the live show though, it turns out that he's pipped me by 0.05 seconds.

In the other race, Louie somehow beats Mike Tindall, despite going down the entire run with his eyes closed, which means I'm up against Mike in the jump. Well, that's me done. No chance. We've never had our jumps measured in practice, but I know my goose is definitely cooked, because Mike is going off the middle ramp and I'm going off the bottom one.

When you think about ski-jumping, you might have had visions of us leaping sixty, seventy metres like Eddie 'The Eagle' Edwards (who's out there with us) used to. In fact, Mike manages eighteen metres, which is further than anyone managed in series one, and twice as far as my effort of nine metres. To put my epic leap in context, that's 5cm further than the world long jump record, and just 242.5 metres shorter than the new ski-jump world-record mark set a couple of weeks later. On telly, it looks more like a plop off the end of a ramp than a jump, because after you take off, you're never more than a couple of metres off the ground. But when you're sitting on the bar at the top of the jump looking down, it does take some bottle to do it, I can tell you.

'I've had a great time' I tell Davina. 'Not really – the whole experience has been terrifying for both me and my family.'

My mate Dom is also eliminated on the opening night, losing in a jump-off against JB. So, for us two, that is that. Well, not quite. There's still a chance one of us will have to come back into the competition if anyone gets injured. Should that happen, both of us are very keen that the other should have the privilege of taking their place.

'It should be you, Phil – you had a better time on this. . .'

'Oh no, you were definitely faster – you're the one who should go back in.'

It's Groundhog Day for the rest of the week: get up, have breakfast, go for a long lunch, then to the pop-up après-ski lodge by the course in the evening for the show, make the odd appearance in the *On the Piste* sister show, then back to the hotel, sleep and repeat.

Having Dawn and Alana out there, and Dom's wife Steph, who is hilarious, and gets on brilliantly with Dawn, helps the time pass. Dawn sees someone on the Digital Spy website forum asking: 'Why are Dom and Phil still out there getting pissed at the bar? Normally, when you're knocked out, you go home.'

Dawn's itching to reply and say we're not actually drunk – even though they shove a pint of beer in my hand when the cameras are on us, it's actually a dry bar. Mind you, Steph does sometimes sneak a nip of rum in for us in a Coke bottle to keep us warm in the sub-zero temperatures. 'Blue Peter' she calls it, as in 'Here's one I made earlier. . .'

The producers don't really want Dom and I to go skiing in case we get injured, but one afternoon we go out with Dawn and Alana anyway. I've had enough after one blue run, so I take their spare gear and go in. Dom carries on, but ends up snow-ploughing all the way down the mountain on his next run, thinking: 'I've lost it – I don't know how to ski anymore.' For all his experience, he's just been worn down by all the accidents over the past month and, as soon as you get a bit of doubt in your mind skiing, that's it, you can't do it.

Thankfully, the rest of the series passes without anyone else getting terminally injured, so our services are not called upon. Joey shocks the world by going all the way and winning the competition, beating Mike Tindall and Louise Hazel into second and third place respectively in the final. Fair play to Joey, he's done brilliantly in the competition, showed lots of nerve and we're all delighted for him. As he puts it in his victory interview with Davina: 'I found it hard to learn things growing up, but being on *The Jump* has proved I can. I've got more skill, well, than I think I have.'

He's a bit confused when he is given a cowbell as his prize, though: 'What is a cowbell, by the way?' he asks. 'Does it mean I need to get a cow?'

As for me, I'm glad it's all over. On the plus side, I've lost about a stone in weight during the past six weeks – I'm not a big eater and we were expending so much energy. And for all the bruises, the show's in-at-the-deep-end approach to training does work, because I'm not a bad skier by the end. It would have been nicer to have started on somewhat gentler slopes, but you do learn a lot quicker by just being thrown in. I won't be rushing to book a skiing holiday any time soon, though.

The best thing to come out of the show is a new friendship with Dom and his wife Steph. A few weeks later they come and stay with us and we compare war wounds. He tells me he came back from Austria with a dose of ringworm, a swollen finger and his shoulder is still giving him gyp from his close encounter with an ice wall.

Maybe I got off quite lightly after all?

EPILOGUE: WHERE I AM

One afternoon early in November 2014, I get a call from Greg to say that Dad's been taken into hospital. I haven't seen Dad for a few months. We've talked on the phone a few times, but he's got that old-school attitude. He never asks me for anything, money or help. He won't call if he's feeling unwell. That's how he is – he wouldn't want to inconvenience anyone even if he's dying. And now he might be.

Dawn and I immediately get in the car and rush up there. I wasn't there when my mum passed away and there's no way I want that to happen again, although Dad has always been adamant that, when the time comes, I shouldn't worry if I'm busy.

When we arrive he's in a room with an oxygen mask on, his eyes closed. All the family, my brother and other relations, are sat there. The doctor tells us it's not looking good. As evening turns to night, everyone's sitting around thinking, 'Oh no, this is it.'

Then all of a sudden, at three in the morning, Dad opens his eyes.

He takes his mask off, surveys all our faces gawping at him and says: 'Look at you lot – none of you have got **** all to say to each other.'

Everyone bursts out laughing. He's right – we've all been sitting for hours in near silence.

Over the next few days, to the surprise of the doctors, his condition improves. I stay a couple of nights with him at the hospital and we get a chance to really talk. We talk about Granddad, his experiences in the Great War, how he intervened to save Dad from enduring similar horrors in the Second World War. We talk about his life with Mum before Greg and I came along, working at the silversmiths together, how he got me back into cricket as a teenager. We laugh at our shared memories. We talk about when Mum died and how I didn't see her too much towards the end. He explains that he was trying to protect me because she was so unwell. She didn't want Greg and me to see her suffer. At the time I didn't really understand that and I've carried that with me all these years. It's always pained me deep down that I didn't really say goodbye. I've never been to my mother's grave since her funeral; I hold her in my heart, so I haven't felt the need to go down there – she wouldn't have wanted me to anyway. My mum told me: 'Be your own man, son. I will always love you.'

Now, I feel like my mum is giving Dad and me this time together so he can put my mind at rest. Our conversations help me to get a few things that have always troubled me in perspective, and make me feel a lot calmer about everything.

He also prepares me for the inevitable. 'Sometimes, when you've got to go, you've got to go,' he tells me. 'I don't want to be like this, boy. Don't feel sad. I'd rather die having a heart attack doing the hundred metres than lying here pissing and shitting myself. I've had a great time. I've seen you boys grow up. I don't want to die, but I'm happy with my lot. I'm going to see your mum now. . .'

Two weeks after his unexpected revival, he's gone.

At the funeral, Greg gives that wonderful eulogy which sums him up so perfectly and has us all laughing and crying. A life well lived, indeed.

In the weeks and months that follow – even amid the terrors of training for *The Jump* – I feel a sense of peace that I've not had since I was very young. Everything that has happened in the past thirty-odd years of my life since Mum died – the tribulations in my twenties and early thirties, the wild behaviour, the self-destructive tendencies, the broken relationships, the massive highs and painful lows – it all just seems to fit into place.

There's no doubt that meeting Dawn changed my life. I was wobbling at that time and without that chance encounter at Goughie's benefit game, I might not be here now. Cricket was coming to an end, divorce, sorting out access to my kids – it was all getting on top of me.

When I was younger I shagged around, cheated on partners, came home and said 'Hello, love' like nothing happened. I thought I was happy, but I wasn't. I was lying to them and myself. At some point, you have to learn from your mistakes, otherwise what's the point? I learnt something very profound: that the only real truth you have is inside your own head. When I lay down at night I wanted to be able to look my partner square in the eye. I wanted someone who I could be with and truly say I love you.

Then Dawn came along and I thought there is a God. Here was a chance to be the person I wanted to be. She's my angel. Without her love, guidance and support, things could have got very messy for me after winning *I'm a Celebrity*.

Imagine, then, how shocked we were when we received a call in 2014 to say that our phone numbers had been found during a police investigation into phone-hacking at *The Sunday Mirror* newspaper. In late 2014, after our numbers had been found, Trinity Mirror plc, the owners of the paper, admitted liability for phone-hacking at all three of its newspaper titles and at the time of writing our case is one of many that is going through the courts. So we are waiting to see if the *Mirror* will admit liability on our case too and then, if they do, we will find out exactly what happened and compensation will be determined.

Back then, we were going out of our minds wondering who was telling journalists such accurate details of our relationship and it seems that, unwittingly, we were. When we were going through bad times, Dawn might leave an angry voicemail or vice versa and all the while it now looks like they were probably listening in. As well as the door-stepping journalists, paparazzi photographers tracking our every move, we fear we were also being hacked. That wound up the pressure to the point that it nearly ruined the best thing in my life. I'm just so thankful we were strong enough to get through it all together because, ultimately, we knew we were made for each other.

Ever since, no such dramas – we've just been very happy together and we're coming up to our tenth wedding anniversary in July 2015.

Dawn tells me I am romantic in that I'm thoughtful and generous, but I'm still in training to walk through a door and remember not to let it swing back into her face. I'm not a big one for giving flowers either – or fur coats like my dad – but I like to think that with me every day's a Saturday.

We're both very sociable and like a party. My dad used to say to me: 'You're always judged by your parties. You might do something wrong, but put a good party on and all will be forgiven.' Dawn and me have hosted some good ones at our house in Kingswood, where we've been since just before that 584-mile walk in 2004.

I still am a lively boy, but without the mania. I don't feel the need to be out every night any more, worrying that if I don't I'll be missing out on something. Some days, I'm happy just being; I don't need to always be doing.

Dawn shares my silly sense of humour and enjoyment of the absurd, which is quite important when you spend a lot of time with me. For instance, at Christmas a couple of years ago, Dawn, Alana and me went to the Egyptian beach resort of Sharm El-Sheikh for a week over Christmas.

It's really good fun, loads of Brits over there, a lot of people around Dawn's and my age. Really good bunch of people and we're all socialising together, going to the bar at night and meeting again around the pool in the morning.

On Christmas Eve, the hotel put on a big dinner. Afterwards, we head to the hotel disco for a little dance. We're expecting it to be a typical little hotel disco, playing *Agadoo* and *Hi Ho Silver Lining*, but it turns out to be a proper club playing pumping house music. *Doof, doof, doof, doof. . .* People have come from everywhere and it's packed. 'Oh, this is great – it's really kicking.'

We've all had a drink during the day by the pool, then met up with a group of ten friends for pre-dinner drinks, then drinks over dinner, so by now, we're all feeling very, um, 'Christmassy'.

In the club, someone suggests a round of tequila shots.

'Oh no,' I say. 'Tequila makes me sick.'

'Sambucas?'

'Alright, yeah, let's have some sambucas.'

By 3am, it's starting to wind down, I'm about eight shots to the good and somewhat slumped at our table. I'm sitting next to a very glamorous, beautifully dressed woman in her sixties who is showing commendable stamina.

People keep shouting me: 'Tuffers! Can I have a photo?'

'Er, whaaat? Yeah.'

I'm doing pictures with blokes sitting on my lap, me sitting on blokes' laps. My only stipulation is: 'No Facebook, no Facebook.'

I've had my little dance, I've had my shots and I'm really quite pissed. But I spy a full shot glass on the table of what I think is sambuca. I'm still a bit thirsty and I think, 'Seems a shame to waste it, one for the road.' I can squeeze one more in after a full day on it.

I pick it up, slam it back and as soon as the liquid hits the back of my tongue, I know it's tequila, and no sooner than it reaches my throat it comes back up again with interest, catching the lady's lovely blouse a glancing blow on the shoulder.

Dawn's seen this and gone: 'Oh my God!'

'I'm so sorry,' I say.

The lady herself very calmly picks up a napkin from the table, carefully wipes her blouse and then picks up another one and leans over and dabs my mouth.

After apologising profusely again, Dawn leads me out of the club to a cheering ovation from all the Brits present. It's like a shambolic walk down the red carpet – they've all got their phones out taking photos and videoing me: 'Goodbye. . . Goodbye. . . Happy Christmas. . . No Facebook!'

On Christmas morning, I wake up feeling like death, but Dawn isn't having me lying in bed all day while the sun's shining outside. So after a tentative breakfast of a glass of juice and a boiled egg, we go down to the beach.

There's a few people with Santa hats on, giving out mince pies. It's a nice atmosphere, but I just want to lie down under a parasol and wait for the hangover to subside. Dawn and Alana have other ideas: 'Right, what shall we do?'

'I'm going to sit here.'

'No, no, come on, let's do something. I know – let's go parasailing.'

'Parasailing? Are you mad?'

'Come on, me and Alana will go up, you can just stay in the boat.'

I'm feeling sick, forget parasailing, how is this a good idea? What is Dawn trying to do to me? But there is no arguing.

We are joined in the boat by a very jolly young couple from London: ''Ello. Merry Christmas!' says the girl. 'Ooh, you're Phil, ain't ya? Oh, my dad loves you on A Question of Sport. . .'

The sea's not that choppy, but try telling my stomach that. I just sit at the front of the boat, sunglasses and hat on, telling myself to hang in there. Half an hour and I'll be back on that sun-lounger.

Dawn goes up, then Alana goes up, the other two people go up – meanwhile I'm going green.

On the way back to the shore, I'm thinking, 'Nearly there, nearly there. . .'

The girl is really excited after parasailing and sparks up a conversation with me. I'm doing my best to answer her questions, and as she's talking to me, I notice that she keeps glancing down at my mid-section. At first I don't think much of it, but she keeps doing it.

'Why does she keep doing that?' I wonder; then, I look down and see, to my utter horror, that my left bollock has fallen out of my swim shorts. And when I say out, right out.

'Oh my God! I'm so sorry,' I say as I hurriedly fumble around, trying to return the missing cannon wheel back to the barracks.

Dawn, who up to now has been more worried about me throwing up, sees what's happened and cracks up laughing. There follows another agonising two minutes before we reach the shore. I've gone bright red and apologise over and over, but the girl seems totally fine about it.

When we finally arrive at their drop-off point, Dawn and Alana are literally rolling about in the boat, crying with laughter, as I issue one last heartfelt apology to the girl: 'Once again, I'm so sorry. I've had a big night, now my nut has fallen out. . .'

'Oh no, don't worry. I've had a wonderful day. I'm in Sharm El-Sheikh on Christmas Day and I've met Phil Tufnell's left bollock. I can't wait till I tell my dad. . .'

Met my left bollock, that's what she says.

'Um, okay, bye. . .'

Like I say, you need to have a sense of humour to, er, hang out with me.

Meanwhile, in my professional life, things have gone better than I ever could have imagined since making the snap decision to retire from cricket. The transition from playing to finding another career in retirement can be very difficult and without *I'm a Celebrity* and everything that followed, I think I would have struggled. I feel very fortunate to have had the opportunities that landed on my lap.

When I was in my twenties, I never could have dreamt that I'd end up working on television or radio, but those early post-jungle experiences presenting *Simply the Best*, sitting next to Wossy on *They Think It's All Over* and the like have stood me in good stead. It was the same when I joined Middlesex after a three-year break from cricket in my teens and did my apprenticeship on the job. Learn by doing the big stuff – sink or swim.

After twelve years in TV and radio, I'm not just ploughing into things without a clue. The more you do it, the better you become, and now I can approach everything with a level of professionalism. I like to think I've proved myself to be pretty good as a captain on *A Question of Sport*, colour commentator on *Test Match Special* and reporter for *The One Show*. If an opportunity comes around again to present a show like *Simply The Best*, I'd have the confidence and experience to do it without the panic I felt back in 2004.

Meanwhile, Paragon, the company my brother Greg and Mike Martin set up back in 2001 (and I remain a shareholder of), is going from strength to strength. It now covers everything from talent management (looking after a roster of well-known cricket and rugby players and broadcasters) to hospitality (every year we welcome 200 people per day to the Phil Tufnell VIP Club at Oval Test matches), event management and brand engagement (I'm not sure what that last one is. . .).

I'm also the proud patron of a number of charities including The Children's Trust based near me in Surrey, the UK's leading charity for children with brain injury. Also, remember in Chapter 2, the London Community Cricket Association, for whom I helped to build a new cricket pavilion via the ITV show *With A Little Help From My Friends* back in 2003? That charity has expanded out of all recognition since then. It is now called The Change Foundation and helps marginalised young people by providing opportunities to play sport and to dance, mentoring, teaching employability skills and life skills. One of their recent initiatives is 'Team Tufnell', a training-for-work programme for young people with a disability and I do whatever I can to help promote the cause, because it's a great organisation that helps to turn kids' lives around.

When I have spare time, I also love to paint and was delighted to be asked to put on two exhibitions of my artworks in 2014, in Birmingham and Brighton.

So that's where I am as I come up towards the big 5-0 in 2016: more happy and settled in my personal life than ever before and enjoying a varied career that continues to throw up surprises, whether it's riding a skeleton at 100kph or purchasing bull scrotum lamps from a penis museum.

I look back on my life so far with a huge smile and almost no regrets, because everything that's happened, good and bad, has led me here. I still feel young at heart and with Dawn by my side I've got so much to look forward to and nothing to fear about turning fifty. I'm looking forward to the next stage.

Naturally, in the months since my dad's death, he's never been far from my thoughts. In early 2015, I gave a talk at the Silversmiths Guild, which was very emotional. The silver trade was like a village – everyone knew each other – and a few people come up to me and say that they remember my dad well and what a lovely chap he was.

Someone recently sent me photos of St John Street as it is now. No. 386, the building Dad used to own and almost gave away when he sold up, is now worth millions. The butcher's shop over the road is still there, with all the original features, just as I remember it. Must pop in and buy a couple of fillet steaks next time I'm passing through Angel.

In April 2015, my brother and I go back to Golders Green Crematorium to bury his ashes alongside my mum's. As I've said, I've never felt the need to visit mum's actual grave before, but now it feels right.

When we arrive there's a small hole with a wooden lid on it next to my mum's plot. An official from the crematorium comes along and says a few words. He then removes the lid covering the hole and holds the cylinder containing my dad's ashes over it. He pushes a release button on top to empty the contents into the hole, while Greg and I stand watching with tears in our eyes. But instead of dropping gently to Dad's intended final resting place, some of the ash billows out and up. The release mechanism doesn't seem to have worked properly and the fella is shaking the canister vigorously before giving it a few whacks on the base, as if he's trying to get ketchup out of a bottle. Meanwhile, we're coughing and spluttering and waving away an ash cloud.

In the car on the way home, I'm still brushing down my suit and picking bits of ash from my teeth.

How my dad would have laughed. He would have laughed and laughed.

INDEX

PICTURE CREDITS

Plate 3
[close up portrait] © Nick Kidd/REX
[on elephant] © Graham Chadwick/EMPICS Sport
[bowling] © David Munden/Popperfoto/Getty Images

Plate 4
[takes wicket of Mark Waugh] ©Johnny Eggit/Getty Images
[jumping mid-air] © Clive Mason/Getty Images
[with champagne] © Patrick Eagar/Getty Images

Plate 5
[bowled out in Cape Town] © Rebecca Naden/PA Archive/Press Association Images
[batting, mid-air] © Phil Walter/EMPICS Sport

Plate 6
[with Jonathan Ross] © Ken McKay/REX
[on mini-cycle] © Ken McKay/REX

Plate 7
[saluting] © ITV/REX
[Bushtucker challenge] © ITV/REX

Plate 8
[with Ant & Dec] © ITV/REX
[with pint] © Cameron Laird/REX

Plate 9
[with sheep] © ITV/REX
[charity walk] © Stuart Atkins/REX

Plate 10
[surfing] © Barry Gomer/REX
[football] © Lee Mills/Action Images

Plate 11
[with Chris Evans] © Ken McKay/REX
[with Meatloaf] © Huw John/REX

Plate 12
[in gorilla costume] © Samir Hussein/Getty Images
[Sausage Week] © Jane Mingay/PA Archive/Press Association Images
[Lawnmower Grand Prix] © David Fisher/REX

Plate 13
[Too Tasty] © Mike Marsland/Getty Images
[Gut Week] © Matt Crossick/PA Archive/Press Association Images
[with paintings] © SNAP/Splash News/Corbis

Plate 14
[with Henry Blofeld] © Gareth Copley/PA Archive/Press Association Images
[with Aggers] © Matthew Lewis-ICC/Getty Images
[QOS] © BBC/Stephen Brooks

Plate 15
[with Katya] © BBC/Guy Levy
[alone] © BBC/Guy Levy

Plate 16
[The Jump] © Todd Antony